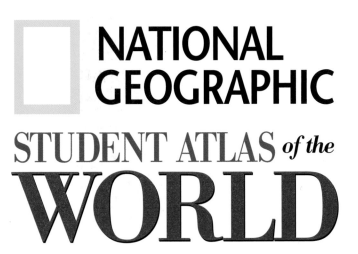

NATIONAL GEOGRAPHIC

STUDENT ATLAS *of the* WORLD

NATIONAL GEOGRAPHIC
Washington, D.C.

About the Earth

The Continents

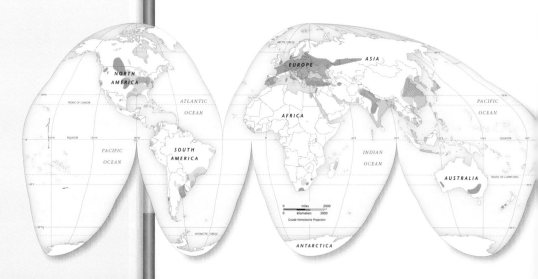

Inside covers:
Measurement Conversion Charts
World Facts

MERCURY

VENUS

EARTH

MARS

SUN

JUPITER

SATURN

URANUS

NEPTUNE

PLUTO

The Earth in Space

At the center of our solar system is the sun, a huge mass of hot gas that is the source of both light and warmth for Earth. Third in a group of nine planets that revolve around the sun, Earth is a terrestrial, or mostly rocky, planet. So are Mercury, Venus, and Mars. Earth is about 93 million miles (150 million kilometers) from the sun, and its journey, or revolution, around the sun takes 365¼ days. Farther away from the sun, five more planets—Jupiter, Saturn, Uranus, and Neptune (all made up primarily of gases) plus tiny, mostly icy Pluto—complete the major heavenly bodies that make up our solar system. The solar system, in turn, is part of the Milky Way galaxy.

▲ *Nine planets* orbit the sun, held in place by its gravitational field. Mercury's orbit (below) is the shortest: 88 Earth days; Pluto's is the longest: 248 Earth years.

SUN

NEPTUNE

PLUTO

MERCURY

URANUS

SATURN

VENUS

EARTH

MARS

JUPITER

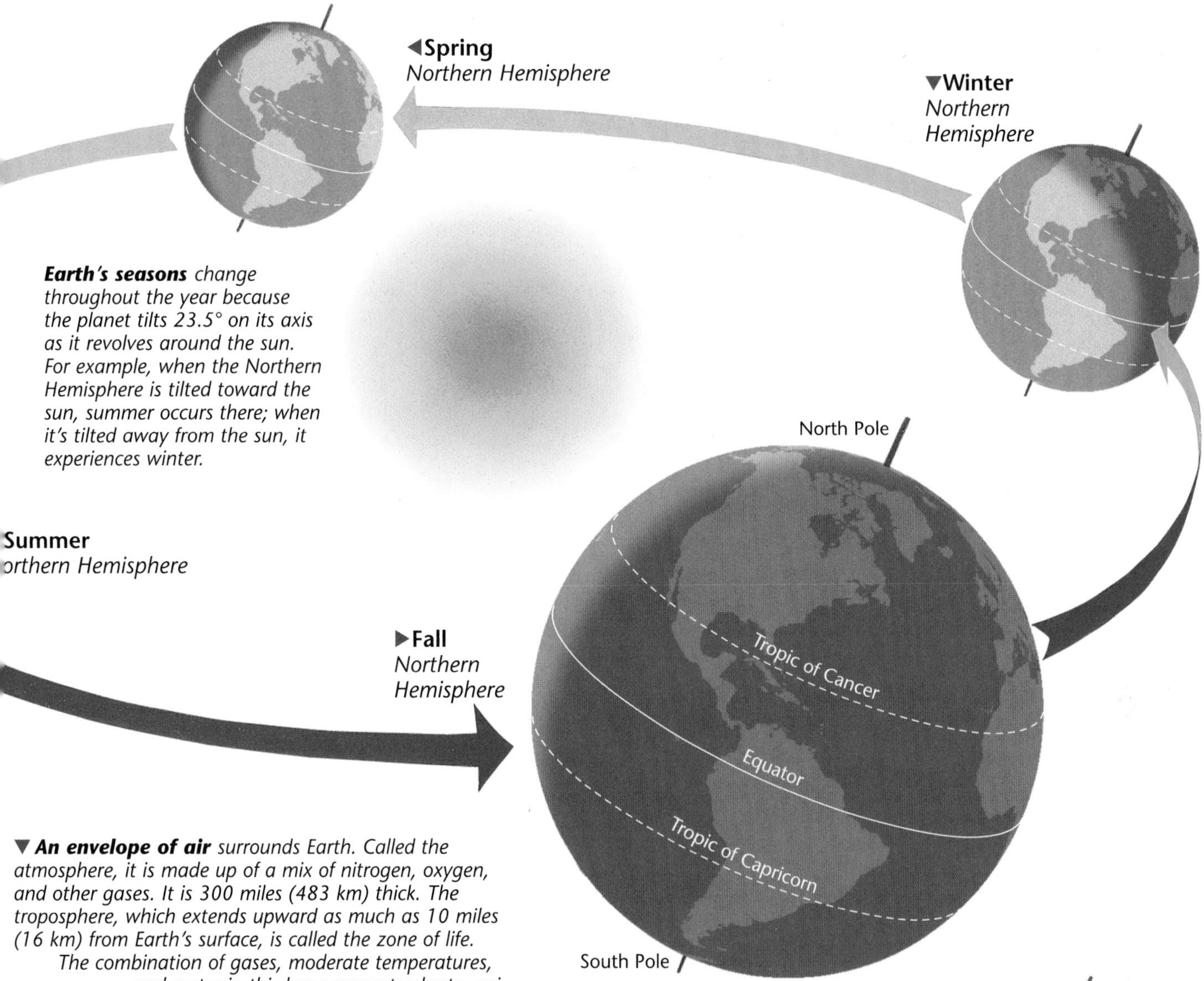

◀Spring
Northern Hemisphere

▼Winter
*Northern
Hemisphere*

Earth's seasons *change
throughout the year because
the planet tilts 23.5° on its axis
as it revolves around the sun.
For example, when the Northern
Hemisphere is tilted toward the
sun, summer occurs there; when
it's tilted away from the sun, it
experiences winter.*

Summer
orthern Hemisphere

▶Fall
*Northern
Hemisphere*

North Pole

Tropic of Cancer

Equator

Tropic of Capricorn

South Pole

▼ *An envelope of air* *surrounds Earth. Called the
atmosphere, it is made up of a mix of nitrogen, oxygen,
and other gases. It is 300 miles (483 km) thick. The
troposphere, which extends upward as much as 10 miles
(16 km) from Earth's surface, is called the zone of life.
The combination of gases, moderate temperatures,
and water in this layer supports plants, animals, and other forms of life on
Earth.*

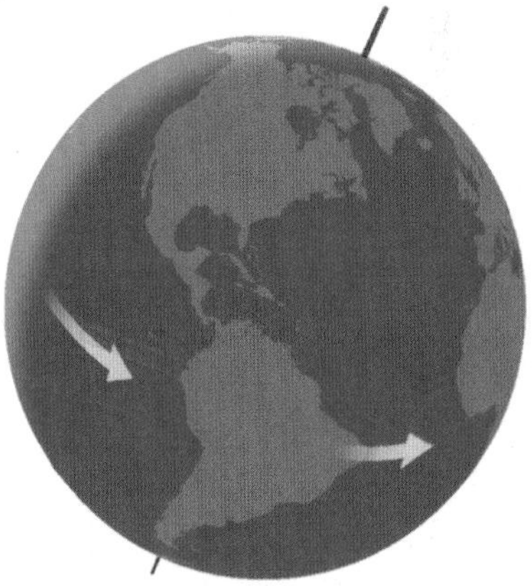

▲ *Earth rotates west to east* *on
its axis, an imaginary line that runs
through Earth's center from Pole to
Pole. Each rotation takes 24 hours,
or one full cycle of day and night.
One complete rotation equals one
Earth day. One complete revolution
around the sun equals one Earth year.*

5

Learning About Maps

MAP PROJECTIONS

Maps tell a story about physical and human systems, places and regions, patterns and relationships. This atlas is a collection of maps that tell a story about Earth.

Understanding that story requires a knowledge of how maps are made and a familiarity with the special language used by cartographers, the people who create maps.

Globes present a model of Earth as it is—a sphere—but they are bulky and can be difficult to use and store. Flat maps are much more convenient, but certain problems result from transferring Earth's curved surface to a flat piece of paper, a process called projection. There are many different types of projections, all of which involve some form of distortion: area, distance, direction, or shape.

(Web Link)

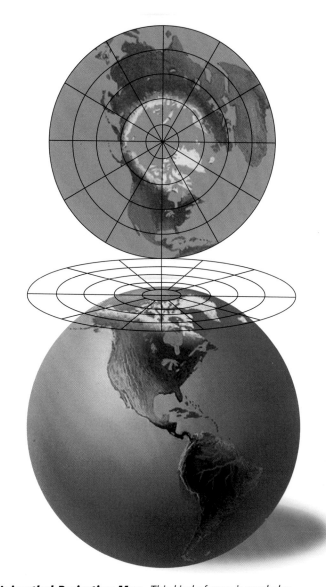

▲ **Azimuthal Projection Map.** *This kind of map is made by projecting a globe onto a flat surface that touches the globe at a single point, such as the North Pole. These maps accurately represent direction along any straight line extending from the point of contact. Away from the point of contact, shape is increasingly distorted.*

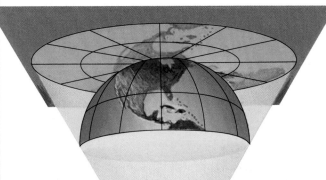

▲ **Making a Projection.** *Imagine a globe that has been cut in half as this one has. If a light is shined into it, the lines of latitude and longitude and the shapes of the continents will cast shadows that can be "projected" onto a piece of paper, as shown here. Depending on how the paper is positioned, the shadows will be distorted in different ways.*

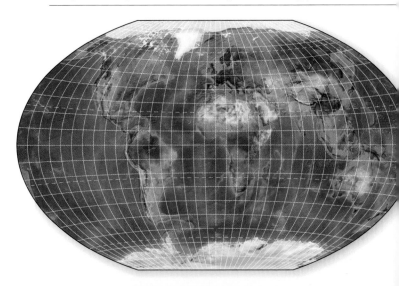

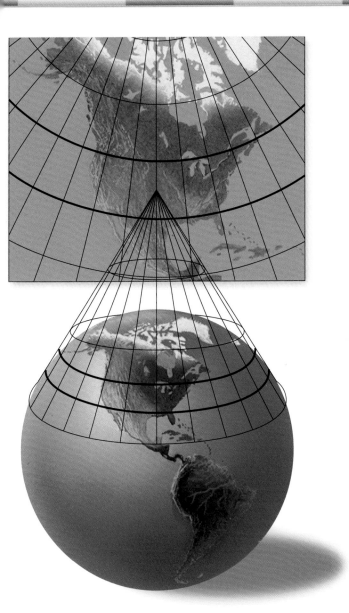

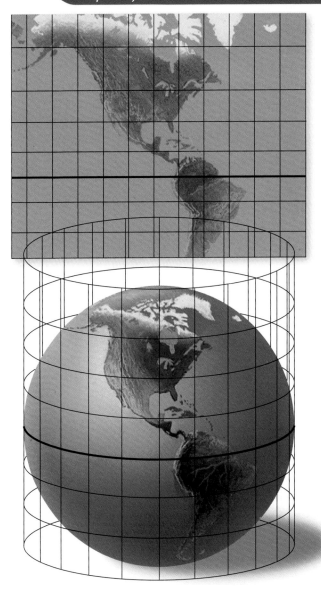

▲ **Conic Projection Map.** *This kind of map is made by projecting a globe onto a cone. The part of Earth being mapped touches the sides of the cone. Lines of longitude appear as straight lines; lines of latitude appear as parallel arcs. Conic projections are often used to map mid-latitude areas with great east-west extent, such as North America.*

▲ **Cylindrical Projection Map.** *A cylindrical projection map is made by projecting a globe onto a cylinder that touches Earth's surface along the Equator. Latitude and longitude lines on this kind of map show true compass directions, which makes it useful for navigation. But there is great distortion in the size of high-latitude landmasses.*

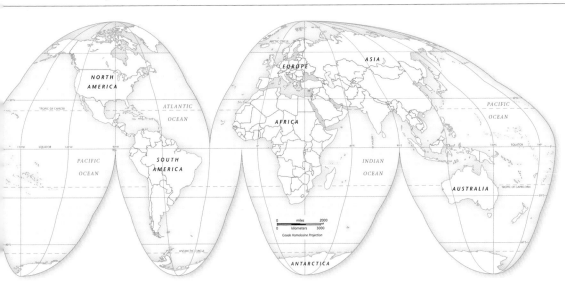

◄ **Other Projections.** *Sometimes cartographers create general purpose world projections, such as the Winkel Tripel (far left), in which distortion of both size and shape is minimized. This creates a reasonably accurate image of Earth. Another general purpose projection is the Goode's Interrupted Homolosine (left), which interrupts ocean areas to preserve the relative size and shape of land areas.*

READING MAPS

People can use maps to find locations, to determine direction or distance, and to understand information about places. Cartographers rely on a special graphic language to communicate through maps.

An imaginary system of lines, called the global grid, helps us locate particular points on Earth's surface. The global grid is made up of lines of latitude and longitude that are measured in degrees, minutes, and seconds. The point where these lines intersect identifies the absolute location of a place. No other place has the exact same address. Web Link

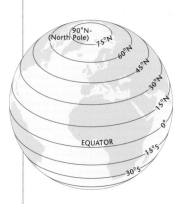

◀ **Latitude.** *Lines of latitude—also called parallels because they are parallel to the Equator—run east to west around the globe and measure location north or south of the Equator. The Equator is 0° latitude.*

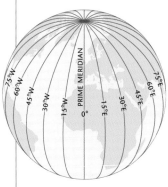

◀ **Longitude.** *Lines of longitude, also called meridians, run from Pole to Pole and measure location east or west of the prime meridian. The prime meridian is 0° longitude, and it runs through Greenwich, near London, England.*

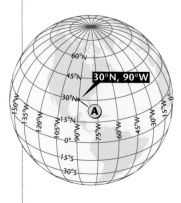

◀ **Global Grid.** *When used together, latitude and longitude form a grid that provides a system for determining the exact, or absolute, location of every place on Earth. For example, the absolute location of point A is 30°N, 90°W.*

▲ **Direction.** *Cartographers put a north arrow or a compass rose, which shows the four cardinal directions—north, south, east, and west—on a map. On this map, point B is northwest (NW) of point A. Northwest is an example of an intermediate direction, which means it is between two cardinal directions. Grid lines can also be used to indicate north.*

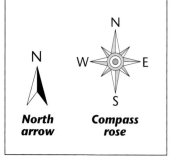

North arrow   Compass rose

▶ **Scale.** *A map represents a part of Earth's surface, but that part is greatly reduced. Cartographers include a map scale to show what distance on Earth is represented by a given length on the map. Scale can be graphic (a bar), verbal, or a ratio.*

To determine how many miles point A is from point B, place a piece of paper on the map above and mark the distance between A and B. Then compare the marks on the paper with the bar scale on the map.

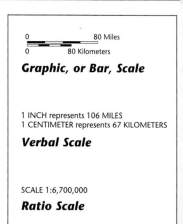

Graphic, or Bar, Scale

1 INCH represents 106 MILES
1 CENTIMETER represents 67 KILOMETERS

Verbal Scale

SCALE 1:6,700,000

Ratio Scale

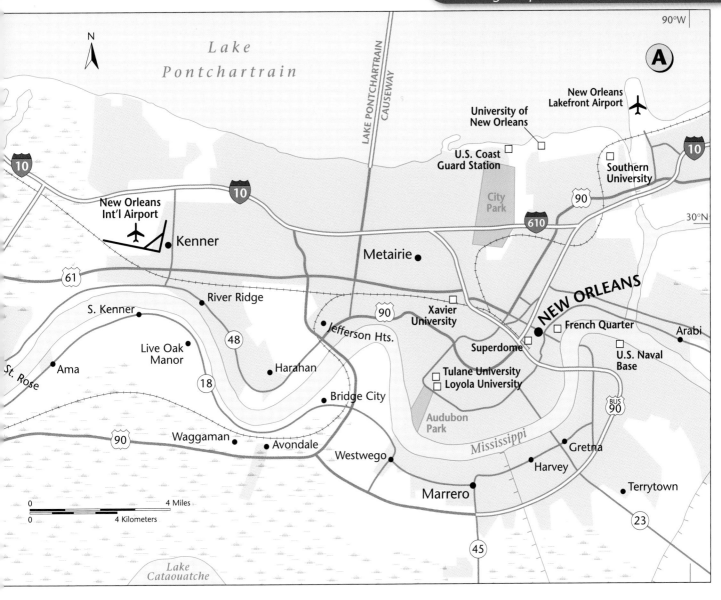

90°W

A

▼ Symbols. *Finally, cartographers use a variety of symbols, which are identified in a map key or legend, to tell us more about the places represented on the map. There are three general types of symbols:*

Point symbols *show exact location of places (such as cities) or quantity (a large dot can mean a more populous city).*

Line symbols *show boundaries or connections (such as roads, canals, and other trade links).*

Area symbols *show the form and extent of a feature (such as a lake, park, or swamp).*

Additional information may be coded in color, size, and shape.

▲ Putting It All Together. *We already know from the map on page 8 which states A and B are located in. But to find out more about city A, we need a larger scale map—one that shows a smaller area in more detail (see above).*

Metropolitan area		Road
Lake or river		Railroad
Park		Runway
Swamp		Airport
Canal		Point of interest
Highway		Town

TYPES OF MAPS

This atlas includes many different types of maps so that a wide variety of information about Earth can be presented. Three of the most commonly used types of maps are physical, political, and thematic.

A **physical map** identifies natural features, such as mountains, deserts, oceans, and lakes. Area symbols of various colors and shadings may indicate height above sea level or, as in the example here, ecosystems. Similar symbols could also show water depth.

A **political map** shows how people have divided the world into countries. Political maps can also show states, counties, or cities within a country. Line symbols indicate boundaries, and point symbols show the locations and sometimes sizes of cities.

Thematic maps use a variety of symbols to show distributions and patterns on Earth. For example, a choropleth map uses shades of color to represent different values. The example here shows the amount of energy consumed each year by various countries. Thematic maps can show many different things, such as patterns of vegetation, land use, and religions.

A **cartogram** is a special kind of thematic map in which the size of a country is based on some statistic other than land area. In the cartogram at far right, population size determines the size of each country. This is why Nigeria—the most populous country in Africa—appears much larger than Sudan, which has more than double the land area of Nigeria (see the political map). Cartograms allow for a quick visual comparison of countries in terms of a selected statistic.

Web Link

This globe is useful for showing Africa's position and size relative to other landmasses, but very little detail is possible at this scale. By using different kinds of maps, mapmakers can show a variety of information in more detail.

Physical Map

Madeira Islands
Canary Islands
Cape Verde Islands
Atlas Mountains
Mediterranean Sea
Dead -1,36 (-416
S A H A R A
Libyan Desert
Nile
Red Se
S A H E L
Niger
AFRICA
White Nile
Blue Nile
Ethic High
Upper Guinea
Gulf of Guinea
0°
Congo
Lake Victoria
Congo Basin
Great Rift Valley
Lake Tanganyika
Lower Guinea
O C E A N
Zambezi
Namib Deser
Kalahari Desert
berg

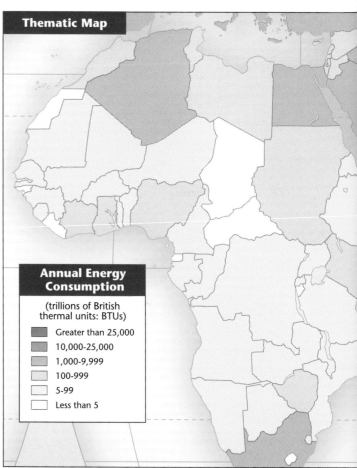

Thematic Map

Annual Energy Consumption

(trillions of British thermal units: BTUs)

	Greater than 25,000
	10,000-25,000
	1,000-9,999
	100-999
	5-99
	Less than 5

Political Map

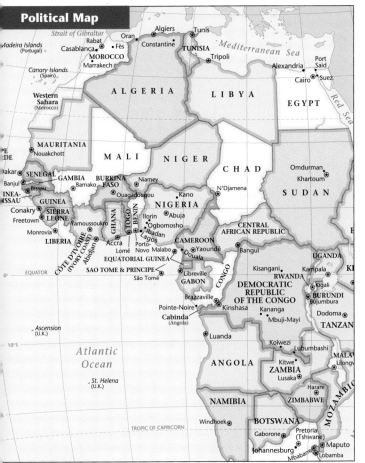

Cartogram

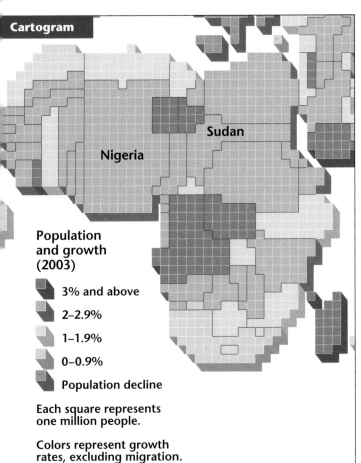

Nigeria

Sudan

Population and growth (2003)

- 3% and above
- 2–2.9%
- 1–1.9%
- 0–0.9%
- Population decline

Each square represents one million people.

Colors represent growth rates, excluding migration.

Satellite Image Maps

Satellites orbiting Earth transmit images of the surface to computers on the ground. These computers translate the information into special maps (below) that use colors to show various characteristics. Such maps are valuable tools for identifying patterns or comparing changes over time.

▼ **Cloud Coverage**

▼ **Topography/Bathymetry**

▼ **Sea Level Variability**

▼ **Sea Surface Temperature**

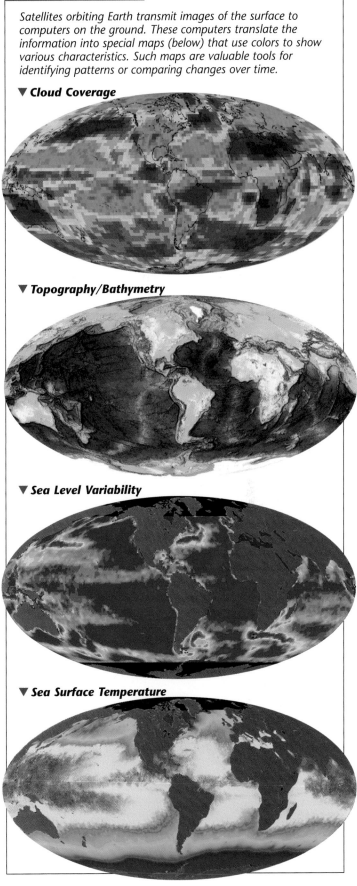

Physical Systems

THE PHYSICAL WORLD

Realms of land and water make up the physical world. More than two-thirds of Earth's surface is covered by water: oceans, lakes, and rivers. The rest is land: continents and islands. People inhabit every continent except Antarctica, which lies frozen beneath a vast ice cap at Earth's South Pole. Each continent is unique, but all show evidence of dynamic forces at work. Some forces build up mountains such as the Rockies, the Andes, and the Himalaya; other forces wear down Earth's surface, creating vast sedimentary plains and lowlands. Powerful rivers such as the Mississippi, the Congo, and the Yangtze (Chang) cut through the land and empty billions of gallons of fresh water into the oceans and seas each day.

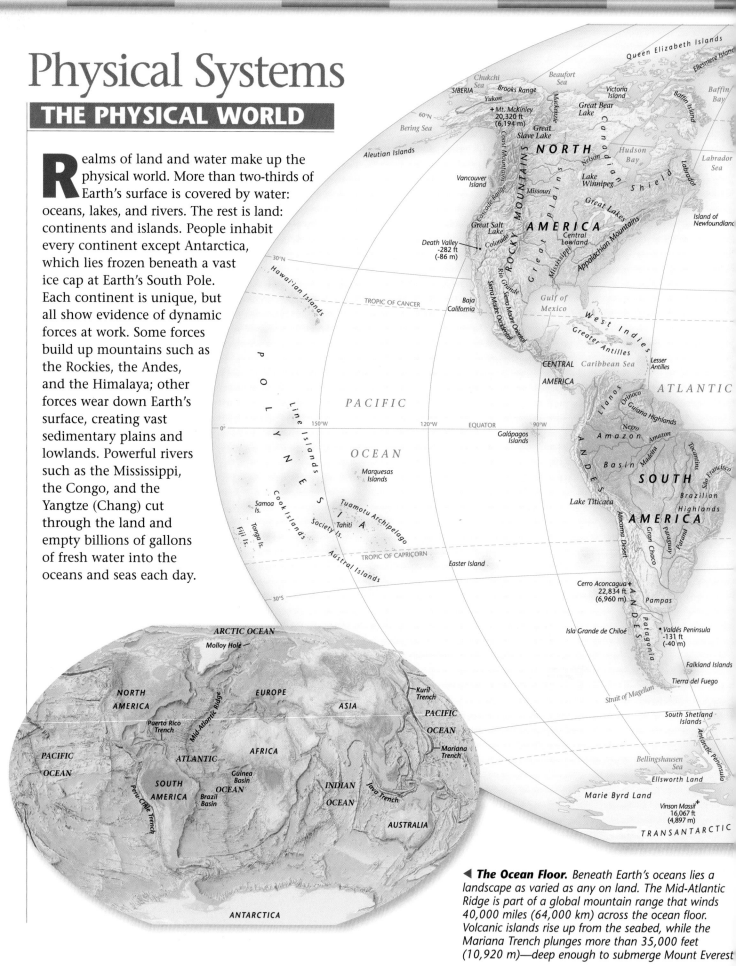

◄ The Ocean Floor. Beneath Earth's oceans lies a landscape as varied as any on land. The Mid-Atlantic Ridge is part of a global mountain range that winds 40,000 miles (64,000 km) across the ocean floor. Volcanic islands rise up from the seabed, while the Mariana Trench plunges more than 35,000 feet (10,920 m)—deep enough to submerge Mount Everest

ARCTIC OCEAN

GREENLAND

Greenland Sea

Svalbard

Novaya Zemlya

Kara Sea

Laptev Sea

East Siberian Sea

ARCTIC CIRCLE

Iceland

Norwegian Sea

Barents Sea

Yenisey

Central Siberian Plateau

Lena

Bering Sea

60°N

British Isles

North Sea

Ob

West Siberian Plain

Angara

Lena

Sea of Okhotsk

Kamchatka Peninsula

Aleutian Is.

Ireland

Great Britain

Baltic Sea

Northern European Plain

Ural Mountains

Irtysh

Ob

Lake Baikal

Amur

Kuril Islands

Hokkaido

Scandinavia

Volga

Altay Mountains

ASIA

GOBI

JAPAN

Sea of Japan (East Sea)

EUROPE

Alps

El'brus 18,510 ft (5,642 m)

The Steppes

Aral Sea

Tian Shan

Taklimakan Desert

Yellow (Huang)

North China Plain

Honshu

Korea

Danube

Caucasus Mts.

Black Sea

Caspian Sea

Zagros Mountains

Kunlun Mountains

Plateau of Tibet

Yellow Sea

East China Sea

Ryukyu Islands

Nampo Shoto

30°N

Azores

Mediterranean Sea

Dead Sea -1,365 ft (-416 m)

Persian Gulf

Indus

HIMALAYA

Brahmaputra

Yangtze (Chang)

Taiwan

PACIFIC

Madeira Islands

Atlas Mountains

ARABIAN PENINSULA

Mt. Everest 29,035 ft (8,850 m)

Ganges

Salween

Hainan

OCEAN

Canary Islands

SAHARA

Libyan Desert

Nile

Red Sea

Arabian Sea

INDIA

Deccan Plateau

Bay of Bengal

Mekong

South China Sea

Luzon

Philippine Sea

Mariana Islands

MICRONESIA

Cape Verde Islands

SAHEL

Niger

White Nile

Blue Nile

Gulf of Aden

Somali Peninsula

Andaman Islands

Indochina Peninsula

Philippine Islands

AFRICA

Ethiopian Highlands

Sri Lanka

Nicobar Is.

Andaman Sea

Malay Peninsula

Marshall Islands

Upper Guinea

Gulf of Guinea

0°

Maldive Islands

60°E

90°E

150°E

EQUATOR

Gilbert Islands

0°

Congo

Lake Victoria

Kilimanjaro 19,340 ft (5,895 m)

Seychelles

INDONESIA

Greater Sunda Islands

Borneo

Celebes

Moluccas

Bismarck Archipelago

New Guinea

MELANESIA

OCEAN

Lower Guinea

Congo Basin

Great Rift Valley

Lake Tanganyika

INDIAN

Sumatra

Java

Solomon Islands

Zambezi

Madagascar

OCEAN

Arafura Sea

Coral Sea

Vanuatu

Fiji Islands

Namib Desert

Mascarene Islands

Great Sandy Desert

Great Dividing Range

New Caledonia

Kalahari Desert

Drakensberg

AUSTRALIA

Lake Eyre -52 ft, (-16 m)

Great Victoria Desert

Central Lowlands

Tasman Sea

30°S

South Sandwich Islands

Kerguélen Islands

Darling

Murray

Mt. Kosciuszko 7,310 ft (2,228 m)

North Island

NEW ZEALAND

Tasmania

South Island

0   miles   2000

0   kilometers   3000

Winkel Tripel Projection

Auckland Islands

ANTARCTIC CIRCLE

60°S

Queen Maud Land

MOUNTAINS

Transantarctic Mountains

Victoria Land

ANTARCTICA

◀ **The Physical World.** Great land-masses called continents break Earth's global ocean into four smaller ones. Each continent is unique in terms of the landforms and rivers that etch its surface and in the ecosystems that lend colors ranging from the deep greens of the tropical forests of northern South America and southeastern Asia to the browns and yellows of the arid lands of Africa and Australia. Most of Antarctica's features are hidden beneath its ice cap.

13 ◀

EARTH'S GEOLOGIC HISTORY

Earth is a dynamic planet. Its outer shell, or crust, is broken into huge pieces called plates. These plates ride on the slowly moving molten rock, or magma, that lies beneath the crust. Their movement constantly changes Earth's surface. For instance, along one convergent boundary—a place where two plates meet—the Indian Plate moves northward, colliding with the Eurasian Plate and heaving up the still growing mountains of the Himalaya. Along another convergent boundary, the Nazca Plate dives beneath the South American Plate in a process called subduction. Volcanoes and underwater earthquakes may occur along subduction zones, sometimes triggering giant waves called tsunamis. Along transform zones, such as California's San Andreas Fault, plates grind past each other, resulting in destructive earthquakes. The Mid-Atlantic Ridge is a divergent boundary where plates are pulling apart, allowing rising molten rock to form new ocean floor. `Web Link`

▼ **Our Changing Planet.** *The Latin phrase terra firma implies planet Earth is solid and unchanging. However, Earth's surface has been anything but unchanging. Geologic evidence suggests that moving plates have collided and moved apart more than once over the course of the planet's long history. As the main map shows, the forces of change show no signs of stopping.*

JUAN DE FUCA PLATE

NORTH AMERICAN PLATE

ROCKY MOUNTAINS

Hawaiian Islands

San Andreas Fault

MID-ATLANTIC RIDGE

CARIBBEAN PLATE

COCOS PLATE

PACIFIC PLATE

EQUATOR

PACIFIC OCEAN

ATLANTIC

EAST PACIFIC RISE

NAZCA PLATE

ANDES

SOUTH AMERICAN PLATE

SCOTIA PLATE

ANTARCTIC PLATE

▶ **Pangaea.**
About 240 million years ago, all of Earth's continents collided to form a vast landmass (now called Pangaea) that stretched from Pole to Pole.

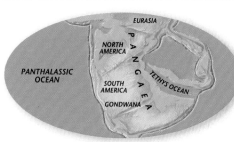

EURASIA

NORTH AMERICA

PANGAEA

PANTHALASSIC OCEAN

SOUTH AMERICA

TETHYS OCEAN

GONDWANA

▶ **Drifting Apart.**
By 94 million years ago, Pangaea had been pulled apart into smaller landmasses. In the warm global climate, dinosaurs evolved into Earth's dominant animal group.

NORTH AMERICA

EURASIA

ATLANTIC OCEAN

PACIFIC OCEAN

PACIFIC OCEAN

SOUTH AMERICA

AFRICA

TETHYS OCEAN

India

AUSTRALIA

ARCTIC OCEAN

NORTH
AMERICAN
PLATE

E U R A S I A N

P L A T E

ALPS

ARABIAN
PLATE

HIMALAYA

Plateau of Tibet

INDIAN

PLATE

PACIFIC
OCEAN

NUBIA

PLATE

Great Rift Valley

SOMALI

PLATE

INDIAN   OCEAN

PHILIPPINE
PLATE

OCEAN

MID-ATLANTIC RIDGE

CAPRICORN
PLATE

PACIFIC
EQUATOR
PLATE

AUSTRALIAN
PLATE

A N T A R C T I C

P L A T E

0   miles   2000

0   kilometers   3000

Winkel Tripel Projection

Plate Tectonics

- Divergent boundary
- Convergent boundary
- Transform zone
- Uncertain boundary
- Earthquake of magnitude 8 or greater on the Richter scale: 1900–present
- Earthquake measuring 6.5 to 7.9 on the Richter scale: 1900–present
- Earthquake generating a deadly tsunami: 1900–present
- Notable volcanic eruption: 1900–present
- Known volcanic eruption during the past 10,000 years
- Volcanic hot spot

◀ **Tectonic boundaries**
mark areas of geologic
change in ocean floors,
along continental margins,
and even through continents,
as in East Africa's Great Rift
Valley. Clusters of volcanoes
and frequent earthquakes
signal areas of instability.

▶**Eve of Destruction.**
By 65 million years
ago, continents were
moving toward their
current positions.
The impact (✱) of an
asteroid in the Gulf
of Mexico probably
extinguished the
dinosaurs and many
other species.

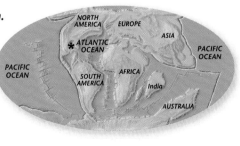

▶**Deep Freeze.**
By 18,000 years
ago, the continents
resembled their
current shapes.
A great ice age
had the far
northern and
southern regions
locked under huge
ice sheets.

EARTH'S LAND & WATER FEATURES

The largest land and water features on Earth are the continents and the oceans, but many other features—large and small—make each place unique. Mountains, plateaus, and plains give texture to the land. The Rockies and the Andes rise high above the lowlands of North and South America. In Asia, the Himalaya and the Plateau of Tibet form the rugged core of Earth's largest continent. These features are the result of powerful forces within Earth pushing up the land. Other landforms, such as canyons and valleys, are created when weathering and erosion wear down parts of Earth's surface.

Dramatic features are not limited to the land. Submarine mountains, appearing like pale blue threads against the deep blue on the satellite map, rise from the seafloor and trace zones of underwater geologic activity. Deep trenches form where plates collide, causing one to dive beneath the other. *Web Link*

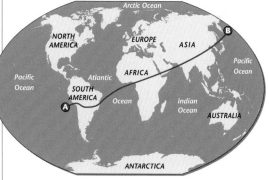

▼ A Slice of Earth.
This cross section of Earth's surface extends from Lake Titicaca near South America's Pacific coast to the Kuril Islands in the northwestern Pacific Ocean. It shows towering mountains, eroded highlands, broad coastal plains, and deep ocean basins.

Elevation (in meters)

8,000
7,000
6,000
5,000
4,000
3,000
2,000
1,000
0
-1,000
-2,000
-3,000
-4,000
-5,000
-6,000
-7,000
-8,000
-9,000

Sea Level

Andes · Lake Titicaca · Gran Chaco · Paraná R. · Brazilian Highlands

SOUTH AMERICA

Pacific Ocean · Peru-Chile Trench · Atlantic Ocean · Brazil Basin · Mid-Atlantic Ridge · Guinea Basin

Niger R. · Adamawa · Blue Nile R. · White Nile R. · Ethiopian Highlands

AFRICA

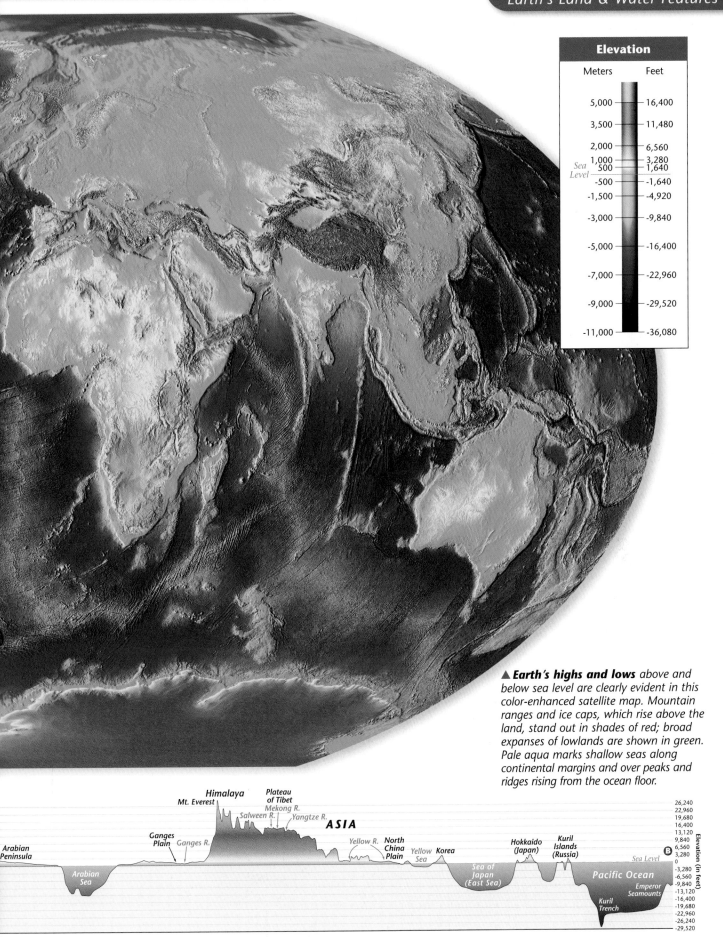

Elevation

Meters	Feet
5,000	16,400
3,500	11,480
2,000	6,560
1,000	3,280
500	1,640
Sea Level	
-500	-1,640
-1,500	-4,920
-3,000	-9,840
-5,000	-16,400
-7,000	-22,960
-9,000	-29,520
-11,000	-36,080

▲ **Earth's highs and lows** above and below sea level are clearly evident in this color-enhanced satellite map. Mountain ranges and ice caps, which rise above the land, stand out in shades of red; broad expanses of lowlands are shown in green. Pale aqua marks shallow seas along continental margins and over peaks and ridges rising from the ocean floor.

Himalaya
Mt. Everest
Plateau of Tibet
Mekong R.
Salween R.
Yangtze R.
ASIA
Ganges Plain
Ganges R.
Yellow R.
North China Plain
Yellow Sea
Korea
Hokkaido (Japan)
Kuril Islands (Russia)
Arabian Peninsula
Arabian Sea
Sea of Japan (East Sea)
Pacific Ocean
Emperor Seamounts
Kuril Trench

Elevation (in feet)
26,240
22,960
19,680
16,400
13,120
9,840
6,560
3,280
Sea Level
0
-3,280
-6,560
-9,840
-13,120
-16,400
-19,680
-22,960
-26,240
-29,520

EARTH'S CLIMATES

Climate is not the same as weather. Climate is the long-term average of conditions in the atmosphere at a particular location on Earth's surface. Weather refers to the momentary conditions of the atmosphere. Climate is important because it influences vegetation and soil development. It also influences people's choices about how and where to live.

There are many different systems for classifying climates. One commonly used system was developed by Russian-born climatologist Wladimir Köppen and later modified by American climatologist Glenn Trewartha. Köppen's system identifies five major climate zones based on average precipitation and temperature, and a sixth zone for highland, or high elevation, areas. Except for continental climate, all climate zones occur in mirror image north and south of the Equator. Web Link

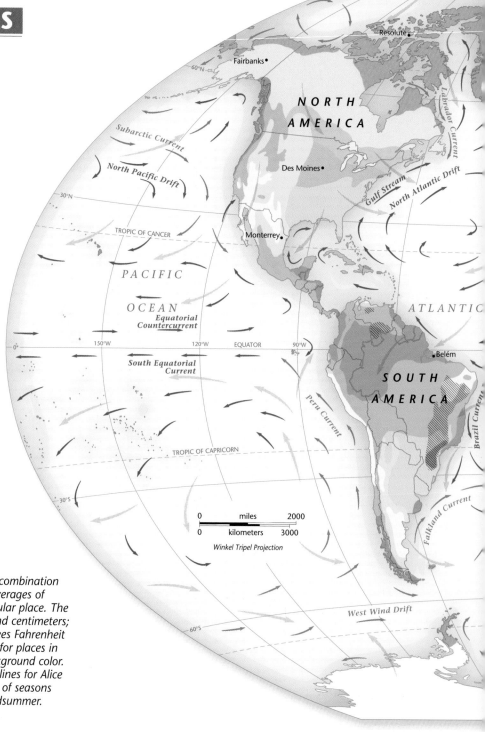

▼ **Climate Graphs.** A climate graph is a combination bar and line graph that shows monthly averages of precipitation and temperature for a particular place. The bar graph shows precipitation in inches and centimeters; the line graph shows temperature in degrees Fahrenheit and Celsius. The graphs below are typical for places in the climate zone represented by their background color. The seeming inversion of the temperature lines for Alice Springs and McMurdo reflects the reversal of seasons south of the Equator, where January is midsummer.

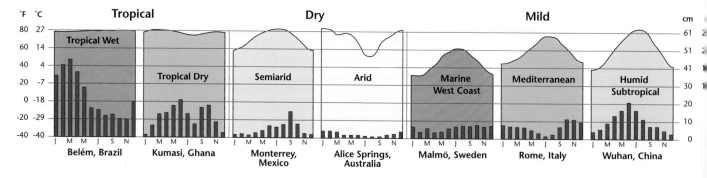

Tropical		Dry		Mild		
Tropical Wet	Tropical Dry	Semiarid	Arid	Marine West Coast	Mediterranean	Humid Subtropical
Belém, Brazil	Kumasi, Ghana	Monterrey, Mexico	Alice Springs, Australia	Malmö, Sweden	Rome, Italy	Wuhan, China

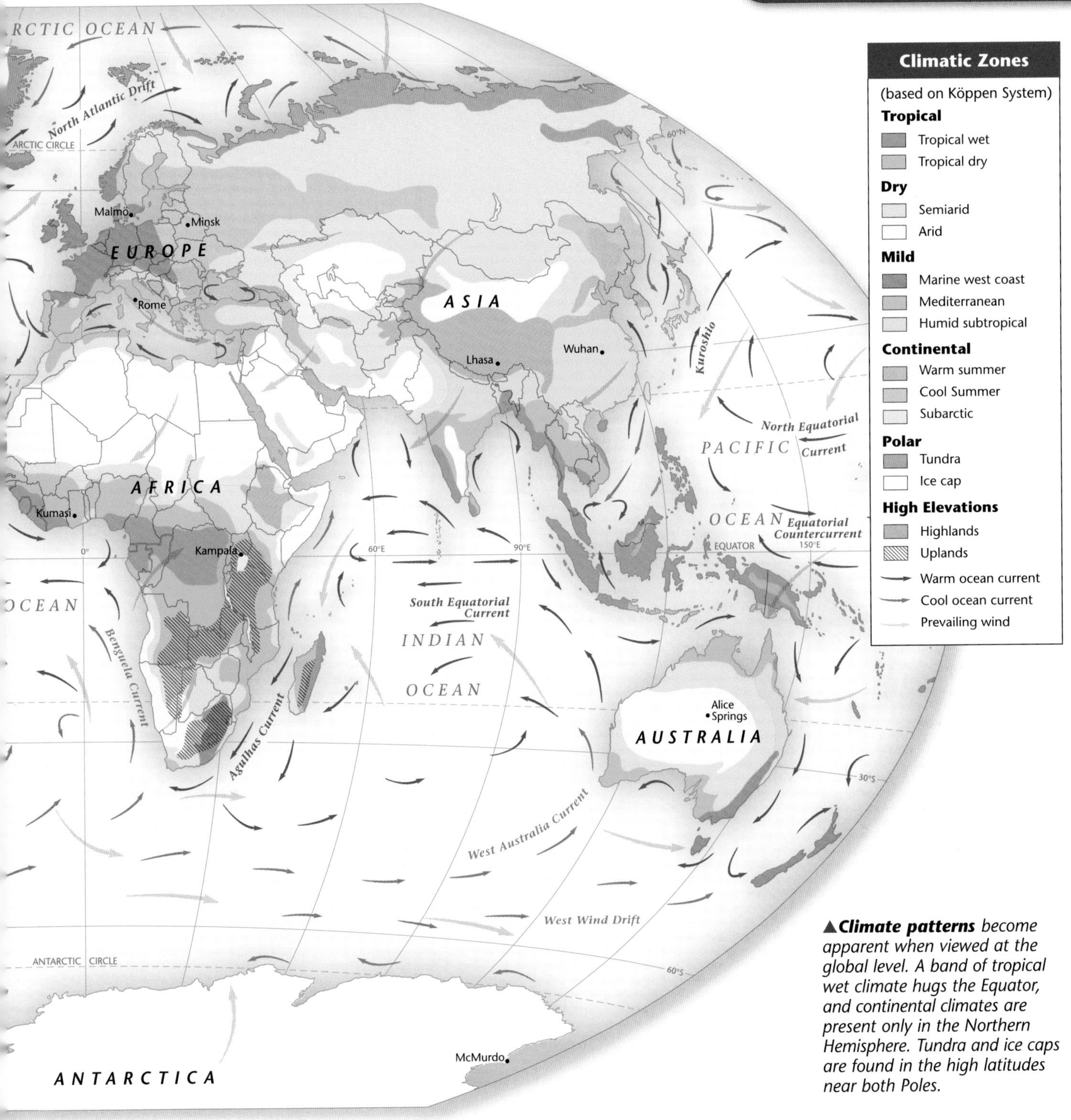

ARCTIC OCEAN
North Atlantic Drift
ARCTIC CIRCLE
Malmö
Minsk
EUROPE
Rome
ASIA
Lhasa
Wuhan
Kuroshio
North Equatorial Current
PACIFIC OCEAN
Equatorial Countercurrent
EQUATOR
AFRICA
Kumasi
Kampala
OCEAN
Benguela Current
Agulhas Current
South Equatorial Current
INDIAN OCEAN
Alice Springs
AUSTRALIA
West Australia Current
West Wind Drift
ANTARCTIC CIRCLE
McMurdo
ANTARCTICA
60°N
60°E
90°E
150°E
0°
30°S
60°S
Climatic Zones
(based on Köppen System)
Tropical
Tropical wet
Tropical dry
Dry
Semiarid
Arid
Mild
Marine west coast
Mediterranean
Humid subtropical
Continental
Warm summer
Cool Summer
Subarctic
Polar
Tundra
Ice cap
High Elevations
Highlands
Uplands
Warm ocean current
Cool ocean current
Prevailing wind

▲***Climate patterns*** *become apparent when viewed at the global level. A band of tropical wet climate hugs the Equator, and continental climates are present only in the Northern Hemisphere. Tundra and ice caps are found in the high latitudes near both Poles.*

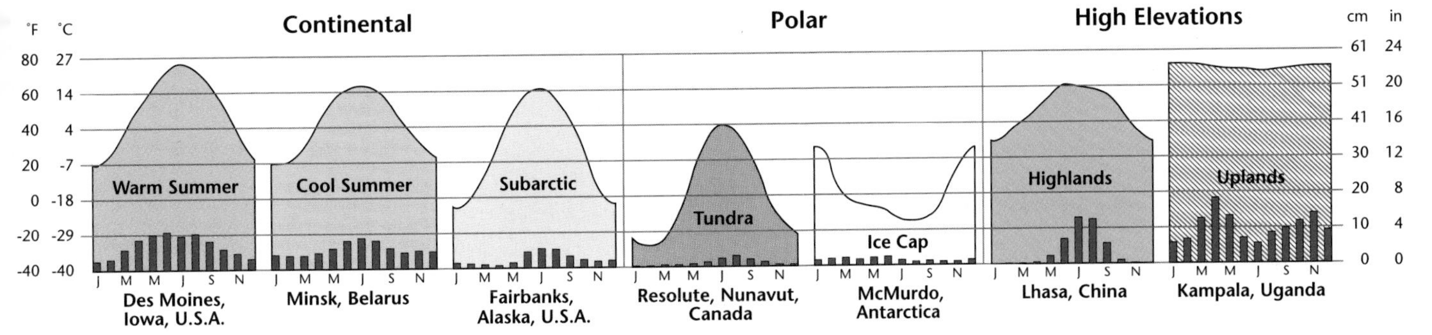

°F °C
80 27
60 14
40 4
20 -7
0 -18
-20 -29
-40 -40
Continental
Polar
High Elevations
cm in
61 24
51 20
41 16
30 12
20 8
10 4
0 0
Warm Summer
Cool Summer
Subarctic
Tundra
Ice Cap
Highlands
Uplands
J M M J S N
Des Moines, Iowa, U.S.A.
Minsk, Belarus
Fairbanks, Alaska, U.S.A.
Resolute, Nunavut, Canada
McMurdo, Antarctica
Lhasa, China
Kampala, Uganda

CLIMATE CONTROLS

The patterns of climate vary widely. Some climates, such as those near the Equator and the Poles, are nearly constant year-round. Others experience great seasonal variations, such as the wet and dry patterns of the tropical dry zone and the monthly average temperature extremes of the subarctic.

Climate patterns are not random. They are the result of complex interactions of basic climate controls: **latitude, elevation, prevailing winds, ocean currents, landforms,** and **location.**

These controls combine in various ways to create the bands of climate that can be seen on the world climate map on pages 18–19 and on the climate maps in the individual continent sections of this atlas. At the local level, however, special conditions may create microclimates that differ from those that are more typical of the region.

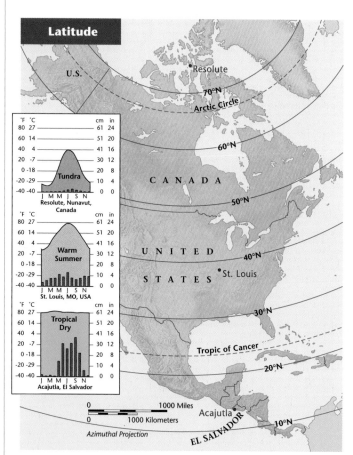

Latitude

▲ *Latitude. Energy from the sun strikes the Equator at a right angle. As latitude (distance north or south of the Equator) increases, the angle becomes increasingly oblique, or slanted. Less energy is received from the sun, and annual average temperatures fall. Therefore, the annual average temperature decreases as latitude increases from Acajutla, El Salvador, to St. Louis, Missouri, to Resolute, Canada.*

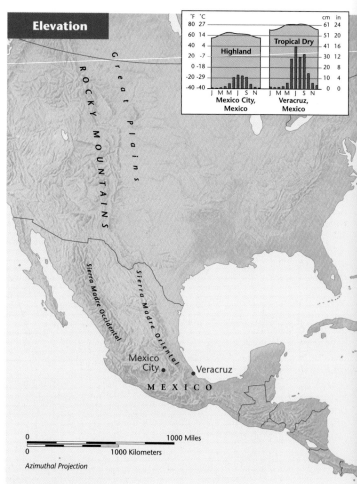

Elevation

▲ *Elevation. Not all locations at the same latitude experience similar climates. Air at higher elevations is cooler and holds less moisture than air at lower elevations. This explains why the climate at Veracruz, Mexico, which is near sea level, is warm and wet, and the climate at Mexico City, which is more than 7,000 feet (2,100 m) above sea level, is cooler and drier.*

Landforms

▶ *Landforms. Air carried by prevailing winds blowing off the ocean is full of moisture. If that air encounters a mountain when it reaches land, it is forced to rise. It becomes cooler, causing precipitation on the windward side of the mountain (see Portland graph). When air descends on the side away from the wind—the leeward side— the air warms and absorbs available moisture. This creates a dry condition known as rain shadow (see Wallowa graph).*

bar

y

w

Prevailing Winds and Ocean Currents

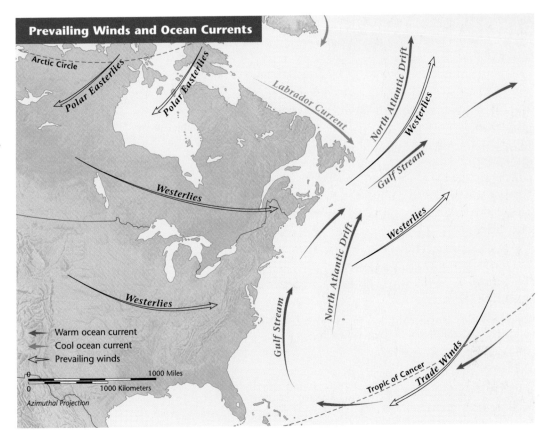

Prevailing Winds and Ocean Currents. *Earth's rotation combined with heat energy from the sun creates patterns of movement in Earth's atmosphere called prevailing winds. In the oceans, similar movements of water are called currents. Prevailing winds and ocean currents bring warm and cold temperatures to land areas. They also bring moisture or take it away. The Gulf Stream and the North Atlantic Drift, for example, are warm-water currents that influence average temperatures in eastern North America and northern Europe. Prevailing winds—trade winds, polar easterlies, and westerlies—also affect temperature and precipitation averages.*

Prevailing Winds and Ocean Currents

- ← Warm ocean current
- ← Cool ocean current
- ← Prevailing winds

1000 Miles
1000 Kilometers
Azimuthal Projection

Location. *Marine locations—places near large bodies of water—have mild climates with little temperature variation because water gains and loses heat slowly (see San Francisco graph). Interior locations—places far from large water bodies—have much more extreme climates. There are great temperature variations because land gains and loses heat rapidly (see Wichita graph). Richmond, which is relatively near the Atlantic Ocean but which is also influenced by prevailing westerly winds blowing across the land, has moderate characteristics of both conditions.*

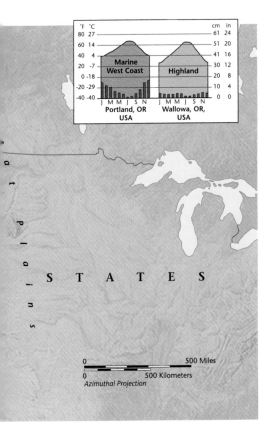

Portland, OR USA — Marine West Coast
Wallowa, OR, USA — Highland

Location

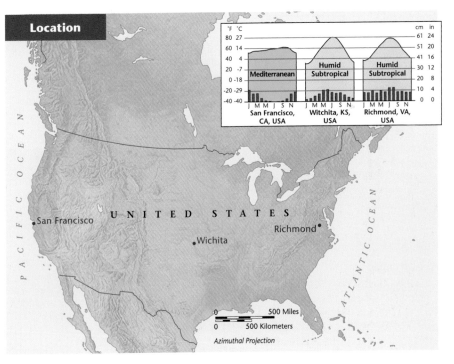

San Francisco, CA, USA — Mediterranean
Witchita, KS, USA — Humid Subtropical
Richmond, VA, USA — Humid Subtropical

500 Miles
500 Kilometers
Azimuthal Projection

EARTH'S NATURAL VEGETATION

Natural vegetation is the plant life that would be found in an area if it were undisturbed by human activity. Natural vegetation varies widely depending on climate and soil conditions. In the rain forest, trees tower as much as 200 feet (60 m) above the forest floor. In the tundra, dwarf species of shrubs and flowers are adaptations to harsh conditions at high latitudes and high elevations.

Vegetation is important to human life. It provides oxygen, food, fuel, products with economic value, even lifesaving medicines. Human activities, however, have greatly affected natural vegetation (see pages 24–25). Huge forests have been cut to provide fuel and lumber. Grasslands have yielded to the plow as people extend agricultural lands. As many as one in eight plants may become extinct as a result of human interference.

Web Link

▼ **Types of Vegetation.** *Vegetation creates a mosaic of colors and textures across Earth's surface. Grasslands dominate in places where there is too little precipitation to support trees. In the wet conditions of the tropics, rain forests and mangroves flourish. Desert shrubs are adapted to dry climates, and tundra plants survive a short growing season. These photographs show some of the plants found in various vegetation regions. Each is keyed to the map by color and number.*

▲ *Tundra*

▲ *Northern coniferous forest*

▲ *Temperate broadleaf forest*

▲ *Desert and dry shrub*

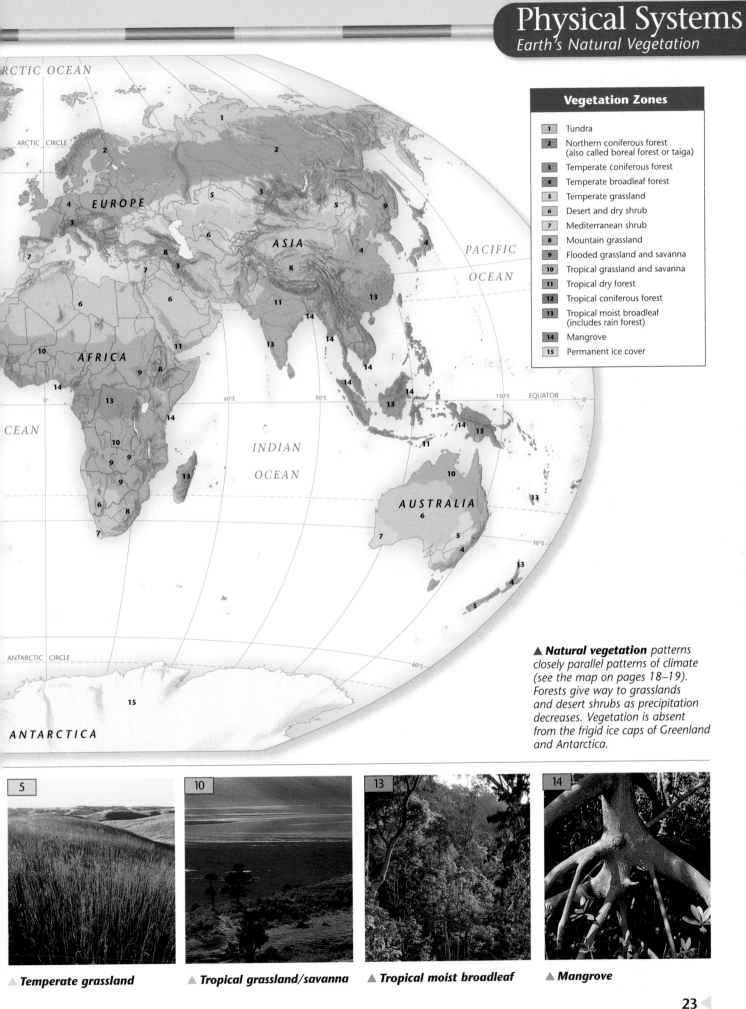

ARCTIC OCEAN

ARCTIC CIRCLE

EUROPE

ASIA

PACIFIC

OCEAN

AFRICA

60°N

EQUATOR

INDIAN

OCEAN

AUSTRALIA

30°S

60°S

ANTARCTIC CIRCLE

ANTARCTICA

OCEAN

0°

60°E

90°E

150°E

0°

Vegetation Zones

1	Tundra
2	Northern coniferous forest (also called boreal forest or taiga)
3	Temperate coniferous forest
4	Temperate broadleaf forest
5	Temperate grassland
6	Desert and dry shrub
7	Mediterranean shrub
8	Mountain grassland
9	Flooded grassland and savanna
10	Tropical grassland and savanna
11	Tropical dry forest
12	Tropical coniferous forest
13	Tropical moist broadleaf (includes rain forest)
14	Mangrove
15	Permanent ice cover

▲ **Natural vegetation** patterns closely parallel patterns of climate (see the map on pages 18–19). Forests give way to grasslands and desert shrubs as precipitation decreases. Vegetation is absent from the frigid ice caps of Greenland and Antarctica.

▲ **Temperate grassland**

▲ **Tropical grassland/savanna**

▲ **Tropical moist broadleaf**

▲ **Mangrove**

ENVIRONMENTAL HOT SPOTS

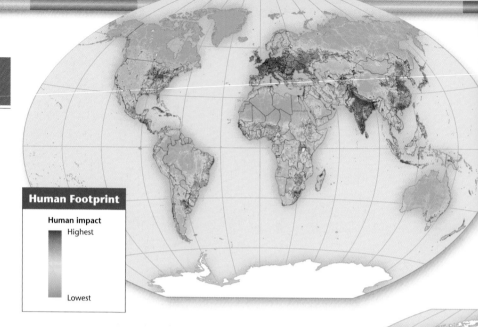

As Earth's human populations increase, pressures on the natural environment also increase.

In industrialized countries, landfills overflow with the volume of trash produced. Industries generate waste and pollution that foul the air and water. Farmers use chemical fertilizers and pesticides that run off into streams and groundwater. Cars release exhaust fumes that pollute the air and perhaps also contribute to global climate change.

In less developed countries, forests are cut, making the land vulnerable to erosion. Fragile grasslands turn to deserts as farmers and herders move onto marginal land as they try to make a living. And cities struggle with issues such as water safety, sanitation, and basic services that accompany the explosive urban growth that characterizes many less developed countries. Web Link

Human Footprint

Human impact

Highest

Lowest

▲ **Human activity** has altered nearly 75 percent of Earth's habitable surface. Referred to as the "human footprint," this disturbance is greatest in areas of high population.

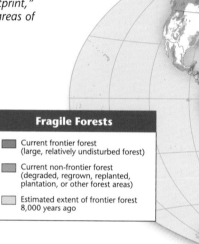

▶ **Forests play** a critical role in Earth's natural systems. They regulate water flow, release oxygen and retain carbon, cycle nutrients, and build soils. But humans have cut, burned, altered, and replaced half of all forests that stood 8,000 years ago.

Fragile Forests

Current frontier forest (large, relatively undisturbed forest)

Current non-frontier forest (degraded, regrown, replanted, plantation, or other forest areas)

Estimated extent of frontier forest 8,000 years ago

▼ **Polluted water** is part of everyday life for these people who live along a contaminated waterway in Kolkata (Calcutta), India. Home to more than 14 million people, the city doesn't have the resources to provide for many of its residents.

▼ **Deforestation** and heavy monsoon rains trigger landslides near Pokhara, Nepal, putting people, their homes, and their livestock at risk.

▲ **An oil spill** off the coast of California closed this beach. Clean-up workers are attempting to reduce the amount of damage to the environment.

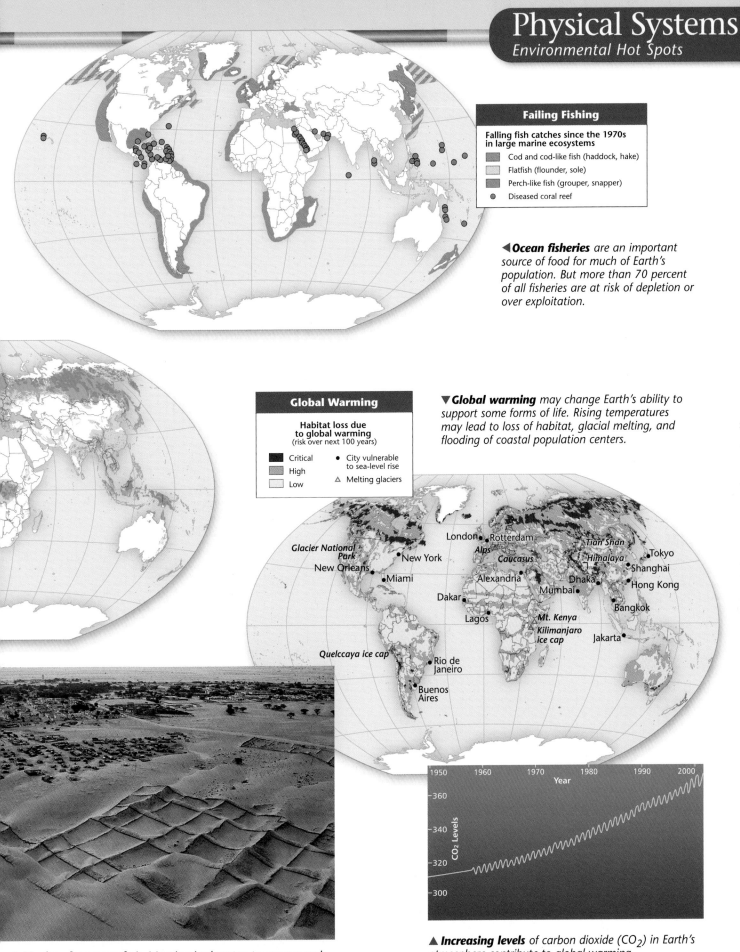

Failing Fishing

Falling fish catches since the 1970s in large marine ecosystems

Cod and cod-like fish (haddock, hake)
Flatfish (flounder, sole)
Perch-like fish (grouper, snapper)
● Diseased coral reef

◄ **Ocean fisheries** *are an important source of food for much of Earth's population. But more than 70 percent of all fisheries are at risk of depletion or over exploitation.*

Global Warming

Habitat loss due to global warming (risk over next 100 years)

Critical
High
Low

● City vulnerable to sea-level rise
△ Melting glaciers

▼ **Global warming** *may change Earth's ability to support some forms of life. Rising temperatures may lead to loss of habitat, glacial melting, and flooding of coastal population centers.*

London
Rotterdam
Alps
Tian Shan
Himalaya
Tokyo
Glacier National Park
New York
Caucasus
Shanghai
New Orleans
Miami
Alexandria
Dhaka
Hong Kong
Dakar
Mumbai
Lagos
Mt. Kenya
Bangkok
Kilimanjaro ice cap
Jakarta
Quelccaya ice cap
Rio de Janeiro
Buenos Aires

1950 1960 1970 1980 1990 2000
Year
360
340
320
300
CO_2 Levels

▲ **Increasing levels** *of carbon dioxide (CO_2) in Earth's atmosphere contribute to global warming.*

▲ **Moving desert sands** *in Mauritania threaten to cover a main road (upper right), which must be cleared daily. People have laid a grid of branches over the sand to try to slow its advance.*

THE POLITICAL WORLD

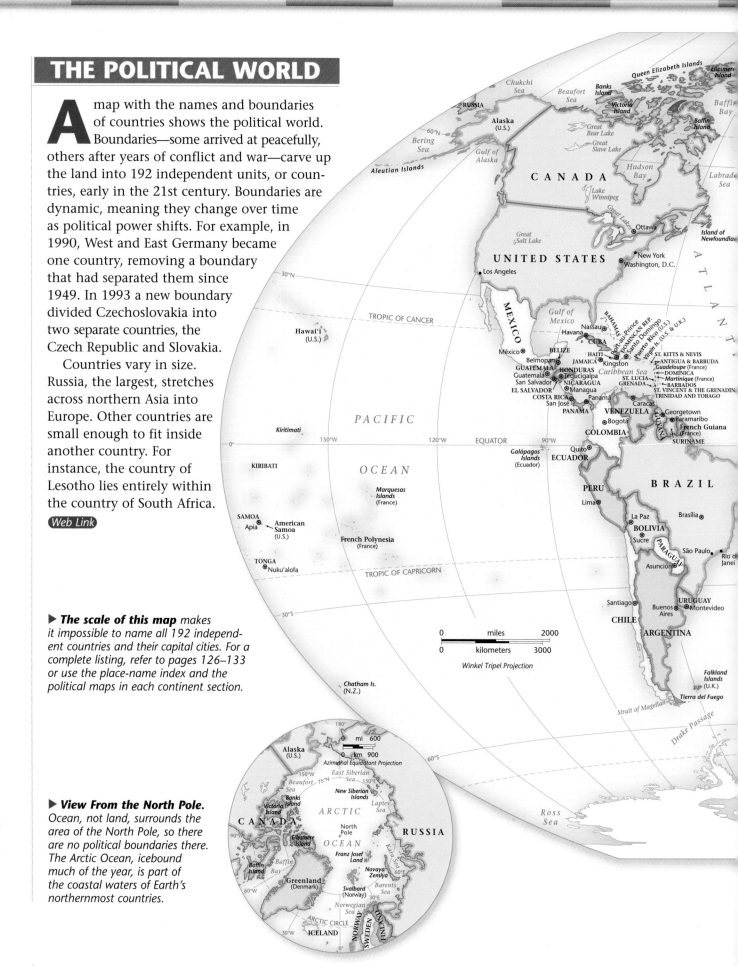

A map with the names and boundaries of countries shows the political world. Boundaries—some arrived at peacefully, others after years of conflict and war—carve up the land into 192 independent units, or countries, early in the 21st century. Boundaries are dynamic, meaning they change over time as political power shifts. For example, in 1990, West and East Germany became one country, removing a boundary that had separated them since 1949. In 1993 a new boundary divided Czechoslovakia into two separate countries, the Czech Republic and Slovakia.

Countries vary in size. Russia, the largest, stretches across northern Asia into Europe. Other countries are small enough to fit inside another country. For instance, the country of Lesotho lies entirely within the country of South Africa.

Web Link

▶ **The scale of this map** makes it impossible to name all 192 independent countries and their capital cities. For a complete listing, refer to pages 126–133 or use the place-name index and the political maps in each continent section.

▶ **View From the North Pole.** Ocean, not land, surrounds the area of the North Pole, so there are no political boundaries there. The Arctic Ocean, icebound much of the year, is part of the coastal waters of Earth's northernmost countries.

▶ **View From the South Pole.** Covered by ice, the continent of Antarctica has been set aside by treaty for scientific research. It has no permanent population and no political boundaries, although 7 countries claim territory there and 19 operate year-round research stations (see map page 125).

WORLD POPULATION

Late in 1999 the United Nations announced that Earth's population had surpassed six billion. Although more than 80 million people are added each year, the rate, or annual percent, at which the population is growing is gradually decreasing. Earth's population has very uneven distribution, with huge clusters in Asia and in Europe. Population density, the number of people living in each square mile (or square kilometer) on average, is high in these regions. For example, there are more than 2,000 people per square mile (800 people per sq km) in Bangladesh. Other areas, such as deserts and Arctic tundra, have less than 2 people per square mile (1 person per sq km). Web Link

▼ **Crowded streets,** like this one in Shanghai, may become commonplace as Earth's population continues to increase and as more people move to urban areas.

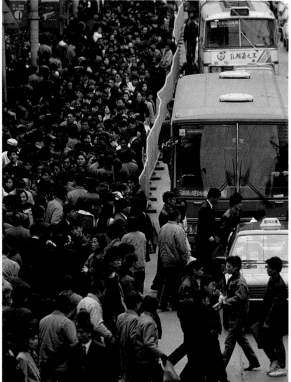

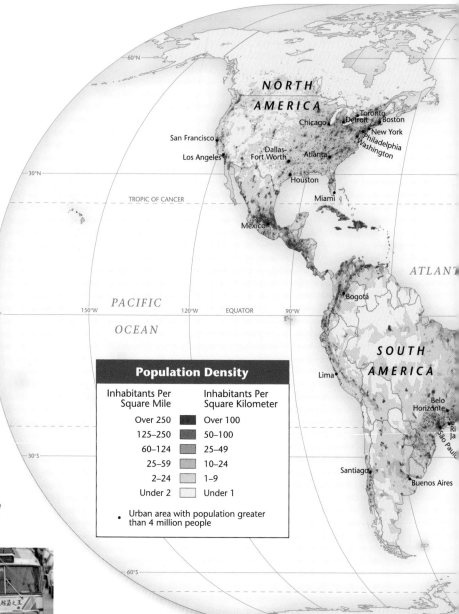

Population Density

Inhabitants Per Square Mile	Inhabitants Per Square Kilometer
Over 250	Over 100
125–250	50–100
60–124	25–49
25–59	10–24
2–24	1–9
Under 2	Under 1

• Urban area with population greater than 4 million people

Population Growth Over Time

The population's rate of increase—the percent by which it changes each year—was slow until industrial and scientific discoveries in the 1800s brought improved health, a more reliable food supply, and other changes that improved the quality of life. Earth's population began to increase rapidly. Although the rate of increase has begun to slow, the United Nations projects that Earth's population will reach almost 9 billion by 2050.

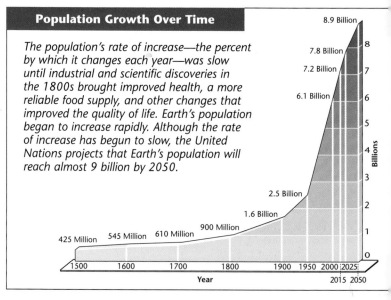

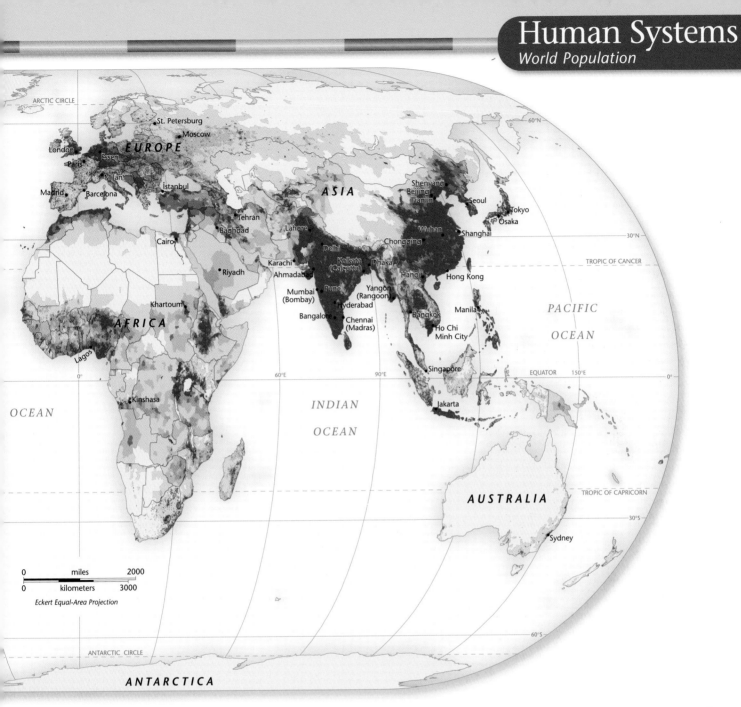

ARCTIC CIRCLE

St. Petersburg
Moscow
London
Paris
Essen
Milan
Madrid
Barcelona
İstanbul
Tehran
Baghdad
Lahore
Cairo
Karachi
Riyadh
Ahmadabad
Delhi
Kolkata (Calcutta)
Dhaka
Mumbai (Bombay)
Pune
Hyderabad
Bangalore
Chennai (Madras)
Khartoum
Yangon (Rangoon)
Hanoi
Hong Kong
Bangkok
Manila
Ho Chi Minh City
Singapore
Jakarta
Kinshasa
Lagos

Shenyang
Beijing
Tianjin
Seoul
Tokyo
Osaka
Wuhan
Shanghai
Chongqing

EUROPE
ASIA
AFRICA
AUSTRALIA
ANTARCTICA

PACIFIC OCEAN
INDIAN OCEAN
OCEAN

Sydney

Kinshasa

60°N
30°N
TROPIC OF CANCER
EQUATOR
TROPIC OF CAPRICORN
30°S
60°S
ANTARCTIC CIRCLE

0°
60°E
90°E
150°E
0°

0   miles   2000
0   kilometers   3000
Eckert Equal-Area Projection

Three Population Pyramids

A population pyramid is a special type of bar graph that shows the distribution of a country's population by sex and age. Italy has a very narrow pyramid, which shows that most people are in middle age. Its population is said to be aging, meaning the median age is increasing. The United States also has a narrow pyramid, but one that shows some growth due to a median age of about 35 years and a young immigrant population. By contrast, Nigeria's pyramid has a broad base, showing it has a young population. More than a third of its people are younger than 15 years.

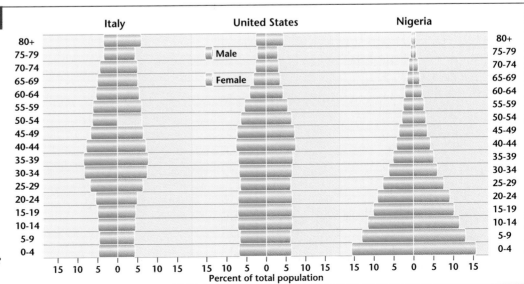

Italy   United States   Nigeria

Male
Female

Percent of total population

WORLD CITIES

Throughout most of history, people have lived spread across the land, first as hunters and gatherers, later as farmers. But urban geographers—people who study cities—predict that sometime in the next decade more people will be living in urban areas than in rural areas. Urban areas include one or more cities and their surrounding suburbs. People living there are employed primarily in industry or in service-related jobs. Large urban areas are sometimes called metropolitan areas. In some countries, such as Belgium, almost all the population lives in cities. But throughout much of Africa south of the Sahara, less than one-third of the people live in urban areas. Even so, some of the world's fastest growing urban areas are towns and small cities in Africa and Asia.

Web Link

Most Populous Urban Areas

In 1950 New York topped a list of only 8 cities with populations of 5 million or more. In 2003 New York had dropped to third behind Tokyo and Mexico City in a list of 46 cities with populations of at least 5 million. By 2015, the list is projected to include 61 cities.

Cities with populations of at least five million for the years:

- 1950
- 1975
- 2003
- 2015

US/Canada	Latin America	Europe	Africa	Asia	Australia/Oceania
1 2 5 8	1 2 8 8	4 4 6 6	0 0 3 4	2 4 24 35	0 0 0 0

Urban and Rural Populations

These graphs show the percentages of people living in urban and rural areas in the world and its various regions. Only Asia and Africa are predominantly rural, although both are experiencing rapid urban growth. Asia, which had only 2 cities of five million or more people in 1950, now has 24.

United States & Canada

79%   21%

Map labels:

NORTH AMERICA

Toronto
Chicago
New York
Philadelphia
Los Angeles
Dallas-Fort Worth
Atlanta
Miami
México

60°N
30°N
TROPIC OF CANCER

Bogotá

ATLANT

PACIFIC OCEAN
150°W   120°W   EQUATOR   90°W
0°

SOUTH AMERICA
Lima
Belo Horizonte
Rio de Janeiro
São Paulo
TROPIC OF CAPRICORN
30°S
Santiago
Buenos Aires
60°S

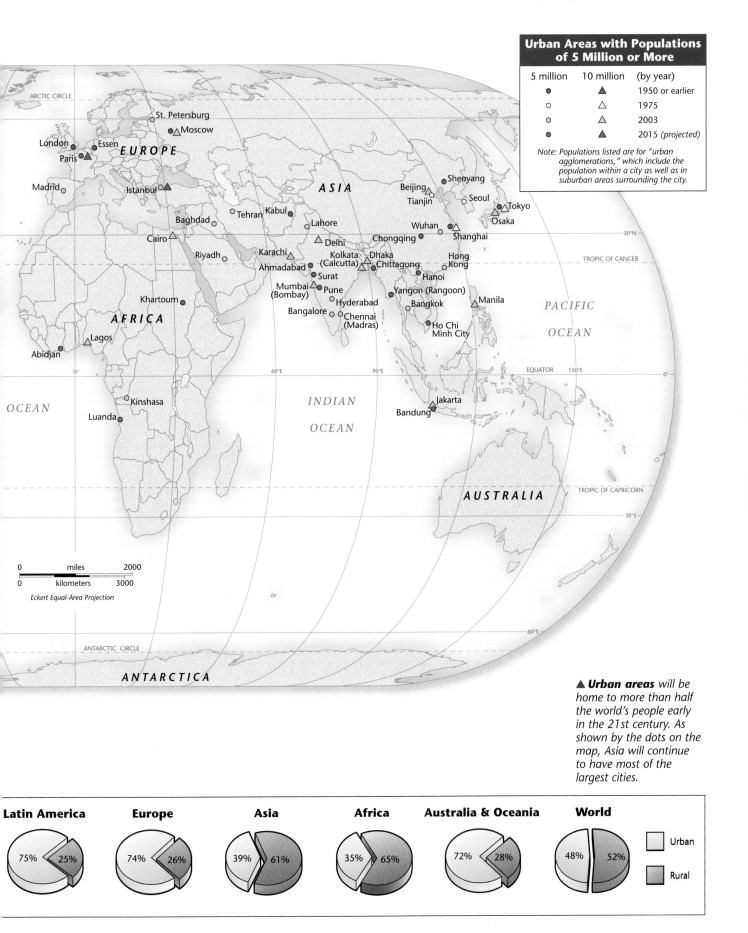

Urban Areas with Populations of 5 Million or More

5 million	10 million	(by year)
●	▲	1950 or earlier
○	△	1975
○	△	2003
●	▲	2015 (projected)

Note: Populations listed are for "urban agglomerations," which include the population within a city as well as in suburban areas surrounding the city.

ARCTIC CIRCLE

St. Petersburg
Moscow
London   Essen   EUROPE
Paris
Madrid   Istanbul   ASIA
Baghdad   Tehran   Kabul   Shenyang
Beijing
Tianjin   Seoul
Cairo   Riyadh   Wuhan   Tokyo
Karachi   Lahore   Chongqing   Osaka
Ahmadabad   Delhi   Shanghai   30°N
Kolkata   Dhaka   TROPIC OF CANCER
(Calcutta)   Chittagong   Hong
Surat   Kong
Mumbai   Pune   Hanoi
(Bombay)   Hyderabad   Yangon (Rangoon)
Khartoum   Bangalore   Chennai   Bangkok   Manila
(Madras)   Ho Chi   PACIFIC
Minh City
AFRICA   OCEAN
Lagos
Abidjan   0°

OCEAN   INDIAN   60°E   90°E   EQUATOR   150°E   0°
Kinshasa   Jakarta
Luanda   OCEAN   Bandung

AUSTRALIA   TROPIC OF CAPRICORN

30°S

| 0 | miles | 2000 |
| 0 | kilometers | 3000 |

Eckert Equal-Area Projection

60°S

ANTARCTIC CIRCLE

ANTARCTICA

▲ **Urban areas** *will be home to more than half the world's people early in the 21st century. As shown by the dots on the map, Asia will continue to have most of the largest cities.*

Latin America	Europe	Asia	Africa	Australia & Oceania	World	
75% / 25%	74% / 26%	39% / 61%	35% / 65%	72% / 28%	48% / 52%	Urban / Rural

WORLD LANGUAGES

Culture is all the shared traits that make different groups of people around the world unique. For example, customs and symbols, food and clothing preferences, housing styles and ways of making a living, and music and art forms are all a part of each group's culture.

Language is one of the most defining characteristics of culture. Language reflects what people value and the way they understand the world. It also reveals how certain groups of people may have common roots at some point in history. For example, English and German are two very different languages, but both are part of the same Indo-European language family. This means that these two languages share certain characteristics that suggest they have evolved from a common ancestor language. Other languages, such as Hungarian, are completely different and seem to be related to almost no other languages.

Patterns on the world language families map (right) also offer clues to the diffusion, or movement, of groups of people. For example, the large area in Africa where Niger-Congo languages are spoken can be explained by the migration of the Bantu people from north-central Africa all the way into southern Africa, beginning around 100 BC. The widespread use of English, extending from the United States to India, reflects the far-reaching effects of British colonial empires. Today, English has become the major language of the Internet.

About 6,000 languages are spoken in the world, but experts think many may become extinct as more people become involved in global trade, communications, and travel.

Web Link

Major Language Families Today

- Afro-Asiatic
- Altaic
- Austro-Asiatic
- Austronesian
- Dravidian
- Indo-European
- Japanese/Korean
- Kam-Tai
- Niger-Congo
- Nilo-Saharan
- Sino-Tibetan
- Uralic
- Other

▼ **The Golden Arches icon** would help you identify this restaurant in Moscow even if you didn't know how to read the Cyrillic alphabet of the Russian language.

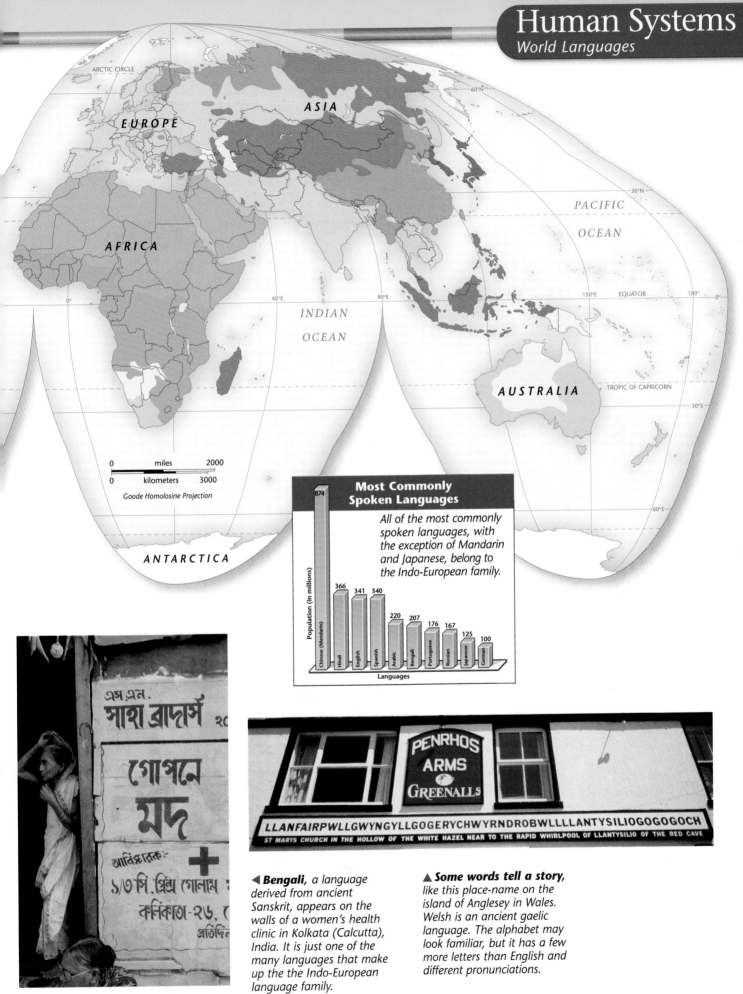

ARCTIC CIRCLE

EUROPE

ASIA

60°N

PACIFIC

OCEAN

30°N

AFRICA

0°   60°E   90°E   150°E   EQUATOR   180°   0°

INDIAN

OCEAN

AUSTRALIA

TROPIC OF CAPRICORN   30°S

| 0 | miles | 2000 |
| 0 | kilometers | 3000 |

Goode Homolosine Projection

ANTARCTICA

60°S

Most Commonly Spoken Languages

All of the most commonly spoken languages, with the exception of Mandarin and Japanese, belong to the Indo-European family.

Population (in millions)

Language	Population
Chinese (Mandarin)	874
Hindi	366
English	341
Spanish	340
Arabic	220
Bengali	207
Portuguese	176
Russian	167
Japanese	125
German	100

Languages

PENRHOS ARMS GREENALLS

LLANFAIRPWLLGWYNGYLLGOGERYCHWYRNDROBWLLLLANTYSILIOGOGOGOCH
ST MARYS CHURCH IN THE HOLLOW OF THE WHITE HAZEL NEAR TO THE RAPID WHIRLPOOL OF LLANTYSILIO OF THE RED CAVE

◄ **Bengali,** *a language derived from ancient Sanskrit, appears on the walls of a women's health clinic in Kolkata (Calcutta), India. It is just one of the many languages that make up the the Indo-European language family.*

▲ **Some words tell a story,** *like this place-name on the island of Anglesey in Wales. Welsh is an ancient gaelic language. The alphabet may look familiar, but it has a few more letters than English and different pronunciations.*

WORLD RELIGIONS

Religious beliefs, a central element of culture throughout the world, vary widely from place to place. Religious beliefs and practices help people deal with the unknown. But people in different places have developed a variety of belief systems.

Universalizing religions, such as Christianity, Islam, and Buddhism, actively seek converts. They have spread throughout the world from their origins in Asia. Other religions, including Judaism, Hinduism, and Shinto, tend to be associated with particular groups of people and are concentrated in certain places. These religions are called ethnic religions. Some groups, especially indigenous, or native, people living in the tropical forests of Africa and South America, believe that spirits inhabit all things in the natural world. Such belief systems are known as animistic religions.

Religion can play an important role in defining cultural identity. Places of worship are often a distinctive part of the cultural landscape. A cathedral, mosque, or temple can reveal much about the people who live in a particular place. Web Link

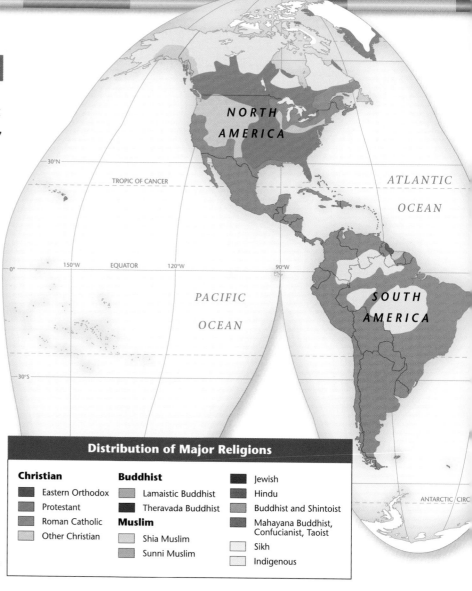

NORTH AMERICA

ATLANTIC OCEAN

30°N

TROPIC OF CANCER

150°W   EQUATOR   120°W   90°W

0°

PACIFIC OCEAN

SOUTH AMERICA

30°S

ANTARCTIC CIRC

Distribution of Major Religions

Christian
- Eastern Orthodox
- Protestant
- Roman Catholic
- Other Christian

Buddhist
- Lamaistic Buddhist
- Theravada Buddhist

Muslim
- Shia Muslim
- Sunni Muslim

- Jewish
- Hindu
- Buddhist and Shintoist
- Mahayana Buddhist, Confucianist, Taoist
- Sikh
- Indigenous

▲ **Most of Hinduism's** 900 million followers live in India and other countries of South Asia. The goddess Durga (above) is regarded as Mother of the Universe and protector of the righteous.

▼ **Jerusalem is holy** to Muslims, Christians, and Jews, a fact that has led to tension and conflict. Below, a Russian orthodox church is silhouetted against the Wailing Wall, while sunlight reflects off the Dome of the Rock mosque.

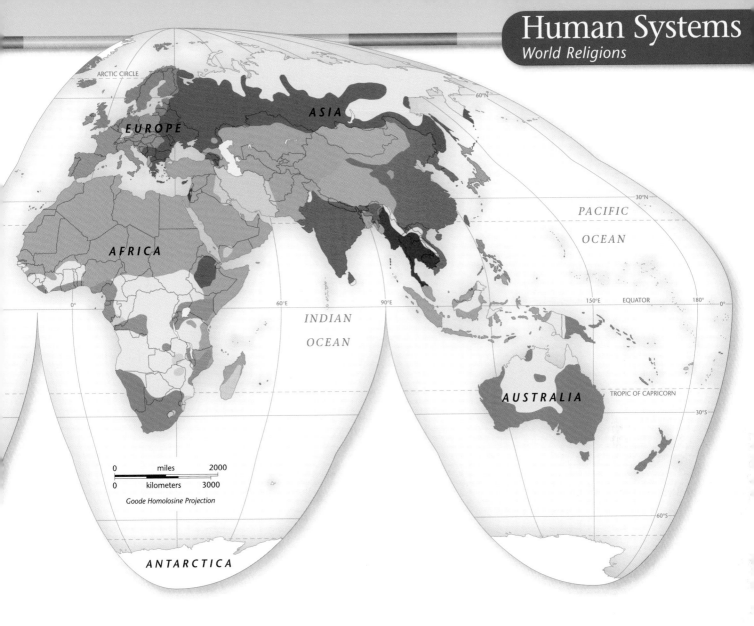

▲ **Muslim worshippers** surround the sacred Kaaba stone, which lies shrouded in black cloth at the center of the Grand Mosque in Mecca. Each year two million Muslims make a *hajj*, or pilgrimage, here to Islam's holiest shrine.

▼ **Statues of Buddha** and temples, such as these built in the 13th century at Wat Chang Hom in northern Thailand, create a unique cultural landscape in southeastern and eastern Asia where most of Buddhism's 350 million followers live.

PREDOMINANT WORLD ECONOMIES

Economic activities are the many different ways that people create products and generate income to meet their needs and wants. Long ago most people lived by hunting and gathering. Today, most engage in a variety of other activities that are commonly grouped into the following categories. Primary activities: agriculture, fishing, forestry; secondary activities: manufacturing and processing industries; tertiary activities: services, such as finance, medicine, education; and quaternary activities: information exchange and e-commerce—buying and selling over the Internet. The more developed economies of the world have shifted from secondary activities toward tertiary and quaternary activities. Less developed economies continue to rely on primary activities. Web Link

NORTH AMERICA
Toronto
New York
Los Angeles
TROPIC OF CANCER
México
ATLANTIC OCEAN
EQUATOR
PACIFIC OCEAN
SOUTH AMERICA
São Paulo
Buenos Aires
ANTARCTIC CIRCLE
30°N
150°W
120°W
90°W
0°
30°S
60°S

Predominant Economies

- • Selected population center
- Agriculture
- Agriculture and forestry
- Fishing
- Forestry (lumber and pulpwood)
- Hunting, fishing and forestry
- Subsistence agriculture
- Little or no economic activity
- Manufacturing
- Nomadic herding
- Stock raising on ranges

▲ **Subsistence Agriculture.** *Many people in developing countries, such as these farmers in Peru, use traditional methods to grow crops for their daily food requirements rather than for commercial sale.*

◀ **Logging.** *Workers ready logs to float down the Columbia River in Washington State. Processing plants will turn the logs into paper products or cut them into lumber for the construction industry.*

▶ **Fishing.** *Tuna is one of the chief commercial fishes as well as a favorite among big game fishermen. Japan is the world's leading harvester of tuna. Albacore, shown here, is one of the top commercial varieties.*

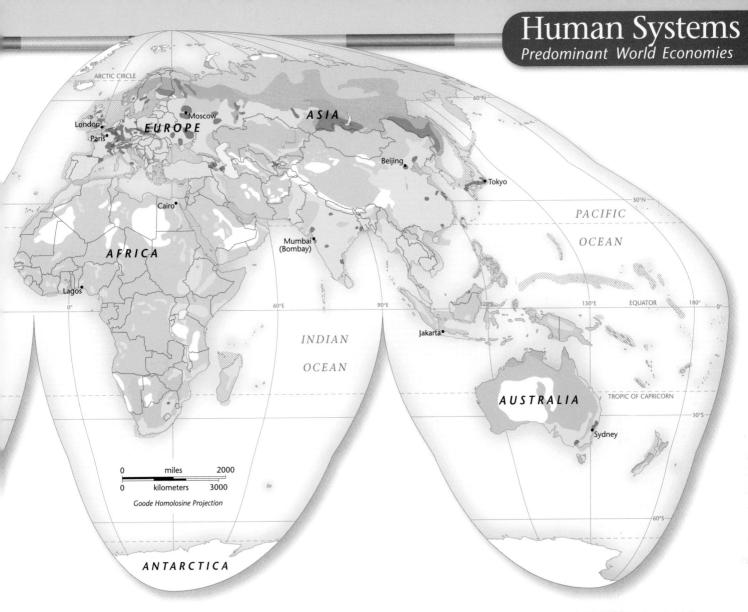

ARCTIC CIRCLE

60°N

EUROPE · Moscow
ASIA
London·
Paris·

Beijing·
·Tokyo

Cairo·
30°N

PACIFIC

Mumbai
(Bombay)·
OCEAN

AFRICA

60°E   90°E   120°E   150°E   EQUATOR   180°   0°
0°

Jakarta·
INDIAN

OCEAN

AUSTRALIA
TROPIC OF CAPRICORN

30°S

·Sydney

| 0 | miles | 2000 |
| 0 | kilometers | 3000 |

Goode Homolosine Projection

60°S

ANTARCTICA

▶ **Education and Communications.** *These services combine to allow students to interact with scientists working in the field. Here students explore the underwater ecology of California's Monterey Bay as part of renowned ocean explorer Robert Ballard's JASON Project.*

▲ **Manufacturing.** *This mill in Slovakia processes raw materials—coal and iron ore—to make steel, which in turn is used by other industries to produce cars, machinery, and other kinds of manufactured goods.*

▶ **The Internet.** *This has opened a whole new way of exchanging information. E-mail connects people in places near and far, while e-commerce allows them to buy and sell products without ever leaving home.*

WORLD FOOD

At the beginning of the 21st century, the world's population numbered 6.3 billion people—more than six billion hungry mouths to feed! Productive cropland, though, like other natural resources, is unevenly distributed. In addition, access to modern farming methods and technology varies from country to country. Some countries produce large surpluses while others struggle to feed their people. Grains such as rice, corn, and wheat provide 80 percent of the world's food energy supply. Web Link

NORTH AMERICA

30°N

TROPIC OF CANCER

ATLANTIC

OCEAN

150°W   EQUATOR   120°W   90°W

0°

PACIFIC

OCEAN

SOUTH AMERICA

30°S

Major Types of Grain

■ Corn
■ Wheat
■ Rice

60°S

ANTARCTIC CIRCLE

▲ *Rice* is an important staple food crop, especially in eastern and southern Asia. Although China produces about one-third of the world's rice, it is also a major importer of rice to feed its population of more than a billion people.

▶ *Corn* originated in the Americas but was carried by Europeans to Europe, Asia, and Africa. Corn is an important food grain for both people and livestock.

◀ *Wheat* is the world's leading export grain. It is a main ingredient in bread and pasta and is grown on every inhabited continent. Each year trade in this grain exceeds 100 million tons.

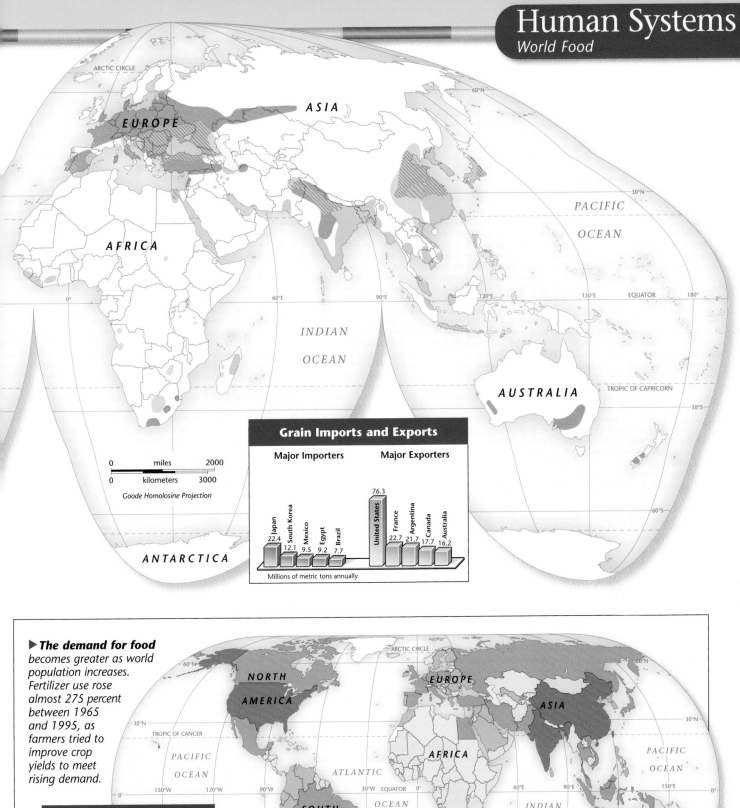

Grain Imports and Exports

Major Importers
- Japan 22.4
- South Korea 12.1
- Mexico 9.5
- Egypt 9.2
- Brazil 7.7

Major Exporters
- United States 76.3
- France 22.7
- Argentina 21.7
- Canada 17.7
- Australia 16.2

Millions of metric tons annually

0 miles 2000
0 kilometers 3000

Goode Homolosine Projection

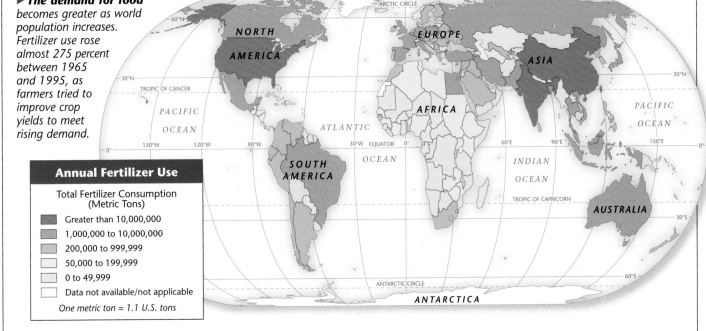

▶ **The demand for food** becomes greater as world population increases. Fertilizer use rose almost 275 percent between 1965 and 1995, as farmers tried to improve crop yields to meet rising demand.

Annual Fertilizer Use

Total Fertilizer Consumption
(Metric Tons)

- Greater than 10,000,000
- 1,000,000 to 10,000,000
- 200,000 to 999,999
- 50,000 to 199,999
- 0 to 49,999
- Data not available/not applicable

One metric ton = 1.1 U.S. tons

WORLD WATER

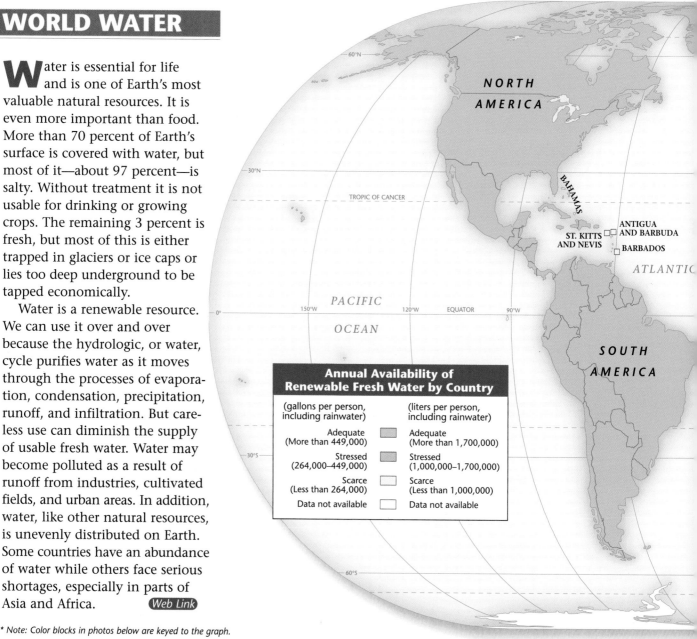

Water is essential for life and is one of Earth's most valuable natural resources. It is even more important than food. More than 70 percent of Earth's surface is covered with water, but most of it—about 97 percent—is salty. Without treatment it is not usable for drinking or growing crops. The remaining 3 percent is fresh, but most of this is either trapped in glaciers or ice caps or lies too deep underground to be tapped economically.

Water is a renewable resource. We can use it over and over because the hydrologic, or water, cycle purifies water as it moves through the processes of evaporation, condensation, precipitation, runoff, and infiltration. But careless use can diminish the supply of usable fresh water. Water may become polluted as a result of runoff from industries, cultivated fields, and urban areas. In addition, water, like other natural resources, is unevenly distributed on Earth. Some countries have an abundance of water while others face serious shortages, especially in parts of Asia and Africa. *(Web Link)*

* *Note: Color blocks in photos below are keyed to the graph.*

NORTH AMERICA

60°N

30°N

TROPIC OF CANCER

BAHAMAS

ST. KITTS AND NEVIS

ANTIGUA AND BARBUDA

BARBADOS

ATLANTIC

PACIFIC OCEAN

150°W   120°W   EQUATOR   90°W

0°

SOUTH AMERICA

30°S

60°S

Annual Availability of Renewable Fresh Water by Country

(gallons per person, including rainwater)		(liters per person, including rainwater)	
Adequate (More than 449,000)		Adequate (More than 1,700,000)	
Stressed (264,000–449,000)		Stressed (1,000,000–1,700,000)	
Scarce (Less than 264,000)		Scarce (Less than 1,000,000)	
Data not available		Data not available	

▲ **Domestic Water Use.** *In much of the less developed world, people haul water daily for household use, as in this village in Central America.*

▲ **Agricultural Water Use.** *Irrigation has made agriculture possible in dry areas such as the San Pedro Valley in Arizona, shown here.*

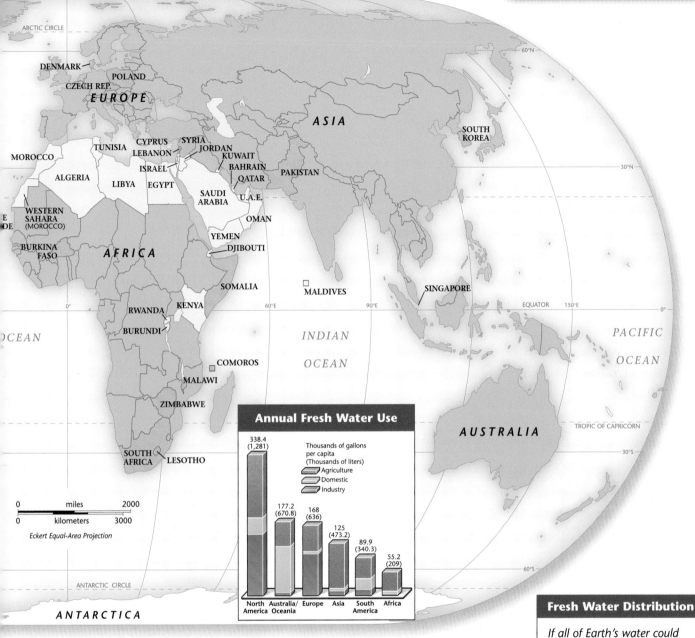

Annual Fresh Water Use

Thousands of gallons per capita
(Thousands of liters)

- Agriculture
- Domestic
- Industry

North America	338.4 (1,281)
Australia/Oceania	177.2 (670.8)
Europe	168 (636)
Asia	125 (473.2)
South America	89.9 (340.3)
Africa	55.2 (209)

0 miles 2000
0 kilometers 3000

Eckert Equal-Area Projection

Fresh Water Distribution

If all of Earth's water could fit into a gallon (4.5 liter) jug, only slightly more than a tablespoon of it would be available fresh water. This graph shows the sources of Earth's fresh water.

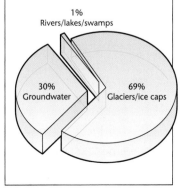

1%
Rivers/lakes/swamps

30%
Groundwater

69%
Glaciers/ice caps

▲ **Industrial Water Use.** Hydroelectric projects, such as this dam in Tucuruí, Brazil, harness running water to generate electricity that powers industry.

▲ **Water Stress.** By using groundwater faster than it is renewed, agriculture in dry areas puts stress on limited water supplies.

41

WORLD ENERGY & MINERAL RESOURCES

Beginning in the 19th century, as the Industrial Revolution spread across Europe and around the world, the demand for energy and mineral resources skyrocketed. Fossil fuels—first coal, then oil— provided the energy that kept the wheels of industry turning. Minerals such as iron ore (essential for the production of steel) and copper (used for electrical wiring) became increasingly important.

Energy and minerals, like all nonrenewable resources, are in limited supply and are unevenly distributed. Countries with major deposits play an important role in the global economy. For example, the Organization of Petroleum Exporting Countries (OPEC) influences the world supply of oil and, therefore, fuel prices.

Web Link

Major fossil fuel deposits

- Coal
- Natural gas
- Oil
- OPEC member

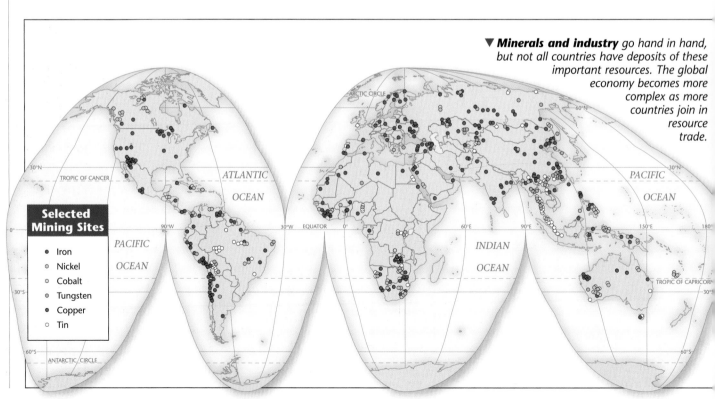

▼ *Minerals and industry* go hand in hand, but not all countries have deposits of these important resources. The global economy becomes more complex as more countries join in resource trade.

Selected Mining Sites

- Iron
- Nickel
- Cobalt
- Tungsten
- Copper
- Tin

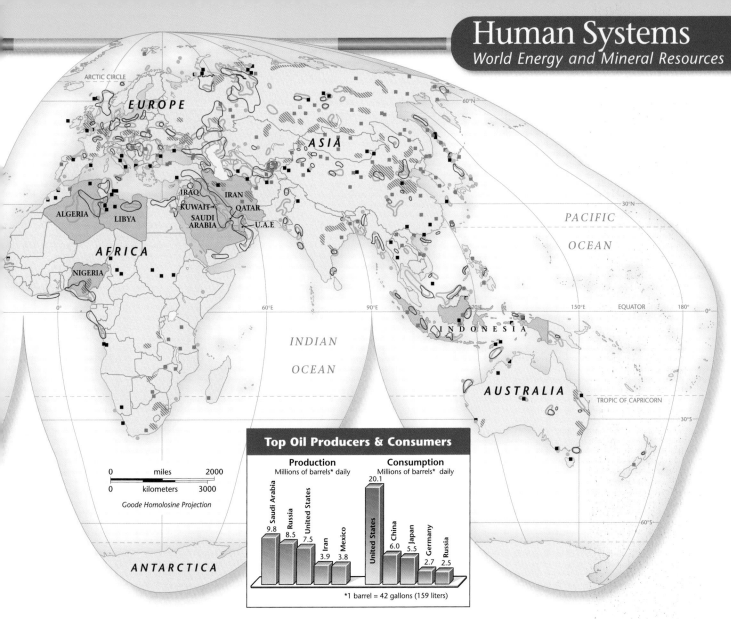

ARCTIC CIRCLE

EUROPE

ASIA

60°N

ALGERIA LIBYA IRAQ IRAN
KUWAIT QATAR
SAUDI ARABIA U.A.E

PACIFIC

OCEAN

30°N

AFRICA

NIGERIA

0° 60°E 90°E 150°E EQUATOR 180°

INDONESIA

INDIAN

OCEAN

AUSTRALIA

TROPIC OF CAPRICORN

30°S

| 0 | miles | 2000 |
| 0 | kilometers | 3000 |

Goode Homolosine Projection

ANTARCTICA

60°S

Top Oil Producers & Consumers

Production
Millions of barrels* daily

Saudi Arabia	Russia	United States	Iran	Mexico
9.8	8.5	7.5	3.9	3.8

Consumption
Millions of barrels* daily

United States	China	Japan	Germany	Russia
20.1	6.0	5.5	2.7	2.5

*1 barrel = 42 gallons (159 liters)

▶ **Reactors** *near Sacramento, California, produce nuclear energy, and solar panels (foreground) capture energy from the sun. These two sources of energy are important alternatives to nonrenewable fossil fuels.*

▲ **A wind energy farm** *near Tehachapi, California, uses windmills to capture the energy of winds blowing off the Pacific Ocean.*

◀ **A geothermal power plant,** *fueled by heat from deep within Earth, produces energy to heat homes in Iceland. Runoff creates a warm pool for bathers.*

▼ **Dependence on oil** *for motor vehicles, industries, and domestic power and heating makes the United States the world's leading consumer of this energy resource.*

43

WORLD CONFLICTS

The world map reveals a complex mosaic of people and cultures. Sometimes these differences can be a source of conflict. For example, when two groups claim the same territory, conflict may result. Or, when major cultural differences such as religion overlap, previously peaceful people may turn to violence. Political differences, opposing value systems, or competition for resources can also create tensions that hold the potential for conflict.

Some conflicts are relatively short-lived, while others last years. For example, when the communist governments of Eastern Europe collapsed, the country of Yugoslavia broke into several new countries. Conflict in Slovenia, which is culturally homogeneous, did not last very long. But Bosnia and Herzegovina faced years of civil war, as groups with different languages, religions, and traditions struggled for control. In the Middle East, territorial disputes between Muslim Palestinians and Jewish Israelis have been a source of turmoil for more than 50 years. And in eastern Asia, ethnic minorities in Myanmar, Indonesia, and the Philippines frequently protest domination by the majority group.

In September 2001, conflict came to the previously safe shores of the United States. In a protest against the global power of the United States, members of a terrorist network known as al Qaeda launched attacks against American symbols of political and economic power. This group and other terrorist cells have also directed attacks in other parts of the world. These actions have resulted in a so-called war on terror, led by the United States. Web Link

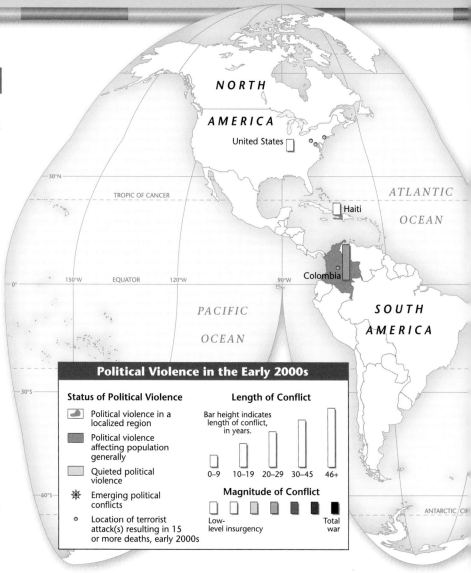

NORTH

AMERICA

United States

ATLANTIC

OCEAN

Haiti

Colombia

PACIFIC

OCEAN

SOUTH

AMERICA

TROPIC OF CANCER

EQUATOR

ANTARCTIC CIR

Political Violence in the Early 2000s

Status of Political Violence

- Political violence in a localized region
- Political violence affecting population generally
- Quieted political violence
- Emerging political conflicts
- Location of terrorist attack(s) resulting in 15 or more deaths, early 2000s

Length of Conflict

Bar height indicates length of conflict, in years.

0–9 10–19 20–29 30–45 46+

Magnitude of Conflict

Low-level insurgency   Total war

▲ *On September 11, 2001,* terrorists used commercial airliners as weapons to attack symbols of U.S. wealth and power in New York City (above) and Washington, D.C.

▼ *Israel is building a wall* (below) between itself and t Palestinian West Bank partly as a defense against terrorist attacks. Both Israelis and Palestinians claim the region as homeland, resulting in ongoing territorial disputes.

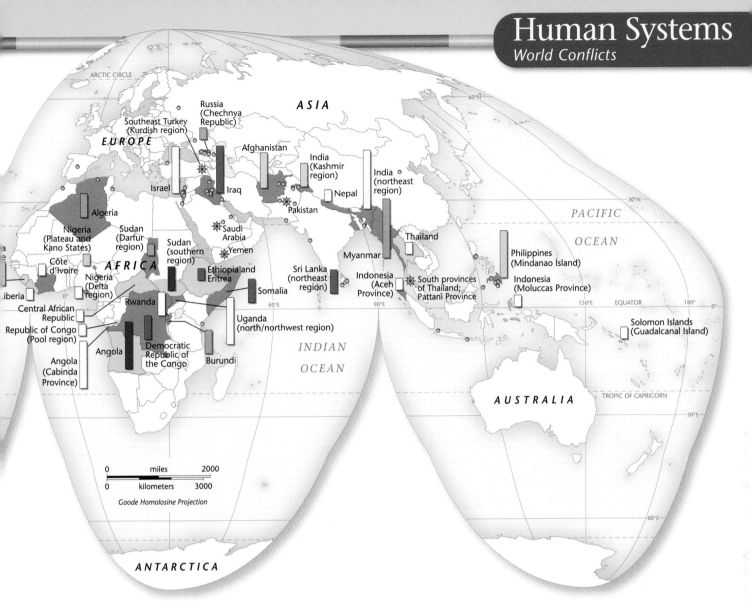

ARCTIC CIRCLE

ASIA

EUROPE

Russia
(Chechnya
Republic)

Southeast Turkey
(Kurdish region)

Afghanistan

India
(Kashmir
region)

India
(northeast
region)

PACIFIC
OCEAN

Israel

Iraq

Nepal

Algeria

Pakistan

Nigeria
(Plateau and
Kano States)

Sudan
(Darfur
region)

Saudi
Arabia

Thailand

Philippines
(Mindanao Island)

Côte
d'Ivoire

AFRICA

Sudan
(southern
region)

Yemen

Sri Lanka
(northeast
region)

Myanmar

Indonesia
(Aceh
Province)

South provinces
of Thailand;
Pattani Province

Indonesia
(Moluccas Province)

iberia

Nigeria
(Delta
region)

Ethiopia and
Eritrea

EQUATOR

Central African
Republic

Rwanda

Somalia

Republic of Congo
(Pool region)

Uganda
(north/northwest region)

INDIAN
OCEAN

Solomon Islands
(Guadalcanal Island)

Angola

Democratic
Republic of
the Congo

Burundi

Angola
(Cabinda
Province)

AUSTRALIA

TROPIC OF CAPRICORN

| 0 | miles | 2000 |
| 0 | kilometers | 3000 |

Goode Homolosine Projection

ANTARCTICA

▲ **The Territory of Jammu and Kashmir** has been a focus of
tension and conflict between predominantly Hindu India and
Muslim Pakistan ever since the partition of British India in 1947.
Here, crowds protest a 2004 election in the city of Srinagar, India.

▼ **Open fighting in Chechnya**, a largely
Muslim region in Russia, broke out in 1994
when it attempted to declare independence.
The war, which led to claims of human rights
abuses by the Russian Army and Chechnyan
fighters, destroyed Groznya, the capital city,
and left the economy in ruins.

WORLD REFUGEES

Every day, people relocate to new cities, new states, or even to new countries. Most move by choice, but some people, called refugees, move to escape war and persecution that make it impossible to remain where they are. Refugees have no choice but to flee to find safety. Such forced movement creates severe hardship especially for families who may have to leave behind all their possessions. They may find themselves in a strange new place where they do not speak the local language, where customs are unfamiliar, and where basic necessities, such as food, water, shelter, sanitation, and medical care, are in short supply.

A specialized agency of the United Nations, the Office of the High Commissioner for Refugees (UNHCR), is responsible for the safety and well-being of refugees worldwide and for ensuring the protection of and respect for their rights. UNHCR works to find solutions to refugee situations through voluntary return to home countries, integration in a host country, or resettlement to another country.

Web Link

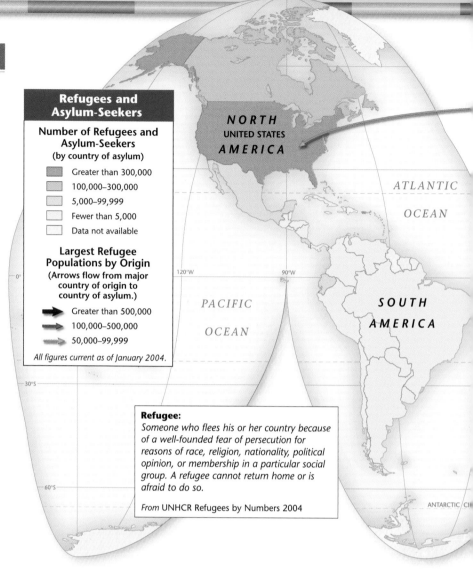

Refugees and Asylum-Seekers

Number of Refugees and Asylum-Seekers
(by country of asylum)

- Greater than 300,000
- 100,000–300,000
- 5,000–99,999
- Fewer than 5,000
- Data not available

Largest Refugee Populations by Origin
(Arrows flow from major country of origin to country of asylum.)

- Greater than 500,000
- 100,000–500,000
- 50,000–99,999

All figures current as of January 2004.

Refugee:
Someone who flees his or her country because of a well-founded fear of persecution for reasons of race, religion, nationality, political opinion, or membership in a particular social group. A refugee cannot return home or is afraid to do so.

From UNHCR Refugees by Numbers 2004

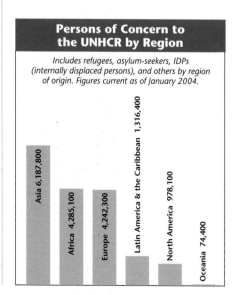

Persons of Concern to the UNHCR by Region

Includes refugees, asylum-seekers, IDPs (internally displaced persons), and others by region of origin. Figures current as of January 2004.

- Asia 6,187,800
- Africa 4,285,100
- Europe 4,242,300
- Latin America & the Caribbean 1,316,400
- North America 978,100
- Oceania 74,400

▲ **Many Kurds,** *a people who live mainly in Iraq and Turkey, fled to the remote mountains of northern Iraq to escape spreading hostilities. This region, referred to as Kurdistan, is the traditional homeland of these stateless people.*

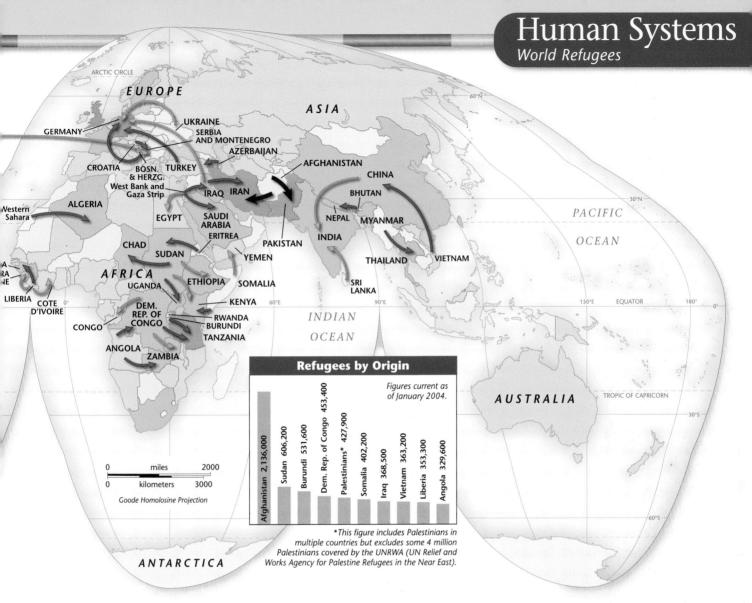

ARCTIC CIRCLE

EUROPE

ASIA

GERMANY
UKRAINE
SERBIA
AND MONTENEGRO
AZERBAIJAN
CROATIA
BOSN.
& HERZG.
TURKEY
West Bank and
Gaza Strip
IRAQ
IRAN
AFGHANISTAN
CHINA
BHUTAN
NEPAL
MYANMAR
Western
Sahara
ALGERIA
EGYPT
SAUDI
ARABIA
ERITREA
PAKISTAN
INDIA
CHAD
SUDAN
YEMEN
THAILAND
VIETNAM
A
RA
NE
AFRICA
UGANDA
ETHIOPIA
SOMALIA
SRI
LANKA
LIBERIA
COTE
D'IVOIRE
KENYA
CONGO
DEM.
REP. OF
CONGO
RWANDA
BURUNDI
TANZANIA
ANGOLA
ZAMBIA

PACIFIC

OCEAN

INDIAN

OCEAN

AUSTRALIA

TROPIC OF CAPRICORN

ANTARCTICA

EQUATOR

0	miles	2000
0	kilometers	3000

Goode Homolosine Projection

Refugees by Origin

Figures current as of January 2004.

- Afghanistan 2,136,000
- Sudan 606,200
- Burundi 531,600
- Dem. Rep. of Congo 453,400
- Palestinians* 427,900
- Somalia 402,200
- Iraq 368,500
- Vietnam 363,200
- Liberia 353,300
- Angola 329,600

*This figure includes Palestinians in multiple countries but excludes some 4 million Palestinians covered by the UNRWA (UN Relief and Works Agency for Palestine Refugees in the Near East).

▲ **Afghan women** *in traditional robes, called burkas, climb on colorful buses for the trip home from refugee camps in Pakistan.*

▲ **Thousands of Sudanese** *refugees have been forced to leave their homes. Some, called internally displaced persons, or IDPs (above), remain in camps within Sudan. Others are refugees who have crossed into Chad to escape rebel forces attacking their villages.*

GLOBALIZATION

The close of the 20th century saw a technology revolution that changed the way people and countries of the world relate to each other. This revolution in technology is an important part of a process known as globalization.

Globalization refers to the complex network of interconnections that link people, companies, and places together without regard for national boundaries. Although it began as early as the 19th century, when countries became increasingly active in international trade, the process of globalization has gained momentum in recent years, affecting many different aspects of daily life.

Because of improvements in communications and transportation, many companies now employ workers in distant countries. Some workers make clothing; some perform accounting tasks; and others work in call centers answering inquiries about product services. Communications improvements also allow banking transactions to take place faster and over greater distances than ever before. Companies that have offices and conduct business in multiple countries around the world are called transnational companies.

One important aspect of today's global communications system is the Internet, a vast system of computer networks that enables people to access information and to communicate around the world in just seconds. Today there are more than 600 million Internet users worldwide, most in North America and Europe. Ideas and images travel over the Internet to distant places, introducing change and making places more and more alike. ⟨Web Link⟩

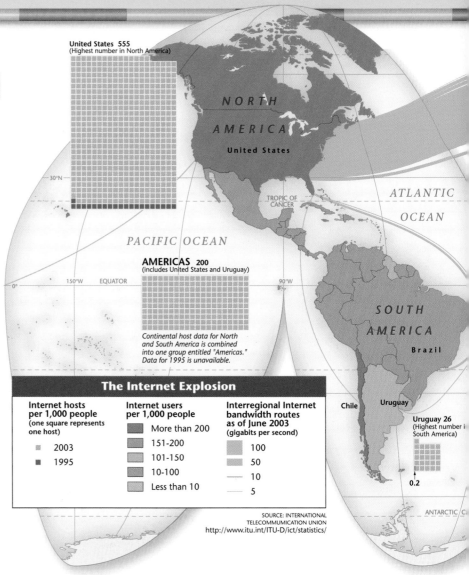

United States 555
(Highest number in North America)

NORTH AMERICA
United States

AMERICAS 200
(includes United States and Uruguay)

Continental host data for North and South America is combined into one group entitled "Americas." Data for 1995 is unavailable.

ATLANTIC OCEAN

PACIFIC OCEAN

SOUTH AMERICA
Brazil

Chile   Uruguay

Uruguay 26
(Highest number in South America)

0.2

ANTARCTIC C

The Internet Explosion

Internet hosts per 1,000 people (one square represents one host)
- 2003
- 1995

Internet users per 1,000 people
- More than 200
- 151-200
- 101-150
- 10-100
- Less than 10

Interregional Internet bandwidth routes as of June 2003 (gigabits per second)
- 100
- 50
- 10
- 5

SOURCE: INTERNATIONAL TELECOMMUMICATION UNION
http://www.itu.int/ITU-D/ict/statistics/

▼ **Maquiladoras,** assembly plants concentrated mainly near the U.S.-Mexico border, rely on low-cost labor to produce finished goods for consumers in the U.S. and around the world. These women in Ciudad Juarez work on audio speakers for export.

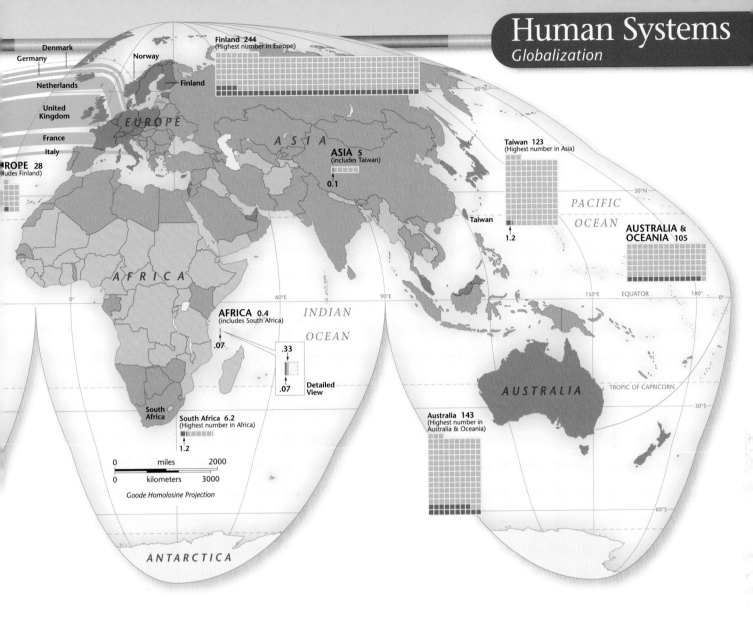

Denmark
Germany
Norway
Netherlands
Finland
United Kingdom
France
Italy

EUROPE
ASIA

Finland 244
(Highest number in Europe)

ROPE 28
(ludes Finland)

ASIA 5
(includes Taiwan)
0.1

Taiwan 123
(Highest number in Asia)

PACIFIC OCEAN

Taiwan
1.2

AUSTRALIA & OCEANIA 105

AFRICA

60°E   90°E

INDIAN OCEAN

AFRICA 0.4
(includes South Africa)
.07

.33
.07
Detailed View

EQUATOR   150°E   180°

AUSTRALIA

TROPIC OF CAPRICORN

South Africa

South Africa 6.2
(Highest number in Africa)
1.2

Australia 143
(Highest number in Australia & Oceania)

0   miles   2000
0   kilometers   3000

Goode Homolosine Projection

ANTARCTICA

▲ **Blending popular and traditional culture,** these young Chinese women share a cell phone while enjoying a cup of tea. Almost 300 million cell phones are used in China, linking people and places for both leisure and work.

Global Cell Phone Usage

The availability of cell phones is one example of the technology divide between more and less developed regions of the world. Being "connected" is essential to participation in the global system that links people and places.

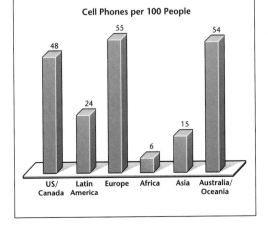

Cell Phones per 100 People

US/Canada	Latin America	Europe	Africa	Asia	Australia/Oceania
48	24	55	6	15	54

CULTURAL DIFFUSION

In the past, when groups of people lived in relative isolation, cultures were quite distinct and varied widely from place to place. Customs, styles, and preferences were handed down from one generation to the next without much change. Such cultures are known as folk cultures.

Today, thanks to high-speed communication, trade, and travel, cultures all around the world encounter and adopt new ideas. This pattern of diffusion introduces new customs, clothing and music trends, food habits, and lifestyles into cultures everywhere at almost the same time. Some people are concerned that this fast-changing trend in popular culture may result in a loss of cultural distinctiveness that makes places unique. For example, fast food chains once found only in the United States can now be seen in major cities around the world. And denim jeans, once a distinctively American clothing style, are worn by young people everywhere in place of more traditional clothing.

An important key to the spread of popular culture is the increasing contact between people and places around the world. Cellular telephones have become popular, not just in the United States and Europe, but also in developing countries where traditional telephone lines are not widely available. Satellite television and cybercafes have helped open the world to styles and trends popular in western countries. And tourists, traveling to places that were once remote and isolated, carry with them new ideas and fashions that are catalysts for bringing about cultural change.

Web Link

International Tourism

International tourist arrivals (in thousands per year)

- More than 40,000
- 4,001–40,000
- 401–4,000
- 100–400
- Less than 100
- No data

▼ **The influence of immigrant cultures** on the American landscape is evident in ethnic communities such as Chinatown in the heart of New York City.

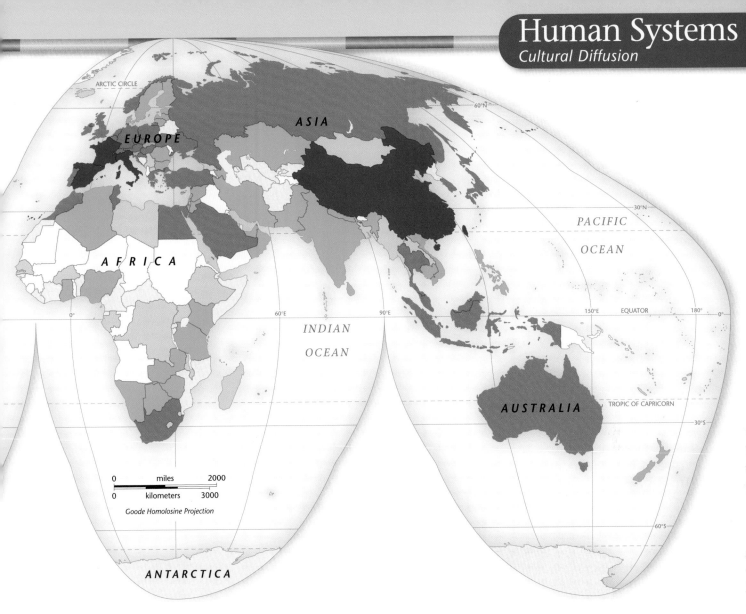

▼ **Women in dark robes** stroll through a mall in Manama, Bahrain. Stores and movie theaters introduce Western fashions and ideas that are in sharp contrast to those of traditional Arab culture.

▲ **Taking a break** from a traditional ceremony, a Maasai warrior in Kenya enjoys a soft drink that was once uniquely American.

TIME ZONES

The *Fiji Times,* a newspaper published in Suva, capital of the Fiji Islands, carries the message "The First Newspaper Published in the World Today" on the front page of each edition. How can this newspaper from a small island country make such a claim? Fiji lies west of the date line, an invisible boundary designated to mark the beginning of each new day. The date line is just part of the system we have adopted to keep track of the passage of days.

For most of human history, people determined time by observing the position of the sun in the sky. Slight differences in time did not matter until, in the mid-19th century, the spread of railroads and telegraph lines changed forever the importance of time. High-speed transportation and communications required schedules, and schedules required that everyone agree on the time.

In 1884, an international conference, convened in Washington, D.C., established an international system of 24 time zones based on the fact that Earth turns from west to east 15 degrees of longitude every hour. Each time zone has a central meridian and is 15 degrees wide, $7\frac{1}{2}$ degrees to either side of the named central meridian.   (Web Link)

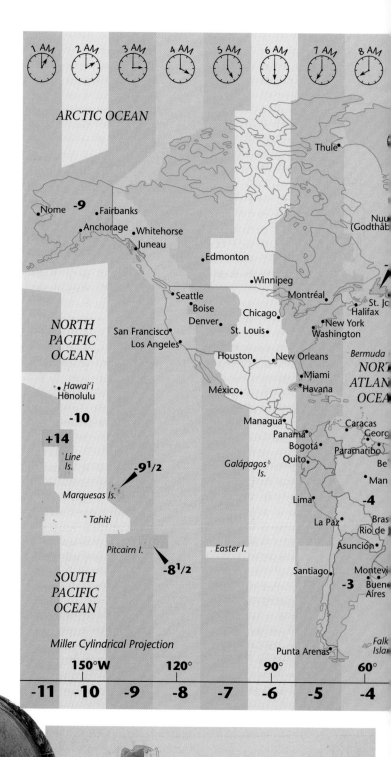

▶ **The prime meridian's** *path is lit up by light bulbs strung across Greenwich Park just north of the Royal Observatory, in England. The photographer used a special lens called a fish-eye to make the park resemble a globe. Of course, on the real Earth, meridians and parallels (lines of longitude and latitude) are imaginary and cannot be seen.*

▲ **A system of standard time** *put trains on schedules, which helped reduce the chance of collisions and the loss of lives and property caused by them.*

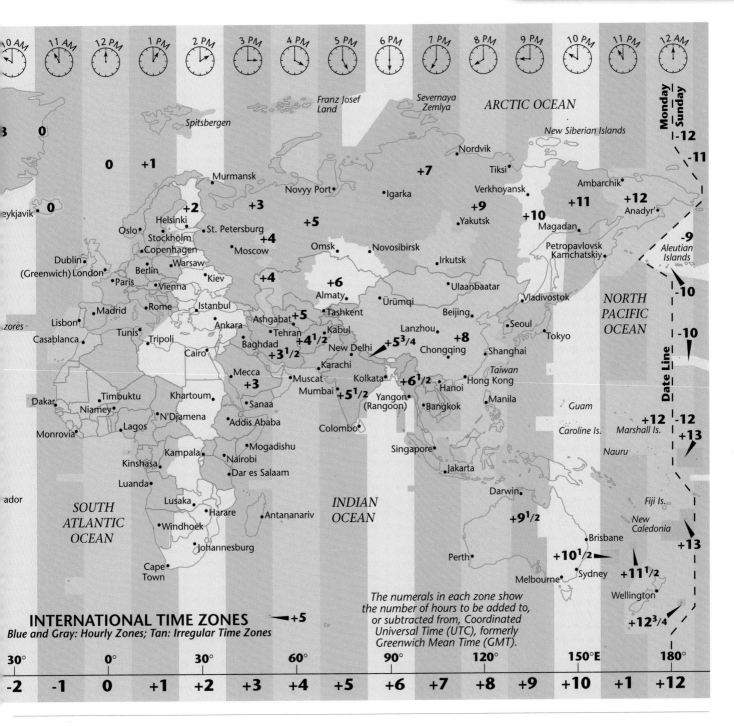

10 AM | 11 AM | 12 PM | 1 PM | 2 PM | 3 PM | 4 PM | 5 PM | 6 PM | 7 PM | 8 PM | 9 PM | 10 PM | 11 PM | 12 AM

Spitsbergen
Franz Josef Land
Severnaya Zemlya
ARCTIC OCEAN
New Siberian Islands

Monday / Sunday
-12
-11

3   0   +1
0   +1
•Murmansk   +7   •Nordvik   •Tiksi   •Ambarchik   +12   Anadyr•
-eykjavik   0   Novyy Port•   •Igarka   +9   •Verkhoyansk   +11   -9
+2   +3   +5   •Yakutsk   +10   •Magadan,   *Aleutian Islands*
Helsinki   Oslo•   •St. Petersburg   +4   •Omsk   •Novosibirsk   Petropavlovsk Kamchatskiy•   -10
Stockholm   •Moscow
•Copenhagen   Warsaw•   •Kiev   +4   +6   •Irkutsk   •Ulaanbaatar   •Vladivostok   **NORTH PACIFIC OCEAN**
Dublin•   Berlin•
(Greenwich) London•   •Vienna   Almaty•   •Ürümqi   Beijing•   •Seoul   -10
•Paris   Rome•   Istanbul•   Tashkent•   Lanzhou•   +8   Tokyo•
•Madrid   •Kiev   Ashgabat•   +5   •Shanghai   Date Line
-zores   Lisbon•   Ankara•   •Tehran   Kabul•   +5¾   •Chongqing
Casablanca•   Tunis•   Tripoli•   Baghdad•   +4½   New Delhi•   *Taiwan*   -10
•Cairo   +3½   •Karachi   Kolkata•   +6½   •Hong Kong
Mecca•   +3   Mumbai•   +5½   Yangon   •Hanoi   •Manila
Dakar•   Khartoum•   (Rangoon)   •Bangkok   *Guam*   +12   -12
•Timbuktu   •Sanaa   Colombo•   *Caroline Is.*   *Marshall Is.*   +13
Niamey•   •N'Djamena   •Addis Ababa   *Nauru*
Monrovia•   •Lagos   Singapore•
Kampala•   •Mogadishu   •Jakarta   •Darwin   *Fiji Is.*
Kinshasa•   •Nairobi   +9½   *New Caledonia*
Luanda•   •Dar es Salaam   **INDIAN OCEAN**   +13
-ador   **SOUTH ATLANTIC OCEAN**   Lusaka•   Harare•   •Antananariv   •Brisbane
•Windhoek   Perth•   +10½   •Sydney   +11½
Cape Town•   •Johannesburg   Melbourne•   Wellington•
+12¾

INTERNATIONAL TIME ZONES
Blue and Gray: Hourly Zones; Tan: Irregular Time Zones →+5

The numerals in each zone show the number of hours to be added to, or subtracted from, Coordinated Universal Time (UTC), formerly Greenwich Mean Time (GMT).

30°	0°	30°	60°	90°	120°	150°E	180°
-2	-1	0	+1	+2	+3	+4	+5	+6	+7	+8	+9	+10	+1	+12

Date Line

The date line (180°) is directly opposite the prime meridian (0°). As Earth rotates, each new day officially begins as the 180° line passes 12 midnight. If you travel west across the date line, you advance one day; if you travel east across the date line, you fall back one day.

Notice on the map how the line zigs to the east as it passes through the South Pacific so that the islands of Fiji will not be split between two different days. Also notice that India is 5½ hours ahead of Coordinated Universal Time (formerly Greenwich Mean Time), and China has only one time zone, even though the country spans more than 60 degrees of longitude. These differences are the result of decisions made at the country level.

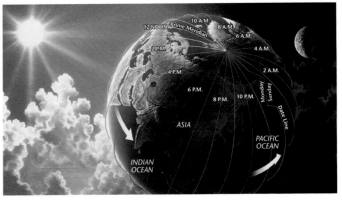

North America

Viewed from high above, North America stretches from the frozen expanses of the Arctic Ocean and Greenland to the lush green of Panama's tropical forests. Hudson Bay and the Great Lakes, fingerprints of long-departed glaciers, dominate the continent's east, while the brown landscapes of the west and southwest tell of dry lands where water is scarce.

Facts & Figures

▶ **Land area:** 9,449,500 sq mi (24,474,000 sq km)

▶ **Population:** 510,051,000

▶ **Highest point:** Mount McKinley (Denali), Alaska: 20,320 ft (6,194 m)

▶ **Lowest point:** Death Valley, California: 282 ft (86 m) below sea level

▶ **Longest river:** Mississippi-Missouri, United States: 3,710 mi (5,971 km)

▶ **Largest lake:** Lake Superior, U.S.-Canada: 31,701 sq mi (82,100 sq km)

▶ **Number of Independent countries:** 23

▶ **Largest country:** Canada: 3,855,101 sq mi (9,984,670 sq km)

▶ **Smallest country:** St. Kitts and Nevis: 104 sq mi (269 sq km)

▶ **Most populous country:** United States: Pop. 293,633,000

▶ **Least populous country:** St. Kitts and Nevis: Pop. 47,000

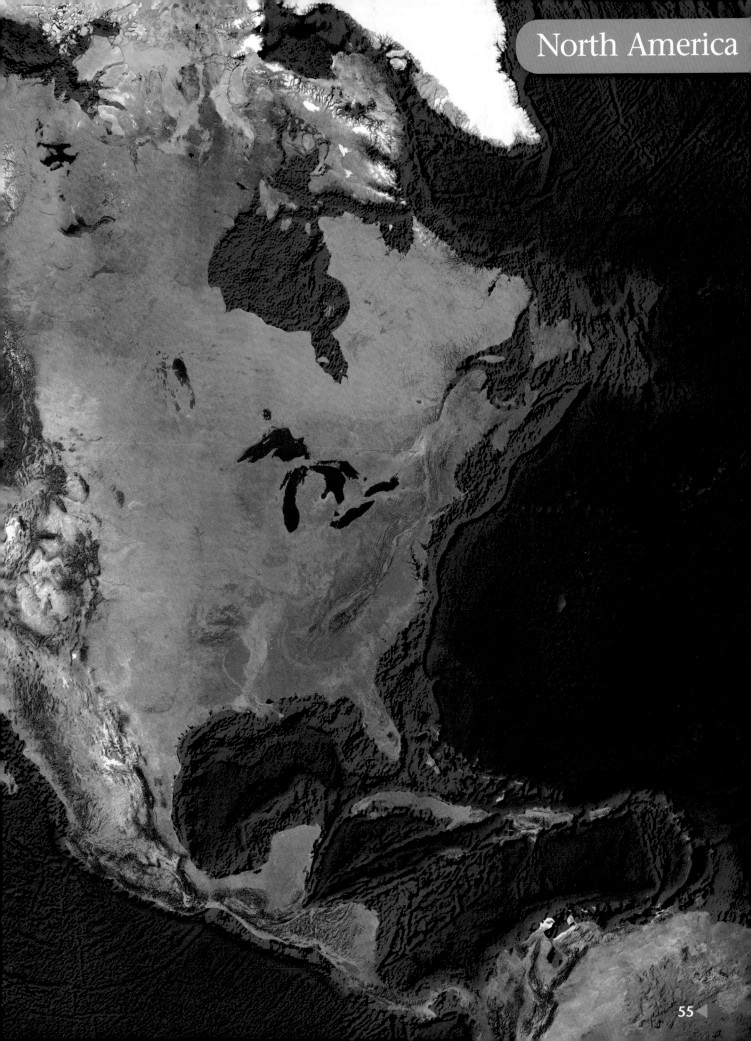

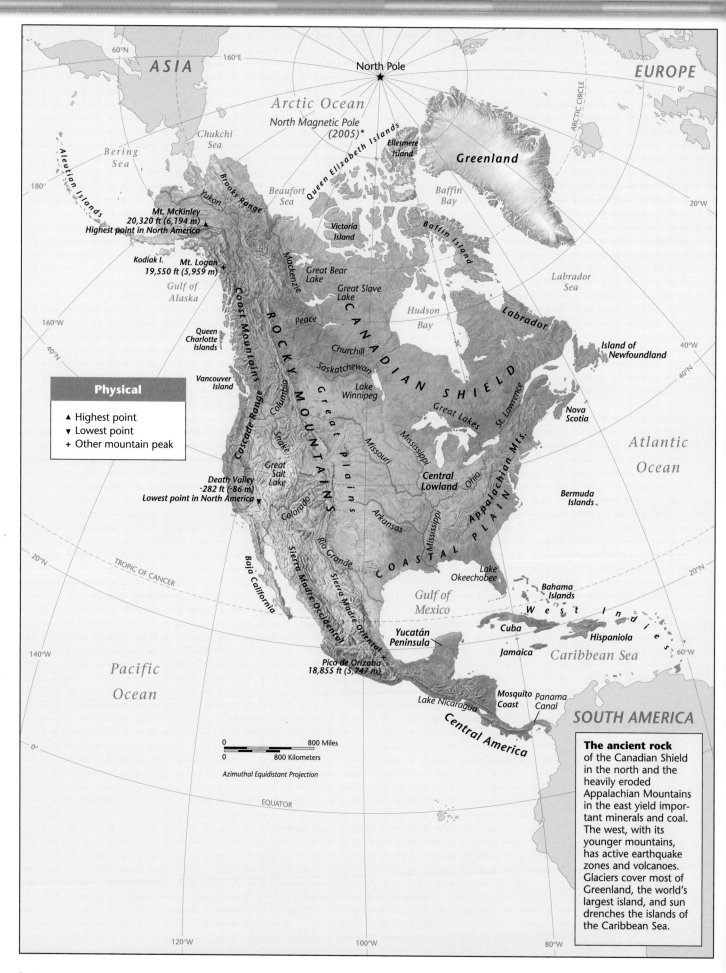

North America

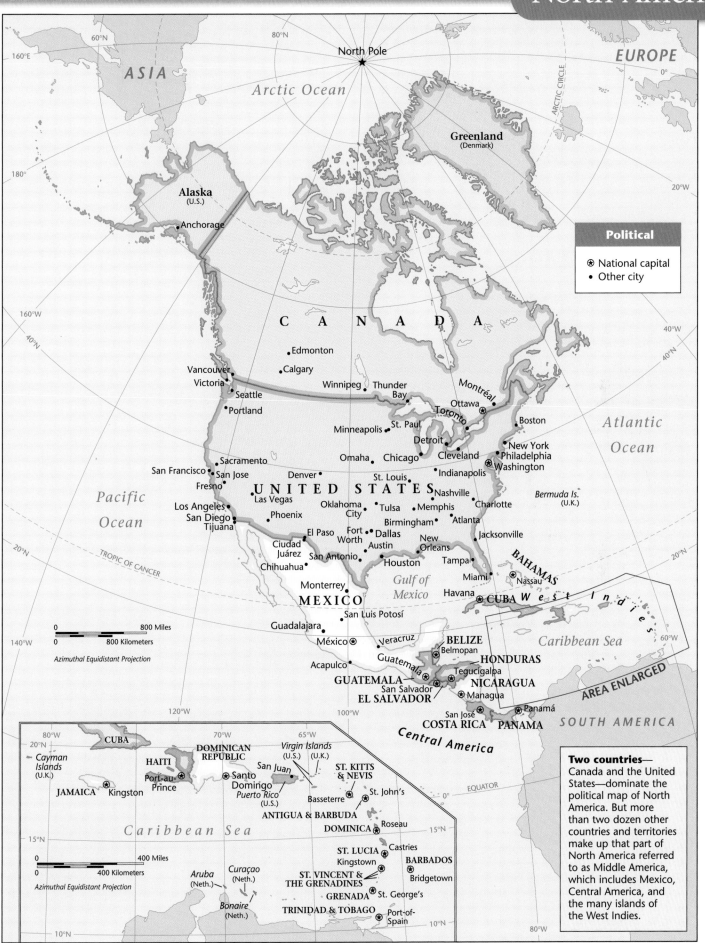

Political
- ⊛ National capital
- • Other city

ASIA

EUROPE

Arctic Ocean

North Pole

160°E

180°

60°N

80°N

0°

ARCTIC CIRCLE

20°W

Greenland
(Denmark)

Alaska
(U.S.)

• Anchorage

40°W

C A N A D A

160°W

40°N

40°N

• Edmonton

• Calgary

Vancouver
Victoria
• Seattle
• Portland

Winnipeg
• Thunder
Bay

Montréal

Ottawa ⊛

Toronto

Boston •

Atlantic
Ocean

Minneapolis
• St. Paul

Detroit •

New York •

Sacramento •

Omaha •
• Chicago

Cleveland •
Philadelphia •
Washington ⊛

San Francisco •
San Jose •
Fresno •

Denver •

St. Louis •

Indianapolis •

Bermuda Is.
(U.K.)

U N I T E D   S T A T E S

Nashville •

Las Vegas •

Oklahoma
City •
• Tulsa
• Memphis

Charlotte •

Los Angeles •
San Diego •
Tijuana •

Phoenix •

Birmingham •
Atlanta •

El Paso •
Fort
Worth • • Dallas
Austin •

New
Orleans •

Jacksonville •

Pacific
Ocean

20°N

TROPIC OF CANCER

Ciudad
Juárez •
San Antonio •

Houston •

Tampa •

BAHAMAS

20°N

Chihuahua •

Gulf of
Mexico

Miami •

Monterrey •

Havana •

Nassau •

⊛ CUBA   W e s t   I n d i e s

MEXICO

San Luis Potosí •

60°W

Guadalajara •

Caribbean Sea

140°W

0   800 Miles
0   800 Kilometers

Azimuthal Equidistant Projection

México ⊛

Veracruz •

BELIZE

Belmopan •

AREA ENLARGED

120°W

100°W

Acapulco •

Guatemala •

HONDURAS

Tegucigalpa •

⊛

GUATEMALA

San Salvador •
EL SALVADOR

NICARAGUA

Managua ⊛

SOUTH AMERICA

San José •

Panamá ⊛

COSTA RICA   PANAMA

Central America

EQUATOR

80°W

20°N

CUBA

70°W

65°W

DOMINICAN
REPUBLIC

Virgin Islands
(U.S.) (U.K.)

Cayman
Islands
(U.K.)

HAITI

Port-au-
Prince ⊛

San Juan •

ST. KITTS
& NEVIS

⊛ Santo
Domingo

JAMAICA   Kingston •

Puerto Rico
(U.S.)

Basseterre ⊛

St. John's •

ANTIGUA & BARBUDA

15°N

C a r i b b e a n   S e a

DOMINICA

Roseau •

15°N

0   400 Miles
0   400 Kilometers

Azimuthal Equidistant Projection

Aruba
(Neth.)

Curaçao
(Neth.)

ST. LUCIA

Castries •

Kingstown •

BARBADOS

ST. VINCENT &
THE GRENADINES

Bridgetown •

Bonaire
(Neth.)

GRENADA   St. George's •

TRINIDAD & TOBAGO

Port-of-
Spain •

10°N

10°N

80°W

Two countries—
Canada and the United
States—dominate the
political map of North
America. But more
than two dozen other
countries and territories
make up that part of
North America referred
to as Middle America,
which includes Mexico,
Central America, and
the many islands of
the West Indies.

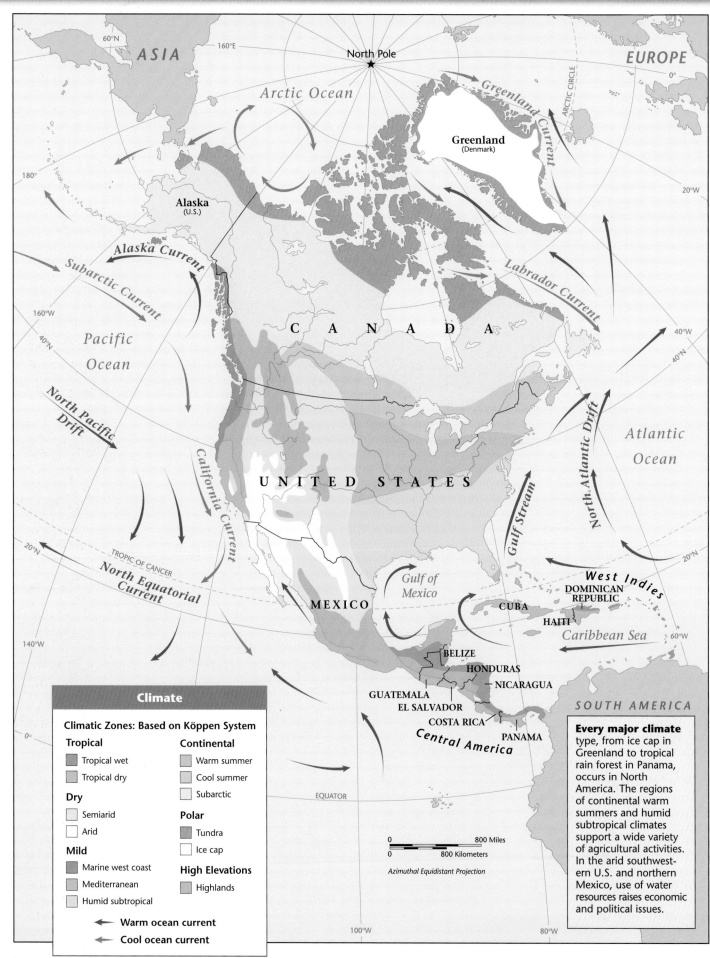

ASIA

160°E

North Pole

EUROPE

60°N

Arctic Ocean

Greenland Current

ARCTIC CIRCLE

0°

Greenland
(Denmark)

20°W

Alaska
(U.S.)

180°

Alaska Current

Subarctic Current

160°W

40°N

Pacific Ocean

C A N A D A

Labrador Current

40°W

40°N

North Pacific Drift

California Current

U N I T E D   S T A T E S

Gulf Stream

North Atlantic Drift

Atlantic Ocean

20°N

TROPIC OF CANCER

North Equatorial Current

MEXICO

Gulf of Mexico

20°N

60°W

West Indies

CUBA

DOMINICAN REPUBLIC

HAITI

Caribbean Sea

140°W

BELIZE

HONDURAS

NICARAGUA

GUATEMALA

EL SALVADOR

COSTA RICA

PANAMA

Central America

SOUTH AMERICA

0°

EQUATOR

100°W

80°W

Climate

Climatic Zones: Based on Köppen System

Tropical
- Tropical wet
- Tropical dry

Dry
- Semiarid
- Arid

Mild
- Marine west coast
- Mediterranean
- Humid subtropical

Continental
- Warm summer
- Cool summer
- Subarctic

Polar
- Tundra
- Ice cap

High Elevations
- Highlands

⬅ Warm ocean current
⬅ Cool ocean current

0   800 Miles
0   800 Kilometers

Azimuthal Equidistant Projection

Every major climate type, from ice cap in Greenland to tropical rain forest in Panama, occurs in North America. The regions of continental warm summers and humid subtropical climates support a wide variety of agricultural activities. In the arid southwestern U.S. and northern Mexico, use of water resources raises economic and political issues.

North America

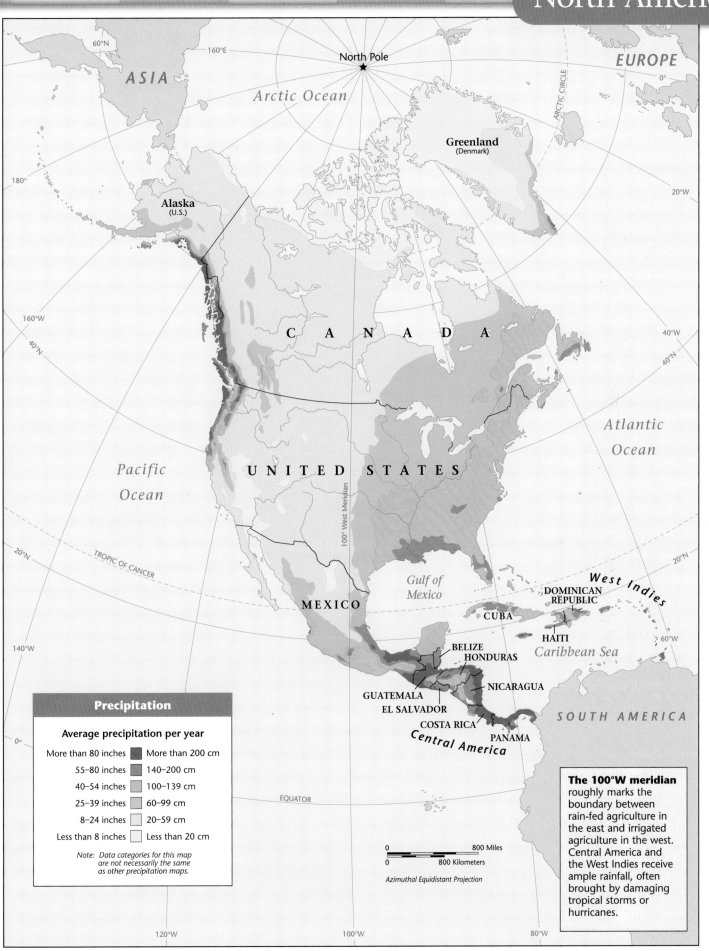

ASIA

Arctic Ocean

North Pole

EUROPE

Greenland
(Denmark)

ARCTIC CIRCLE

Alaska
(U.S.)

C A N A D A

*Pacific
Ocean*

U N I T E D   S T A T E S

100° West Meridian

*Atlantic
Ocean*

TROPIC OF CANCER

*Gulf of
Mexico*

West Indies

DOMINICAN
REPUBLIC

CUBA

HAITI

M E X I C O

Caribbean Sea

BELIZE
HONDURAS

GUATEMALA

NICARAGUA

EL SALVADOR

SOUTH AMERICA

COSTA RICA

PANAMA

Central America

EQUATOR

Precipitation

Average precipitation per year

More than 80 inches		More than 200 cm
55–80 inches		140–200 cm
40–54 inches		100–139 cm
25–39 inches		60–99 cm
8–24 inches		20–59 cm
Less than 8 inches		Less than 20 cm

*Note: Data categories for this map
are not necessarily the same
as other precipitation maps.*

0   800 Miles

0   800 Kilometers

Azimuthal Equidistant Projection

The 100°W meridian
roughly marks the
boundary between
rain-fed agriculture in
the east and irrigated
agriculture in the west.
Central America and
the West Indies receive
ample rainfall, often
brought by damaging
tropical storms or
hurricanes.

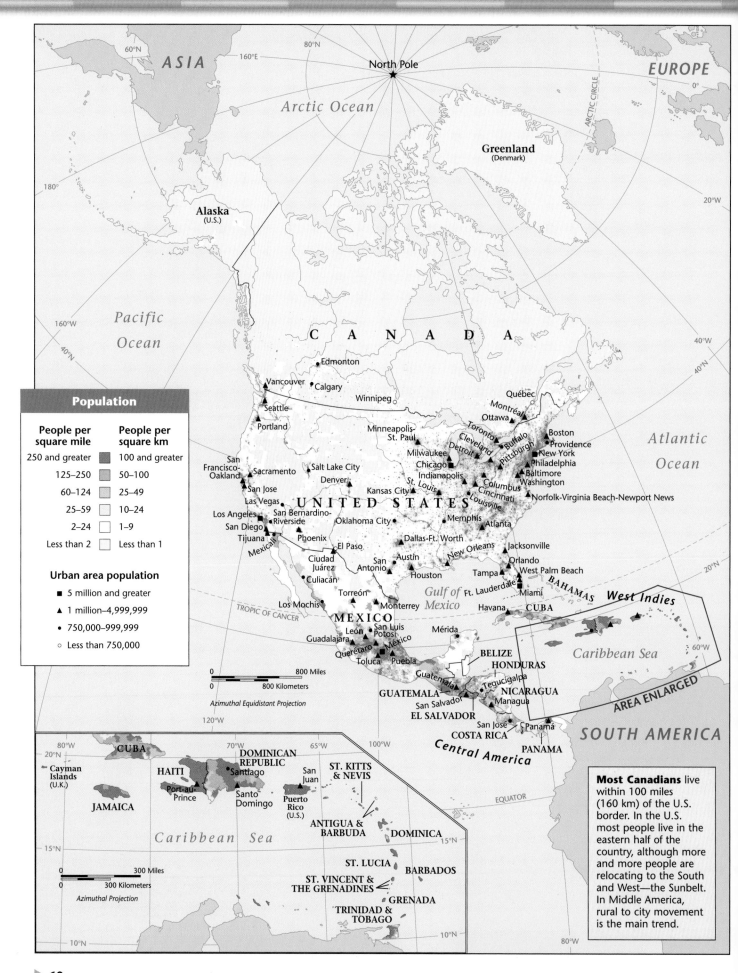

Population

People per square mile | **People per square km**
- 250 and greater — 100 and greater
- 125–250 — 50–100
- 60–124 — 25–49
- 25–59 — 10–24
- 2–24 — 1–9
- Less than 2 — Less than 1

Urban area population
- ■ 5 million and greater
- ▲ 1 million–4,999,999
- ● 750,000–999,999
- ○ Less than 750,000

ASIA

EUROPE

North Pole

Arctic Ocean

Greenland
(Denmark)

Alaska
(U.S.)

Pacific Ocean

C A N A D A

Atlantic Ocean

Edmonton
Vancouver
Calgary
Seattle
Winnipeg
Portland
Québec
Montréal
Ottawa
Minneapolis-St. Paul
Toronto
Buffalo
Boston
Providence
Milwaukee
Cleveland
Pittsburgh
New York
Detroit
Philadelphia
Chicago
Baltimore
San Francisco-Oakland
Sacramento
Salt Lake City
Denver
Indianapolis
Columbus
Washington
San Jose
Kansas City
St. Louis
Cincinnati
Louisville
Norfolk-Virginia Beach-Newport News
Las Vegas
U N I T E D   S T A T E S
Los Angeles
San Bernardino-Riverside
Oklahoma City
Memphis
Atlanta
San Diego
Tijuana
Phoenix
Mexicali
Dallas-Ft. Worth
New Orleans
Jacksonville
El Paso
Ciudad Juárez
Austin
Orlando
West Palm Beach
Culiacán
San Antonio
Houston
Tampa
Ft. Lauderdale
Torreón
Miami
Los Mochis
Monterrey
Gulf of Mexico
Havana
CUBA
BAHAMAS
West Indies
MEXICO
Mérida
Caribbean Sea
León
San Luis Potosí
AREA ENLARGED
Guadalajara
Querétaro
México
BELIZE
Toluca
Puebla
HONDURAS
SOUTH AMERICA
Guatemala
Tegucigalpa
NICARAGUA
GUATEMALA
San Salvador
Managua
EL SALVADOR
San José
Panamá
COSTA RICA
PANAMA
Central America

TROPIC OF CANCER

0 ————— 800 Miles
0 ————— 800 Kilometers

Azimuthal Equidistant Projection

120°W
100°W

CUBA
Cayman Islands
(U.K.)
HAITI
DOMINICAN REPUBLIC
Santiago
San Juan
ST. KITTS & NEVIS
Port-au-Prince
Santo Domingo
Puerto Rico
(U.S.)
JAMAICA
ANTIGUA & BARBUDA
DOMINICA
Caribbean Sea
ST. LUCIA
BARBADOS
ST. VINCENT & THE GRENADINES
GRENADA
TRINIDAD & TOBAGO

0 ————— 300 Miles
0 ————— 300 Kilometers

Azimuthal Projection

EQUATOR

Most Canadians live within 100 miles (160 km) of the U.S. border. In the U.S. most people live in the eastern half of the country, although more and more people are relocating to the South and West—the Sunbelt. In Middle America, rural to city movement is the main trend.

North America

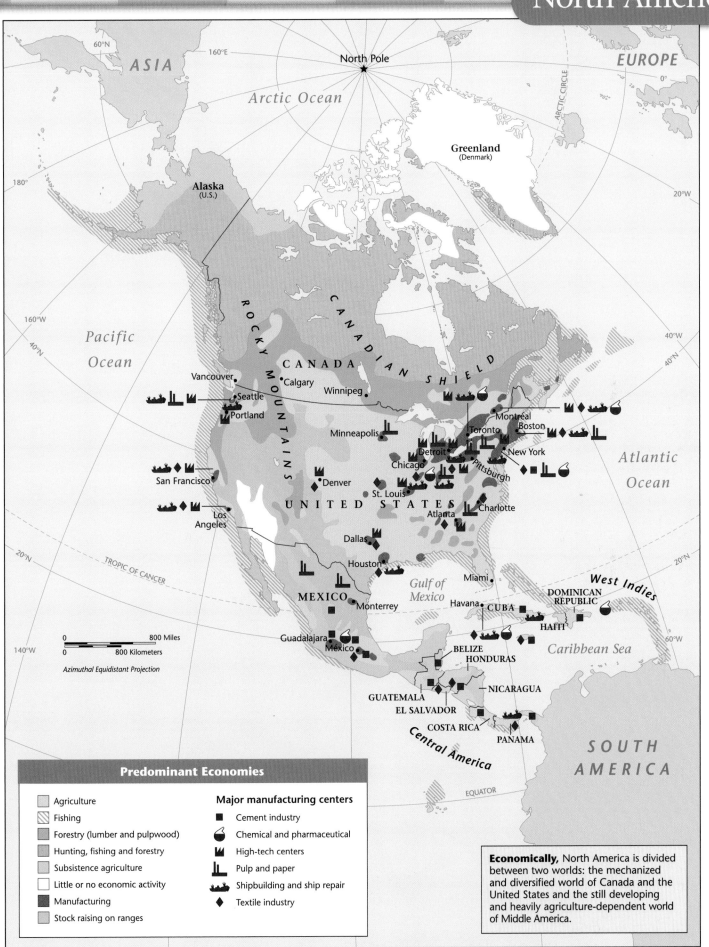

Predominant Economies

| Agriculture |
| Fishing |
| Forestry (lumber and pulpwood) |
| Hunting, fishing and forestry |
| Subsistence agriculture |
| Little or no economic activity |
| Manufacturing |
| Stock raising on ranges |

Major manufacturing centers

- ■ Cement industry
- Chemical and pharmaceutical
- High-tech centers
- Pulp and paper
- Shipbuilding and ship repair
- ◆ Textile industry

Economically, North America is divided between two worlds: the mechanized and diversified world of Canada and the United States and the still developing and heavily agriculture-dependent world of Middle America.

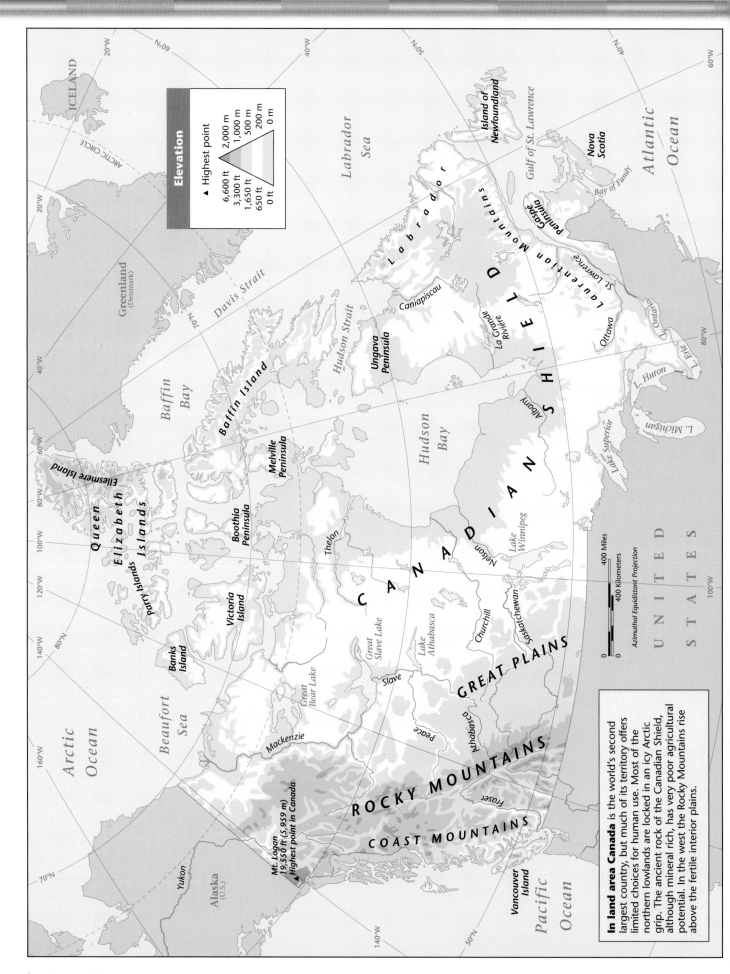

Elevation

▲ Highest point

2,000 m	6,600 ft
1,000 m	3,300 ft
500 m	1,650 ft
200 m	650 ft
0 m	0 ft

ICELAND

ARCTIC CIRCLE

Greenland
(Denmark)

Labrador Sea

Island of Newfoundland

Gulf of St. Lawrence

Nova Scotia

Bay of Fundy

Gaspé Peninsula

St. Lawrence

Atlantic Ocean

Labrador

Laurentian Mountains

Davis Strait

Baffin Bay

Baffin Island

Hudson Strait

Caniapiscau

Ungava Peninsula

La Grande Rivière

Ottawa

L. Ontario

L. Erie

Queen Elizabeth Islands

Ellesmere Island

Parry Islands

Melville Peninsula

Boothia Peninsula

C A N A D I A N   S H I E L D

Albany

Hudson Bay

Lake Superior

L. Huron

L. Michigan

Victoria Island

Banks Island

Thelon

Lake Winnipeg

Nelson

Great Bear Lake

Great Slave Lake

Lake Athabasca

Churchill

Saskatchewan

G R E A T   P L A I N S

Slave

Mackenzie

Peace

Athabasca

R O C K Y   M O U N T A I N S

Fraser

C O A S T   M O U N T A I N S

Vancouver Island

Mt. Logan
19,550 ft (5,959 m)
Highest point in Canada

Yukon

Alaska
(U.S.)

Arctic Ocean

Beaufort Sea

Pacific Ocean

U N I T E D   S T A T E S

400 Miles
400 Kilometers
Azimuthal Equidistant Projection

In land area Canada is the world's second largest country, but much of its territory offers limited choices for human use. Most of the northern lowlands are locked in an icy Arctic grip. The ancient rock of the Canadian Shield, although mineral rich, has very poor agricultural potential. In the west the Rocky Mountains rise above the fertile interior plains.

North America
Canada

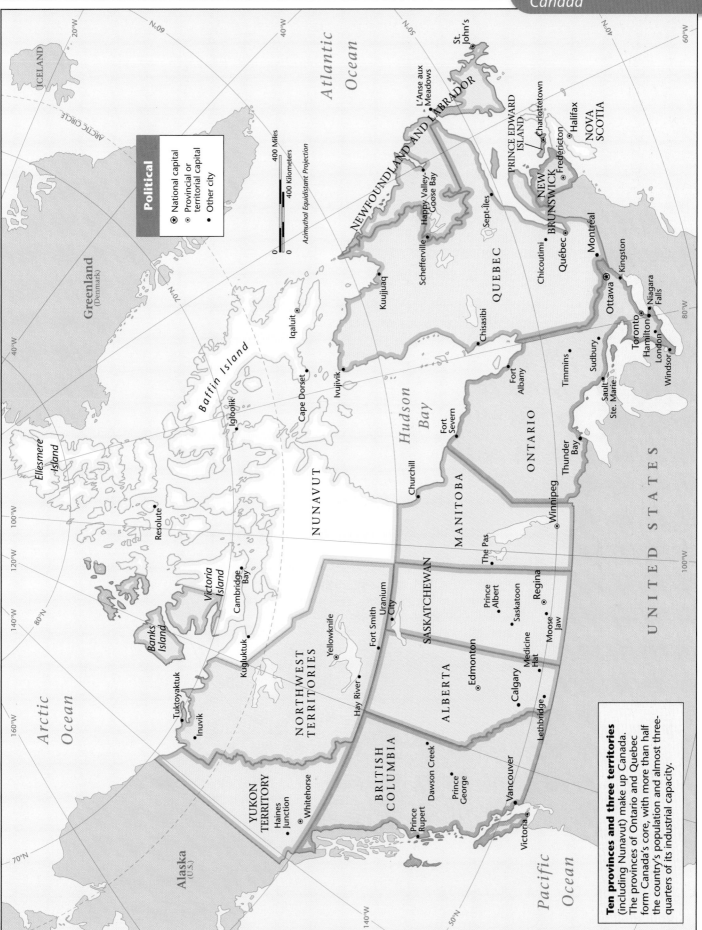

Political
- ⊛ National capital
- ⊙ Provincial or territorial capital
- • Other city

400 Miles
400 Kilometers

Azimuthal Equidistant Projection

ICELAND

Greenland
(Denmark)

Atlantic Ocean

St. John's

L'Anse aux Meadows

NEWFOUNDLAND AND LABRADOR

Charlottetown

PRINCE EDWARD ISLAND

Halifax

NOVA SCOTIA

Fredericton

NEW BRUNSWICK

Happy Valley-Goose Bay

Schefferville

Sept-Îles

QUEBEC

Chicoutimi

Québec

Montréal

Kingston

Kuujjuaq

Ottawa

Niagara Falls

Toronto

Hamilton

London

Windsor

Chisasibi

Sudbury

Timmins

Sault Ste. Marie

ONTARIO

Thunder Bay

Fort Albany

Fort Severn

Baffin Island

Iqaluit

Igloolik

Cape Dorset

Ivujivik

Hudson Bay

Churchill

Winnipeg

MANITOBA

The Pas

Ellesmere Island

Greenland

Resolute

NUNAVUT

Victoria Island

Cambridge Bay

Banks Island

Kugluktuk

Yellowknife

Fort Smith

Uranium City

SASKATCHEWAN

Prince Albert

Saskatoon

Regina

Moose Jaw

Medicine Hat

NORTHWEST TERRITORIES

Hay River

Tuktoyaktuk

Inuvik

ALBERTA

Edmonton

Calgary

Lethbridge

BRITISH COLUMBIA

Dawson Creek

Prince George

Prince Rupert

Vancouver

Victoria

YUKON TERRITORY

Haines Junction

Whitehorse

Arctic Ocean

Alaska (U.S.)

Pacific Ocean

U N I T E D   S T A T E S

Ten provinces and three territories (including Nunavut) make up Canada. The provinces of Ontario and Quebec form Canada's core, with more than half the country's population and almost three-quarters of its industrial capacity.

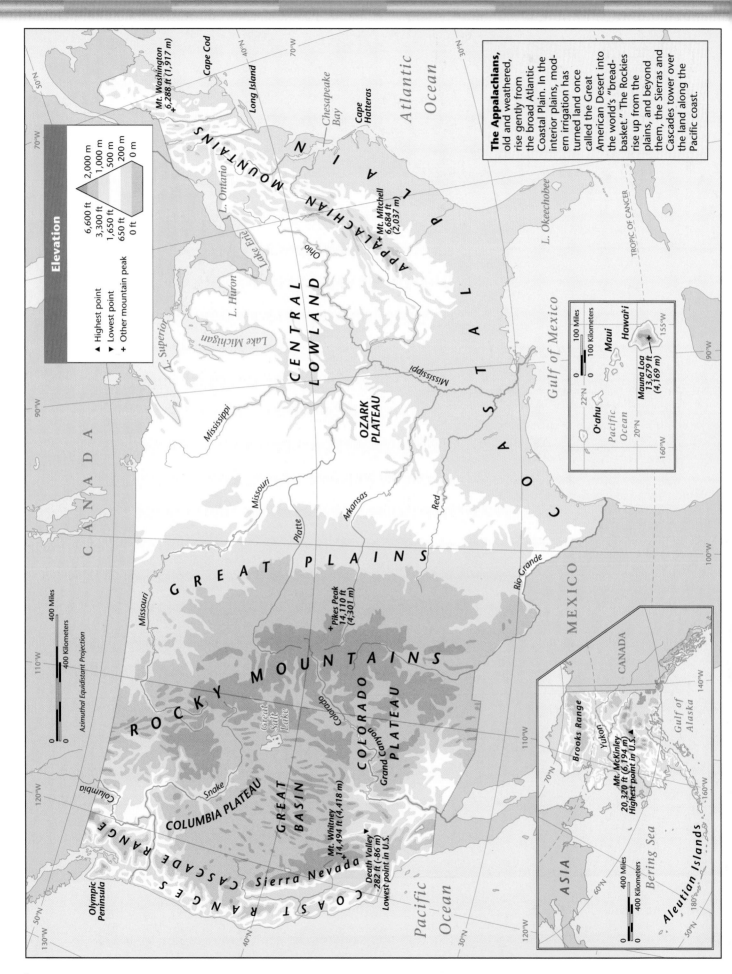

Elevation

2,000 m
1,000 m
500 m
200 m
0 m

6,600 ft
3,300 ft
1,650 ft
650 ft
0 ft

▲ Highest point
▼ Lowest point
+ Other mountain peak

The Appalachians, old and weathered, rise gently from the broad Atlantic Coastal Plain. In the interior plains, modern irrigation has turned land once called the Great American Desert into the world's "breadbasket." The Rockies rise up from the plains, and beyond them, the Sierras and Cascades tower over the land along the Pacific coast.

CANADA

ATLANTIC Ocean

Mt. Washington 6,288 ft (1,917 m) +

Cape Cod

Long Island

Chesapeake Bay

Cape Hatteras

L. Ontario

Lake Erie

L. Huron

L. Superior

Lake Michigan

APPALACHIAN MOUNTAINS

CENTRAL LOWLAND

COASTAL PLAIN

OZARK PLATEAU

Ohio

Mississippi

Missouri

Mississippi

Platte

Arkansas

Red

Rio Grande

Mt. Mitchell 6,684 ft (2,037 m) +

L. Okeechobee

TROPIC OF CANCER

Gulf of Mexico

MEXICO

GREAT PLAINS

+ Pikes Peak 14,110 ft (4,301 m)

ROCKY MOUNTAINS

COLORADO PLATEAU

Great Salt Lake

Colorado

Grand Canyon

Snake

Columbia

COLUMBIA PLATEAU

GREAT BASIN

CASCADE RANGE

COAST RANGES

Sierra Nevada

Olympic Peninsula

Mt. Whitney 14,494 ft (4,418 m)

Death Valley -282 ft (-86 m) Lowest point in U.S. ▼

Pacific Ocean

400 Miles
400 Kilometers
Azimuthal Equidistant Projection

Hawai'i

Maui

O'ahu

Pacific Ocean

Mauna Loa 13,679 ft (4,169 m) +

100 Miles
100 Kilometers

ASIA

CANADA

Brooks Range

Yukon

Mt. McKinley 20,320 ft (6,194 m) Highest point in U.S. ▲

Gulf of Alaska

Bering Sea

Aleutian Islands

400 Miles
400 Kilometers

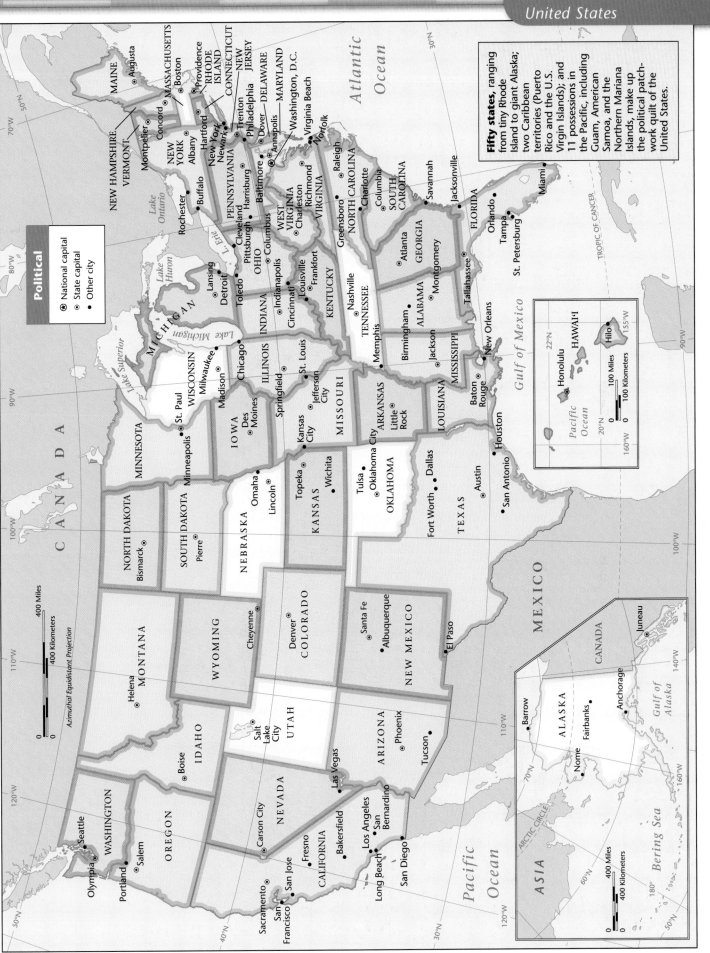

Fifty states, ranging from tiny Rhode Island to giant Alaska; two Caribbean territories (Puerto Rico and the U.S. Virgin Islands); and 11 possessions in the Pacific, including Guam, American Samoa, and the Northern Mariana Islands, make up the political patchwork quilt of the United States.

Political
⊛ National capital
◎ State capital
• Other city

Atlantic Ocean

TROPIC OF CANCER

Pacific Ocean

CANADA

MEXICO

Gulf of Mexico

HAWAI'I
Honolulu
Hilo
Pacific Ocean
0 100 Miles
0 100 Kilometers
22°N
20°N
155°W
160°W

ASIA
ALASKA
Barrow
Nome
Fairbanks
Anchorage
Juneau
CANADA
Gulf of Alaska
Bering Sea
ARCTIC CIRCLE
0 400 Miles
0 400 Kilometers

MAINE
Augusta
NEW HAMPSHIRE
VERMONT
Montpelier
Concord
MASSACHUSETTS
Boston
Providence
RHODE ISLAND
CONNECTICUT
NEW JERSEY
Trenton
Philadelphia
DELAWARE
Dover
MARYLAND
Annapolis
Washington, D.C.
Hartford
Albany
NEW YORK
Newark
New York
PENNSYLVANIA
Harrisburg
Baltimore
Virginia Beach
Norfolk
Buffalo
Rochester
Lake Ontario
L. Erie
Cleveland
Pittsburgh
OHIO
Columbus
WEST VIRGINIA
Charleston
Richmond
VIRGINIA
Raleigh
NORTH CAROLINA
Charlotte
Greensboro
Columbia
SOUTH CAROLINA
Savannah
Jacksonville
FLORIDA
Orlando
Tampa
St. Petersburg
Miami

Lansing
Detroit
Toledo
MICHIGAN
Lake Michigan
Lake Huron
Lake Superior
WISCONSIN
Milwaukee
Madison
St. Paul
MINNESOTA
Minneapolis
IOWA
Des Moines
Chicago
ILLINOIS
INDIANA
Indianapolis
Cincinnati
Louisville
Frankfort
KENTUCKY
Nashville
TENNESSEE
Memphis
Springfield
St. Louis
MISSOURI
Jefferson City
Kansas City
Topeka
KANSAS
Wichita
Little Rock
ARKANSAS
Birmingham
ALABAMA
Montgomery
Atlanta
GEORGIA
Tallahassee
MISSISSIPPI
Jackson
LOUISIANA
Baton Rouge
New Orleans
Houston

NORTH DAKOTA
Bismarck
SOUTH DAKOTA
Pierre
NEBRASKA
Omaha
Lincoln
MONTANA
Helena
WYOMING
Cheyenne
Denver
COLORADO
Santa Fe
Albuquerque
NEW MEXICO
El Paso
Tulsa
Oklahoma City
OKLAHOMA
Fort Worth
Dallas
Austin
San Antonio
TEXAS

WASHINGTON
Olympia
Seattle
Portland
Salem
OREGON
IDAHO
Boise
NEVADA
Carson City
Las Vegas
UTAH
Salt Lake City
ARIZONA
Phoenix
Tucson
CALIFORNIA
Sacramento
San Francisco
San Jose
Fresno
Bakersfield
Los Angeles
San Bernardino
Long Beach
San Diego

400 Miles
400 Kilometers
Azimuthal Equidistant Projection

80°W
70°W
60°W
90°W
100°W
110°W
120°W
130°W
30°N
40°N
50°N
60°N
70°N

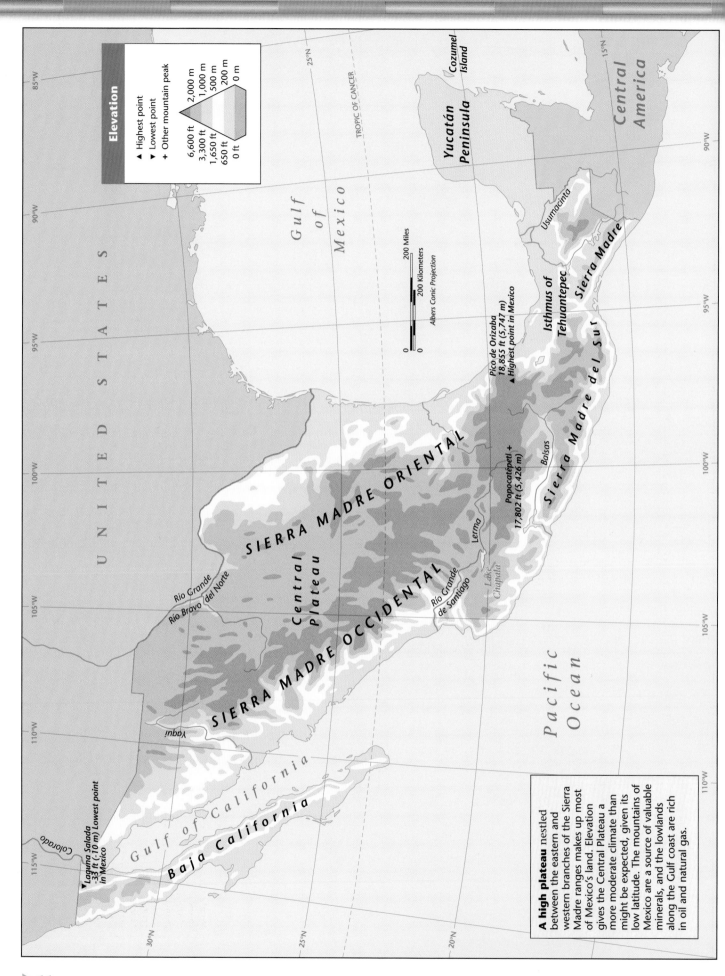

Elevation

▲ Highest point
▼ Lowest point
+ Other mountain peak

6,600 ft — 2,000 m
3,300 ft — 1,000 m
1,650 ft — 500 m
650 ft — 200 m
0 ft — 0 m

United States

Gulf of Mexico

TROPIC OF CANCER

Yucatán Peninsula

Cozumel Island

Central America

Usumacinta

Sierra Madre

Isthmus of Tehuantepec

200 Miles
200 Kilometers
Albers Conic Projection

Pico de Orizaba
18,855 ft (5,747 m)
▲ Highest point in Mexico

SIERRA MADRE ORIENTAL

Balsas

Popocatépetl +
17,802 ft (5,426 m)

Sierra Madre del Sur

Central Plateau

Lerma

Rio Grande
Río Bravo del Norte

Río Grande de Santiago

Lake Chapala

SIERRA MADRE OCCIDENTAL

Yaqui

Pacific Ocean

Gulf of California

Baja California

Colorado

▼ Laguna Salada
-33 ft (-10 m) Lowest point in Mexico

A high plateau nestled between the eastern and western branches of the Sierra Madre ranges makes up most of Mexico's land. Elevation gives the Central Plateau a more moderate climate than might be expected, given its low latitude. The mountains of Mexico are a source of valuable minerals, and the lowlands along the Gulf coast are rich in oil and natural gas.

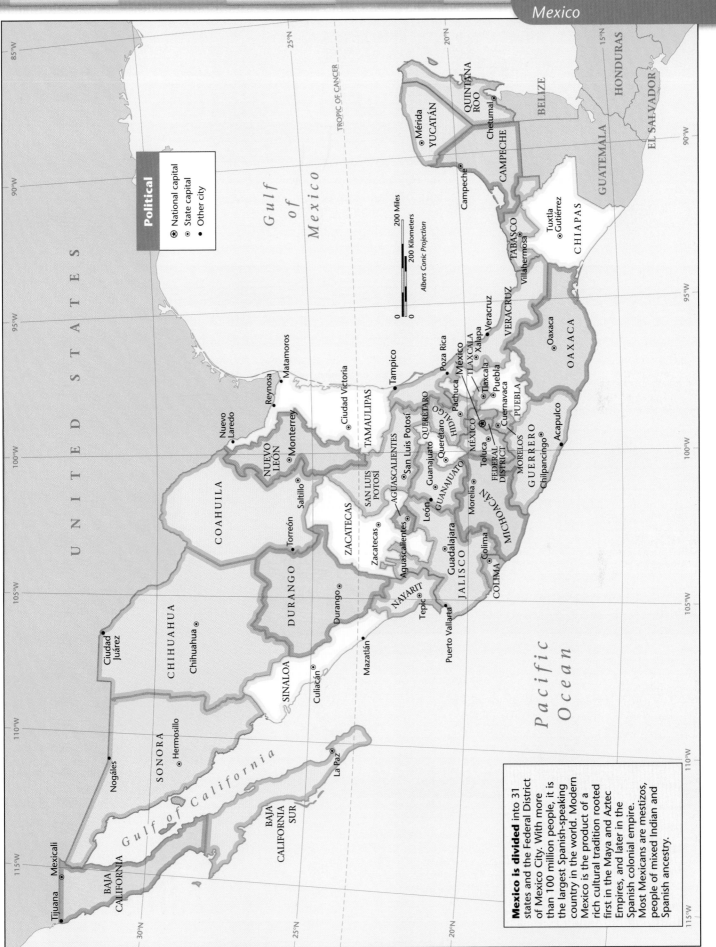

Political
⊛ National capital
◉ State capital
• Other city

United States

Gulf of Mexico

Pacific Ocean

Gulf of California

200 Miles
200 Kilometers
Albers Conic Projection

TROPIC OF CANCER

BELIZE
GUATEMALA
HONDURAS
EL SALVADOR

QUINTANA ROO
Chetumal
Mérida ◉ YUCATÁN
CAMPECHE
Campeche ◉
TABASCO
Villahermosa ◉
Tuxtla Gutiérrez ◉ CHIAPAS

VERACRUZ
Veracruz
Xalapa ◉
Poza Rica •
TLAXCALA
Tlaxcala ◉
Puebla ◉
PUEBLA
Cuernavaca ◉
Oaxaca ◉ OAXACA
Acapulco •

México ⊛
MÉXICO
Toluca ◉
FEDERAL DISTRICT
MORELOS
GUERRERO
Chilpancingo ◉

Pachuca ◉
HIDALGO
QUERÉTARO
Querétaro ◉

Tampico •
Ciudad Victoria ◉
TAMAULIPAS

Matamoros •
Reynosa •

Nuevo Laredo •
Monterrey ◉
NUEVO LEÓN

Saltillo ◉
COAHUILA

Torreón •

San Luis Potosí ◉
SAN LUIS POTOSÍ

AGUASCALIENTES
Aguascalientes ◉

ZACATECAS
Zacatecas ◉

Guanajuato ◉
GUANAJUATO
León •

Morelia ◉
MICHOACÁN

Guadalajara ◉
JALISCO

Colima ◉
COLIMA

NAYARIT
Tepic ◉

Puerto Vallarta •

DURANGO
Durango ◉

CHIHUAHUA
Chihuahua ◉

Ciudad Juárez •

SINALOA
Culiacán ◉

Mazatlán •

SONORA
Hermosillo ◉

Nogáles •

La Paz •

BAJA CALIFORNIA SUR

BAJA CALIFORNIA

Mexicali ◉
Tijuana •

Mexico is divided into 31 states and the Federal District of Mexico City. With more than 100 million people, it is the largest Spanish-speaking country in the world. Modern Mexico is the product of a rich cultural tradition rooted first in the Maya and Aztec Empires, and later in the Spanish colonial empire. Most Mexicans are mestizos, people of mixed Indian and Spanish ancestry.

Natural Hazards

Natural Hazards: Selected Statistics

Hurricanes

This list names North America's eight strongest recorded hurricanes as of 2004. In other parts of the world hurricanes are called cyclones and typhoons.

1980 Allen: 165 mph/265 kmph*

1969 Camille: 165 mph/265 kmph

1950 Dog: 160 mph/257 kmph

1988 Gilbert: 160 mph/257 kmph

1977 Anita: 150 mph/241 kmph

1961 Carla: 150 mph/241 kmph

1979 David: 150 mph/241 kmph

1955 Janet: 150 mph//241 kmph

*maximum wind speed recorded

Tornadoes

The following states had the highest average annual number of tornadoes from 1950 to 1998.

Texas: 125

Oklahoma: 52

Florida: 49

Kansas: 48

Nebraska: 38

Iowa: 31

Illinois: 28

Missouri: 25

Louisiana: 24

Mississippi: 24

Earthquakes

This list shows the number of earthquakes in North America in the 20th century that had a magnitude of 8.0 to 9.9 on the Richter scale.

Mexico: 8

Alaska (U.S.): 7

Guatemala: 2

British Columbia (Canada): 1

California (U.S.): 1

Dominican Republic: 1
(see map page 57)

Panama: 1

The forces of nature inspire awe. They can also bring damage and destruction, especially when people locate homes and businesses in places that are at risk of experiencing violent storms, earthquakes, volcanoes, floods, wildfires, or other natural hazards.

Tornadoes, violent, swirling storms with winds that can exceed 200 miles (300 km) per hour, strike the U.S. more than 800 times each year. Hurricanes, massive low-pressure storms that form over warm ocean waters, bring destructive winds and rain primarily to the Gulf of Mexico and the southeastern mainland. Melting spring snows and heavy rains trigger flooding; periods of drought make other regions vulnerable to wildfires. These and other hazards of nature are not limited to this continent. Natural hazards pose serious threats to lives and property wherever people live.

▼ **Wildfires.** Putting lives and property at great risk, wildfires destroy millions of acres of forest each year. At the same time, fires help renew ecosystems by removing debris and encouraging seedling growth.

▲ **Volcanoes.** From deep inside Earth, molten rock, called magma, rises and breaks through the surface, sometimes quietly, but more often violently, shooting billowing ash clouds as shown here at Mount St. Helens, in Washington State.

▶ **Floods.** Towns and farmland that occupy fertile plains along rivers are always in danger from floods. In 1993 the great Mississippi River floods devastated millions of people in the midwestern United States.

Web Link for information on natural hazards: www.usgs.gov/hazards/#hazinfo

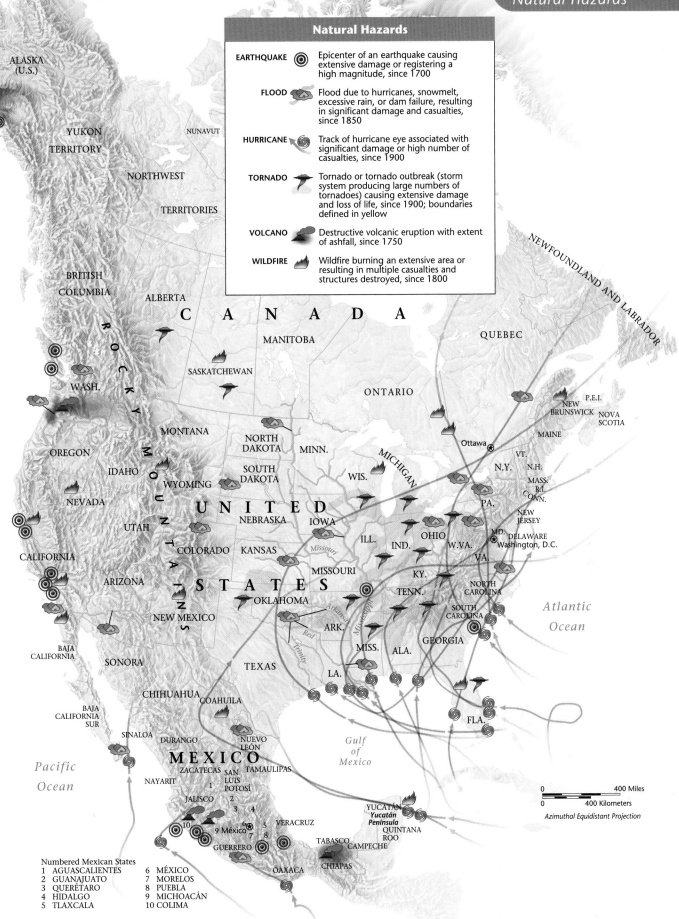

Natural Hazards

EARTHQUAKE — Epicenter of an earthquake causing extensive damage or registering a high magnitude, since 1700

FLOOD — Flood due to hurricanes, snowmelt, excessive rain, or dam failure, resulting in significant damage and casualties, since 1850

HURRICANE — Track of hurricane eye associated with significant damage or high number of casualties, since 1900

TORNADO — Tornado or tornado outbreak (storm system producing large numbers of tornadoes) causing extensive damage and loss of life, since 1900; boundaries defined in yellow

VOLCANO — Destructive volcanic eruption with extent of ashfall, since 1750

WILDFIRE — Wildfire burning an extensive area or resulting in multiple casualties and structures destroyed, since 1800

ALASKA (U.S.)

YUKON TERRITORY

NUNAVUT

NORTHWEST TERRITORIES

BRITISH COLUMBIA

ALBERTA

CANADA

MANITOBA

SASKATCHEWAN

QUEBEC

NEWFOUNDLAND AND LABRADOR

ONTARIO

WASH.

OREGON

IDAHO

MONTANA

NORTH DAKOTA

MINN.

MICHIGAN

NEW BRUNSWICK

P.E.I.

NOVA SCOTIA

MAINE

Ottawa

NEVADA

WYOMING

SOUTH DAKOTA

WIS.

N.Y.

VT.

N.H.

MASS.

R.I.

CONN.

PA.

CALIFORNIA

UTAH

UNITED

NEBRASKA

IOWA

ILL.

IND.

OHIO

W.VA.

NEW JERSEY

MD. DELAWARE
Washington, D.C.

ARIZONA

COLORADO

KANSAS

STATES

MISSOURI

Missouri

OKLAHOMA

KY.

TENN.

VA.

NORTH CAROLINA

Atlantic Ocean

NEW MEXICO

Arkansas

Red

Trinity

ARK.

Mississippi

MISS.

ALA.

GEORGIA

SOUTH CAROLINA

BAJA CALIFORNIA

SONORA

TEXAS

LA.

FLA.

CHIHUAHUA

COAHUILA

BAJA CALIFORNIA SUR

SINALOA

DURANGO

NUEVO LEÓN

Gulf of Mexico

Pacific Ocean

MEXICO

ZACATECAS

SAN LUIS POTOSÍ

TAMAULIPAS

NAYARIT

1

JALISCO

2

3

4

10

6

9 México

5

7

8

VERACRUZ

YUCATÁN

Yucatán Peninsula

QUINTANA ROO

CAMPECHE

GUERRERO

TABASCO

OAXACA

CHIAPAS

0   400 Miles
0   400 Kilometers

Azimuthal Equidistant Projection

Numbered Mexican States
1 AGUASCALIENTES
2 GUANAJUATO
3 QUERÉTARO
4 HIDALGO
5 TLAXCALA
6 MÉXICO
7 MORELOS
8 PUEBLA
9 MICHOACÁN
10 COLIMA

South America

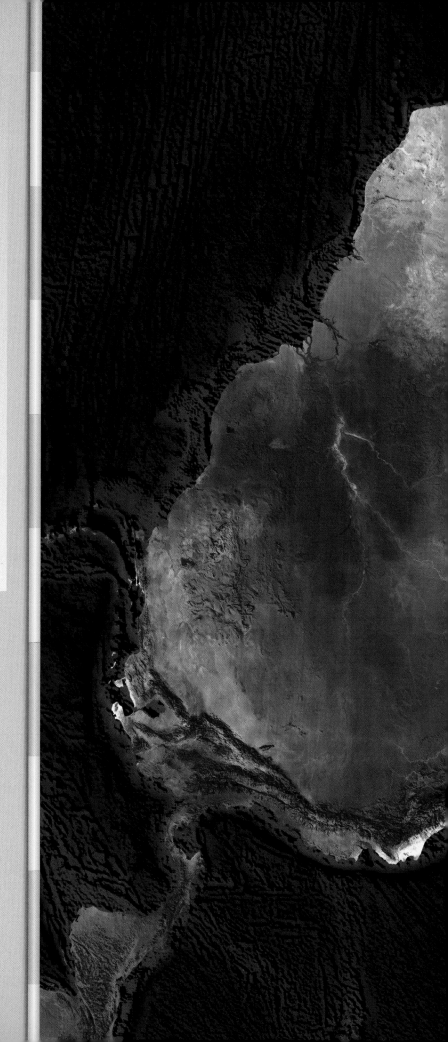

From the towering, snow-capped Andes in the west to the steamy rain forest of the Amazon Basin in the north, and from the fertile grasslands of the Pampas to the arid Atacama Desert along the Pacific coast, South America is a continent of extremes. North to south the continent extends from the tropical waters of the Caribbean Sea to the windblown islands of Tierra del Fuego. Its longest river, the Amazon, carries more water than any other river in the world.

Facts & Figures

▸ **Land area:** 6,880,500 sq mi (17,819,000 sq km)

▸ **Population:** 364,992,000

▸ **Highest point:** Aconcagua, Argentina: 22,834 ft (6,960 m)

▸ **Lowest point:** Valdés Peninsula, Argentina: 131 ft (40 m) below sea level

▸ **Longest river:** Amazon: 4,000 mi (6,437 km)

▸ **Largest lake:** Lake Titicaca, Bolivia-Peru: 3,200 sq mi (8,290 sq km)

▸ **Number of independent countries:** 12

▸ **Largest country:** Brazil: 3,300,169 sq mi (8,547,403 sq km)

▸ **Smallest country:** Suriname: 63,037 sq mi (163,265 sq km)

▸ **Most populous country:** Brazil: Pop. 179,091,000

▸ **Least populous country:** Suriname: Pop. 449,000

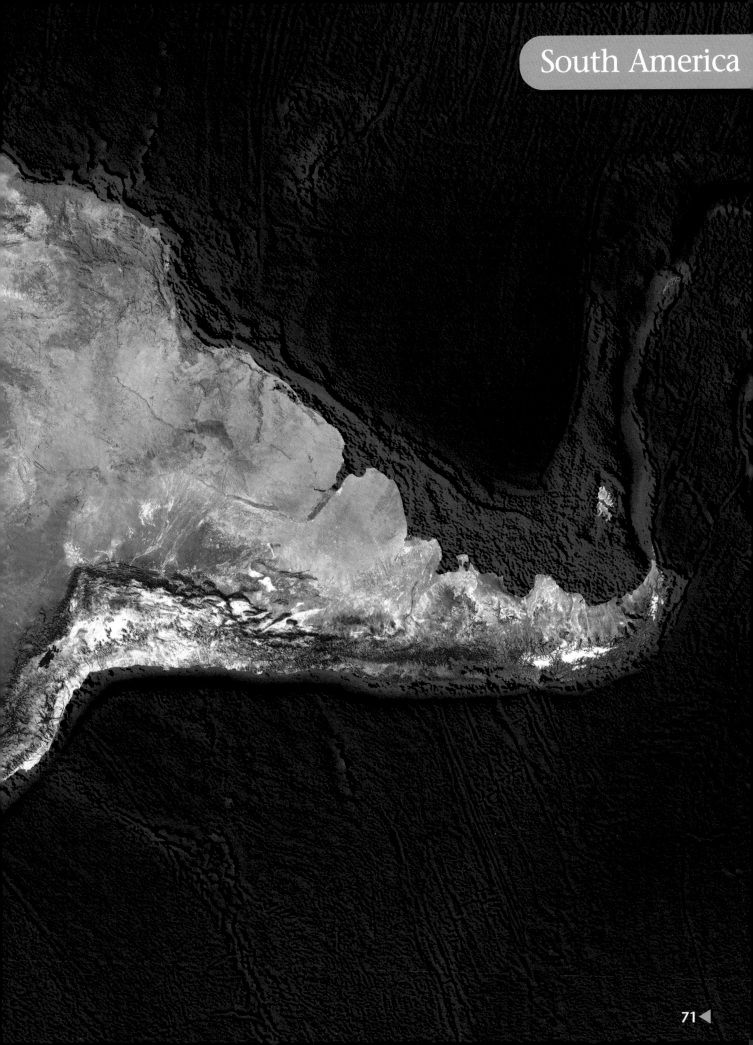

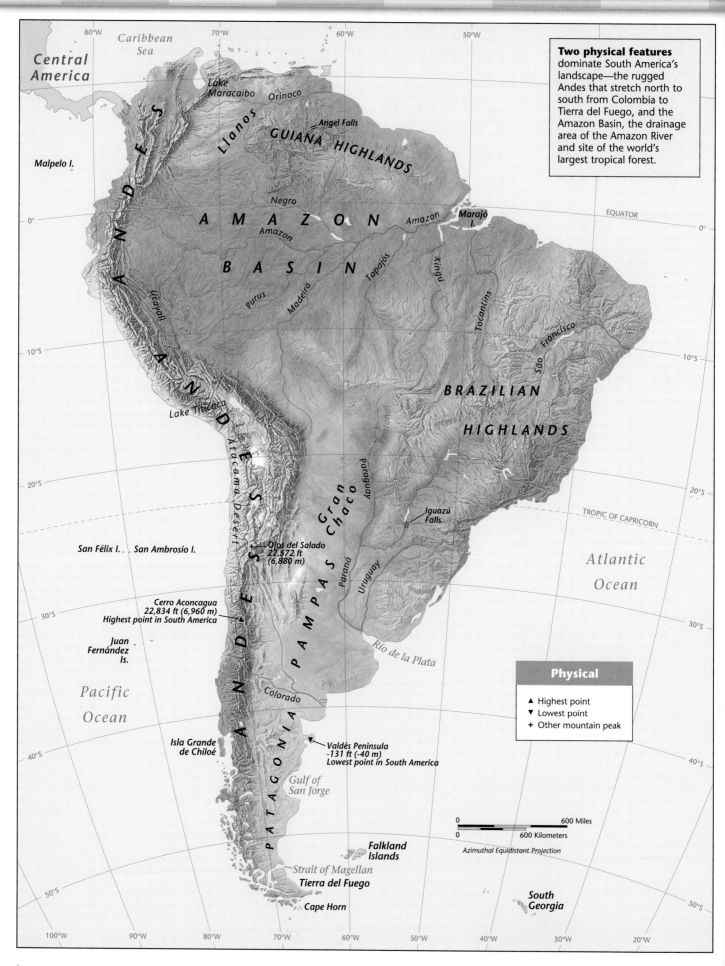

Central
America

Caribbean
Sea

Lake
Maracaibo

Orinoco

Malpelo I.

Llanos

GUIANA HIGHLANDS

Angel Falls

Two physical features
dominate South America's
landscape—the rugged
Andes that stretch north to
south from Colombia to
Tierra del Fuego, and the
Amazon Basin, the drainage
area of the Amazon River
and site of the world's
largest tropical forest.

Negro

A M A Z O N

Amazon

Amazon

Marajó
I.

EQUATOR

0°

0°

B A S I N

Ucayali

Purus

Madeira

Tapajós

Xingu

Tocantins

São
Francisco

10°S

10°S

Lake Titicaca

BRAZILIAN

HIGHLANDS

A
N
D
E
S

Atacama Desert

20°S

20°S

Pantanal

Gran
Chaco

Paraguay

TROPIC OF CAPRICORN

San Félix I.   San Ambrosio I.

Ojos del Salado
22,572 ft
(6,880 m)

Iguazú
Falls

Atlantic
Ocean

Cerro Aconcagua
22,834 ft (6,960 m)
Highest point in South America

Paraná

Uruguay

30°S

30°S

Juan
Fernández
Is.

P A M P A S

A
N
D
E
S

Pacific
Ocean

Colorado

Río de la Plata

Physical

▲ Highest point
▼ Lowest point
+ Other mountain peak

Isla Grande
de Chiloé

P A T A G O N I A

Valdés Peninsula
-131 ft (-40 m)
Lowest point in South America

40°S

40°S

Gulf of
San Jorge

0   600 Miles

0   600 Kilometers

Azimuthal Equidistant Projection

Falkland
Islands

Strait of Magellan

Tierra del Fuego

50°S

50°S

Cape Horn

**South
Georgia**

100°W   90°W   80°W   70°W   60°W   50°W   40°W   30°W   20°W

80°W   70°W   60°W   50°W

South America

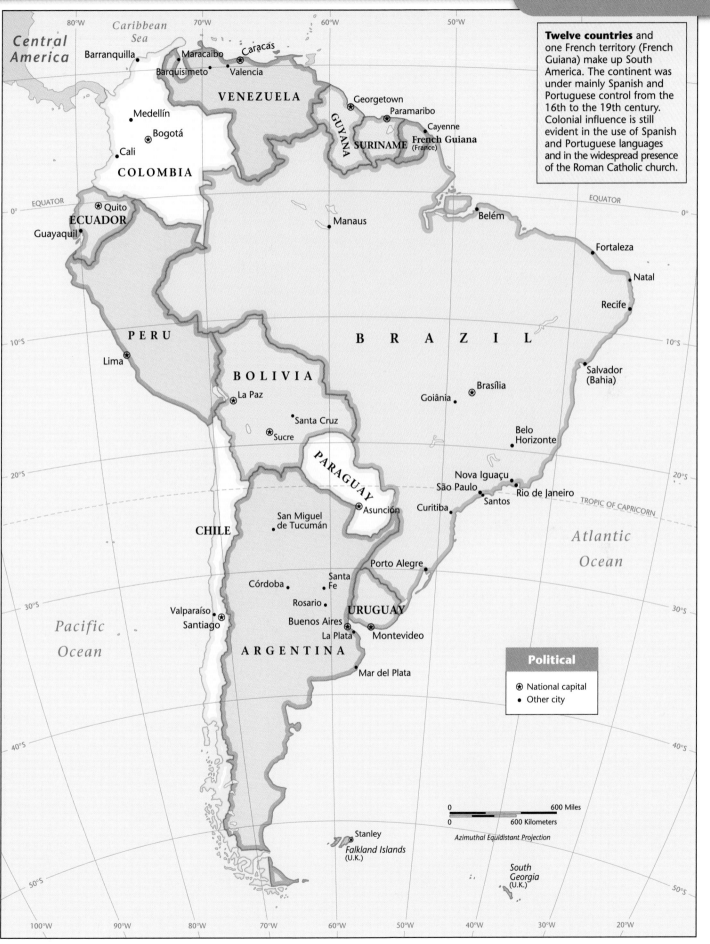

Twelve countries and one French territory (French Guiana) make up South America. The continent was under mainly Spanish and Portuguese control from the 16th to the 19th century. Colonial influence is still evident in the use of Spanish and Portuguese languages and in the widespread presence of the Roman Catholic church.

Central America

Caribbean Sea

Barranquilla
Maracaibo
Caracas
Barquisimeto
Valencia
VENEZUELA
Medellín
Bogotá
Cali
COLOMBIA
Georgetown
Paramaribo
GUYANA
SURINAME
Cayenne
French Guiana (France)

EQUATOR
ECUADOR
Quito
Guayaquil
Manaus
Belém

Fortaleza
Natal
PERU
Recife
Lima
BRAZIL
BOLIVIA
Salvador (Bahia)
La Paz
Santa Cruz
Sucre
Goiânia
Brasília
Belo Horizonte
PARAGUAY
Nova Iguaçu
São Paulo
Rio de Janeiro
Santos
Asunción
Curitiba
TROPIC OF CAPRICORN
CHILE
San Miguel de Tucumán
Atlantic Ocean
Porto Alegre
Córdoba
Santa Fe
Rosario
URUGUAY
Valparaíso
Buenos Aires
Santiago
La Plata
Montevideo
Pacific Ocean
ARGENTINA
Mar del Plata

Political
⊛ National capital
• Other city

0   600 Miles
0   600 Kilometers
Azimuthal Equidistant Projection

Stanley
Falkland Islands (U.K.)
South Georgia (U.K.)

73

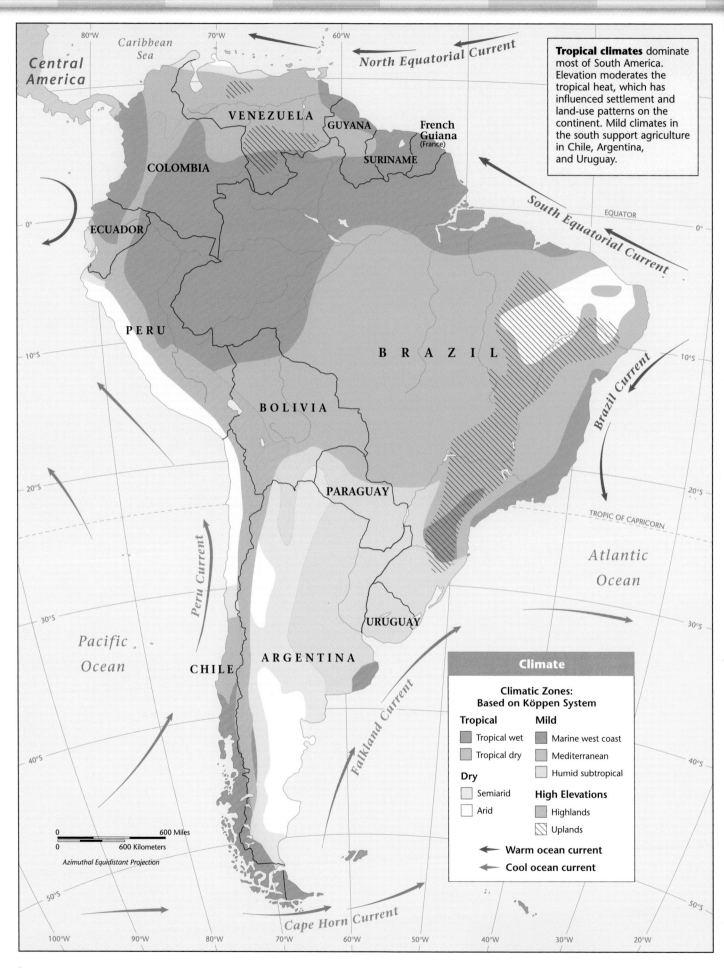

Caribbean Sea

Central America

North Equatorial Current

Tropical climates dominate most of South America. Elevation moderates the tropical heat, which has influenced settlement and land-use patterns on the continent. Mild climates in the south support agriculture in Chile, Argentina, and Uruguay.

VENEZUELA

GUYANA

French Guiana (France)

COLOMBIA

SURINAME

ECUADOR

South Equatorial Current

EQUATOR

PERU

B R A Z I L

Brazil Current

BOLIVIA

PARAGUAY

TROPIC OF CAPRICORN

Atlantic Ocean

Peru Current

Pacific Ocean

URUGUAY

CHILE

ARGENTINA

Falkland Current

Cape Horn Current

0   600 Miles
0   600 Kilometers
Azimuthal Equidistant Projection

Climate

**Climatic Zones:
Based on Köppen System**

Tropical
Tropical wet
Tropical dry

Mild
Marine west coast
Mediterranean
Humid subtropical

Dry
Semiarid
Arid

High Elevations
Highlands
Uplands

→ Warm ocean current
→ Cool ocean current

South America

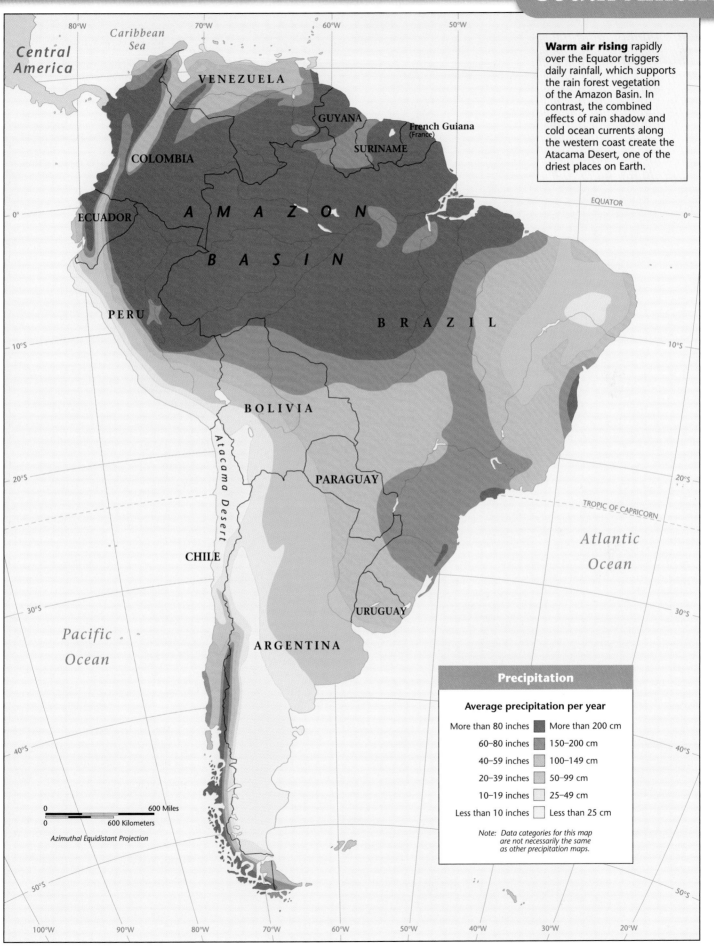

Warm air rising rapidly over the Equator triggers daily rainfall, which supports the rain forest vegetation of the Amazon Basin. In contrast, the combined effects of rain shadow and cold ocean currents along the western coast create the Atacama Desert, one of the driest places on Earth.

Central America

Caribbean Sea

VENEZUELA

GUYANA

SURINAME

French Guiana
(France)

COLOMBIA

EQUATOR

ECUADOR

A M A Z O N

B A S I N

PERU

B R A Z I L

BOLIVIA

Atacama Desert

PARAGUAY

TROPIC OF CAPRICORN

Atlantic Ocean

CHILE

URUGUAY

Pacific Ocean

ARGENTINA

0   600 Miles
0   600 Kilometers

Azimuthal Equidistant Projection

Precipitation

Average precipitation per year

More than 80 inches	More than 200 cm
60–80 inches	150–200 cm
40–59 inches	100–149 cm
20–39 inches	50–99 cm
10–19 inches	25–49 cm
Less than 10 inches	Less than 25 cm

Note: Data categories for this map are not necessarily the same as other precipitation maps.

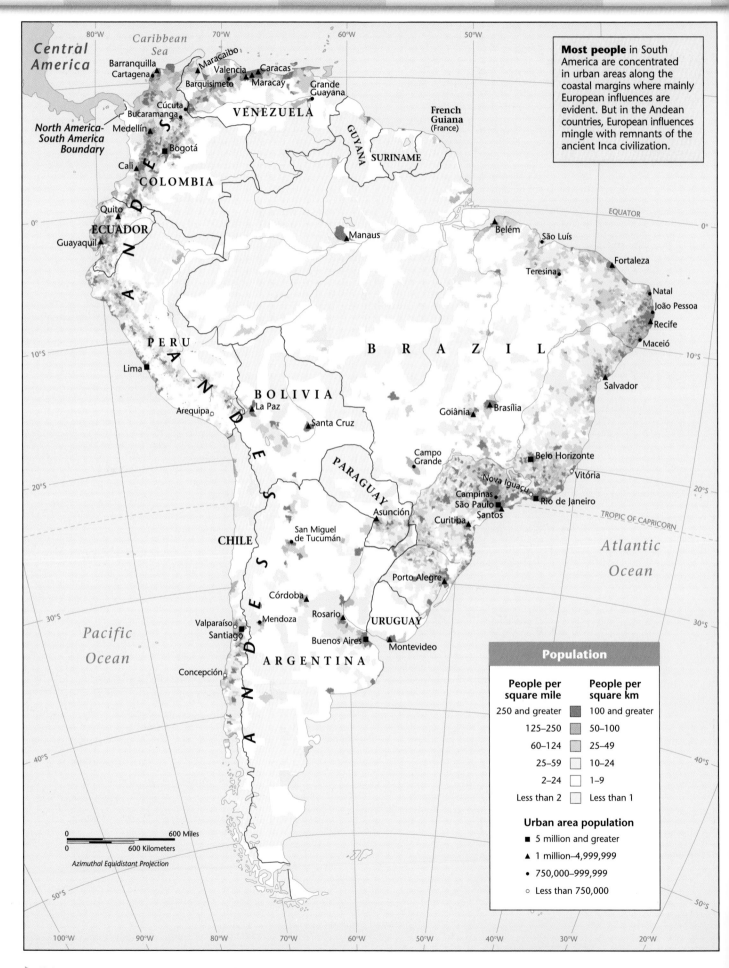

Most people in South America are concentrated in urban areas along the coastal margins where mainly European influences are evident. But in the Andean countries, European influences mingle with remnants of the ancient Inca civilization.

North America-South America Boundary

Central America

Caribbean Sea

VENEZUELA

GUYANA

SURINAME

French Guiana (France)

COLOMBIA

ECUADOR

PERU

BOLIVIA

BRAZIL

PARAGUAY

CHILE

ARGENTINA

URUGUAY

Pacific Ocean

Atlantic Ocean

EQUATOR

TROPIC OF CAPRICORN

Barranquilla
Cartagena
Maracaibo
Valencia
Caracas
Maracay
Barquisimeto
Grande Guayana
Cúcuta
Bucaramanga
Medellín
Bogotá
Cali
Quito
Guayaquil
Manaus
Belém
São Luís
Fortaleza
Teresina
Natal
João Pessoa
Recife
Maceió
Lima
Salvador
Arequipa
La Paz
Santa Cruz
Goiânia
Brasília
Campo Grande
Belo Horizonte
Vitória
Nova Iguaçu
Campinas
São Paulo
Santos
Rio de Janeiro
Asunción
Curitiba
San Miguel de Tucumán
Porto Alegre
Córdoba
Rosario
Valparaíso
Santiago
Mendoza
Buenos Aires
Montevideo
Concepción

ANDES

Population

People per square mile	**People per square km**
250 and greater	100 and greater
125–250	50–100
60–124	25–49
25–59	10–24
2–24	1–9
Less than 2	Less than 1

Urban area population

■ 5 million and greater
▲ 1 million–4,999,999
● 750,000–999,999
○ Less than 750,000

0 — 600 Miles
0 — 600 Kilometers
Azimuthal Equidistant Projection

South America

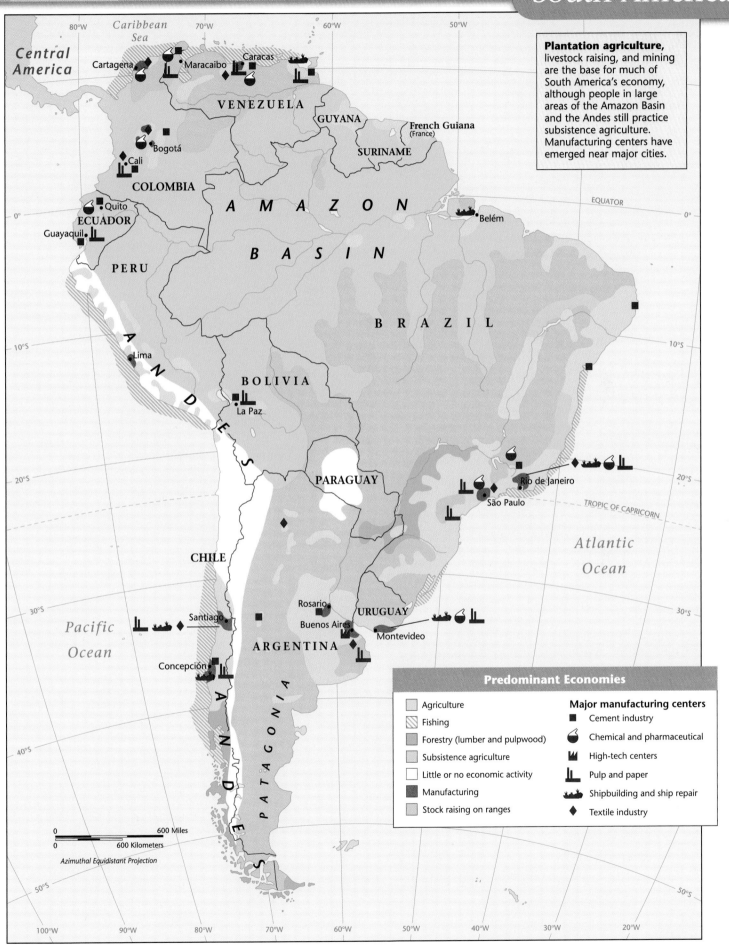

Plantation agriculture, livestock raising, and mining are the base for much of South America's economy, although people in large areas of the Amazon Basin and the Andes still practice subsistence agriculture. Manufacturing centers have emerged near major cities.

Caribbean Sea

Central America

Cartagena
Maracaibo
Caracas
VENEZUELA
GUYANA
French Guiana (France)
SURINAME
Bogotá
Cali
COLOMBIA
Quito
ECUADOR
Guayaquil
PERU
Lima
A M A Z O N
B A S I N
EQUATOR
Belém
BRAZIL
BOLIVIA
La Paz
PARAGUAY
Rio de Janeiro
São Paulo
TROPIC OF CAPRICORN
Atlantic Ocean
CHILE
Rosario
URUGUAY
Santiago
Buenos Aires
Montevideo
ARGENTINA
Pacific Ocean
Concepción
A N D E S
P A T A G O N I A

0°
0°

10°S
10°S

20°S
20°S

30°S
30°S

40°S

50°S
50°S

80°W
70°W
60°W
50°W
100°W
90°W
80°W
70°W
60°W
50°W
40°W
30°W
20°W

0   600 Miles
0   600 Kilometers
Azimuthal Equidistant Projection

Predominant Economies

Agriculture

Fishing

Forestry (lumber and pulpwood)

Subsistence agriculture

Little or no economic activity

Manufacturing

Stock raising on ranges

Major manufacturing centers

■ Cement industry

Chemical and pharmaceutical

High-tech centers

Pulp and paper

Shipbuilding and ship repair

◆ Textile industry

Amazon Rain Forest

AREA ENLARGED

SOUTH AMERICA

The Amazon rain forest, which covers approximately 2.7 million square miles (7 million sq km), is the world's largest tropical forest. Located mainly in Brazil, the Amazon rain forest accounts for more than 20 percent of all the world's tropical forests. Known in Brazil as the selva, the rain forest is a vast storehouse of biological diversity, filled with plants and animals both familiar and exotic. According to estimates, at least half of all species are found in tropical forests, but many of these species have not yet been identified.

Tropical forests contain many valuable resources, including cacao (chocolate), nuts, spices, rare hardwoods, and plant extracts used to make medicines. Some drugs used in treating cancer and heart disease come from plants found only in tropical forests. But human intervention—logging, mining, and clearing land for crops and grazing—has put tropical forests at great risk. In Brazil, roads cut into the rain forest have opened the way for settlers, who clear away the forest only to discover soil too poor in nutrients to sustain agriculture for more than a few years. Land usually is cleared by a method called slash-and-burn, which contributes to global warming by releasing great amounts of carbon dioxide into the atmosphere.

Tropical Forests

Tropical rain forests grow in parts of every continent except Europe and Antarctica. Together, the tropical forests of South America and Africa make up three-quarters of the world's total. Brazil alone has more than 300 million acres (120 million hectares)—more than any other country.

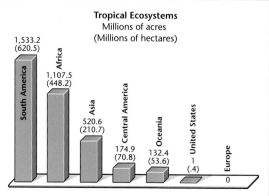

Tropical Ecosystems
Millions of acres
(Millions of hectares)

- South America: 1,533.2 (620.5)
- Africa: 1,107.5 (448.2)
- Asia: 520.6 (210.7)
- Central America: 174.9 (70.8)
- Oceania: 132.4 (53.6)
- United States: 1 (.4)
- Europe: 0

▶ *Price of progress. Clearing trees to make way for expanding economic activities leads to widespread environmental destruction. Slash-and-burn agriculture exposes fragile soils to heat and torrential rains, and the runoff from mining operations pollutes streams and rivers. In an effort to reverse this trend, some countries and international organizations have set up national parks, reserves, and other protected areas.*

Web Link for information on rain forests: http://www.srl.caltech.edu/personnel/krubal/rainforest/Edit560s6/www/facts.ht

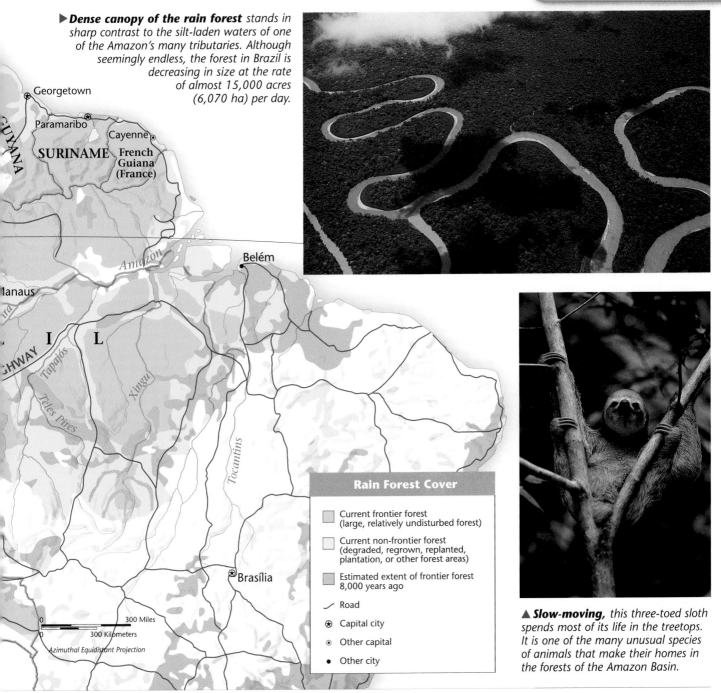

▶ **Dense canopy of the rain forest** *stands in sharp contrast to the silt-laden waters of one of the Amazon's many tributaries. Although seemingly endless, the forest in Brazil is decreasing in size at the rate of almost 15,000 acres (6,070 ha) per day.*

Georgetown

Paramaribo

SURINAME

Cayenne

French Guiana (France)

GUYANA

Amazon

Belém

Manaus

B R A Z I L

Tapajós

HIGHWAY

Xingu

Teles Pires

Tocantins

Brasília

0   300 Miles

0   300 Kilometers

Azimuthal Equidistant Projection

Rain Forest Cover

■	Current frontier forest (large, relatively undisturbed forest)
□	Current non-frontier forest (degraded, regrown, replanted, plantation, or other forest areas)
■	Estimated extent of frontier forest 8,000 years ago
/	Road
⊛	Capital city
⊙	Other capital
•	Other city

▲ **Slow-moving,** *this three-toed sloth spends most of its life in the treetops. It is one of the many unusual species of animals that make their homes in the forests of the Amazon Basin.*

▲ **Slash-and-burn** *is a method used in the tropics for clearing land for farms. But the soil is poor in nutrients, and good yields are short-lived.*

▲ **Mining operations,** *such as this tin mine, remove forests to gain access to mineral deposits.*

79 ◀

Europe

Smaller than every other continent except Australia, Europe is a mosaic of islands and peninsulas. In fact, Europe itself is one big peninsula, jutting westward from the huge land-mass of Asia and nearly touching Africa to the south. Europe's ragged coastline measures more than one and a half times the length of the Equator—38,279 miles (61,603 km) to be exact—giving 31 of its 44 countries direct access to the sea.

Facts & Figures

▶ **Land area:** 3,837,400 sq mi (9,938,000 sq km)

▶ **Population:** 728,392,000

▶ **Highest point:** Mount El'brus, Russia: 18,510 ft (5,642 m)

▶ **Lowest point:** Caspian Sea: 92 ft (28 m) below sea level

▶ **Longest river:** Volga, Russia: 2,290 mi (3,685 km)

▶ **Largest lake entirely in Europe:** Ladoga, Russia: 6,853 sq mi (17,703 sq km)

▶ **Number of independent countries:** 44 (including Russia)

▶ **Largest country entirely in Europe:** Ukraine 233,090 sq mi (603,700 sq km)

▶ **Smallest country:** Vatican City: 0.2 sq mi (0.4 sq km)

▶ **Most populous country entirely in Europe:** Germany: Pop. 82,621,000

▶ **Least populous country:** Vatican City: Pop. 1,000

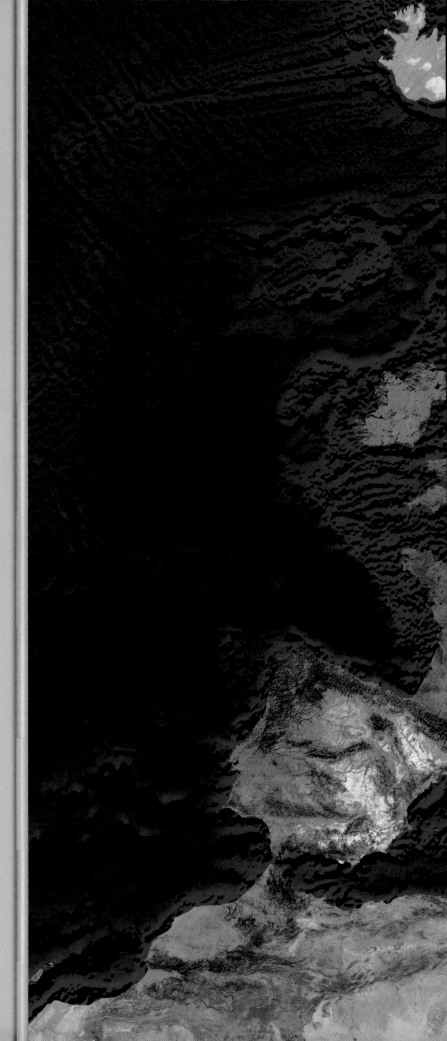

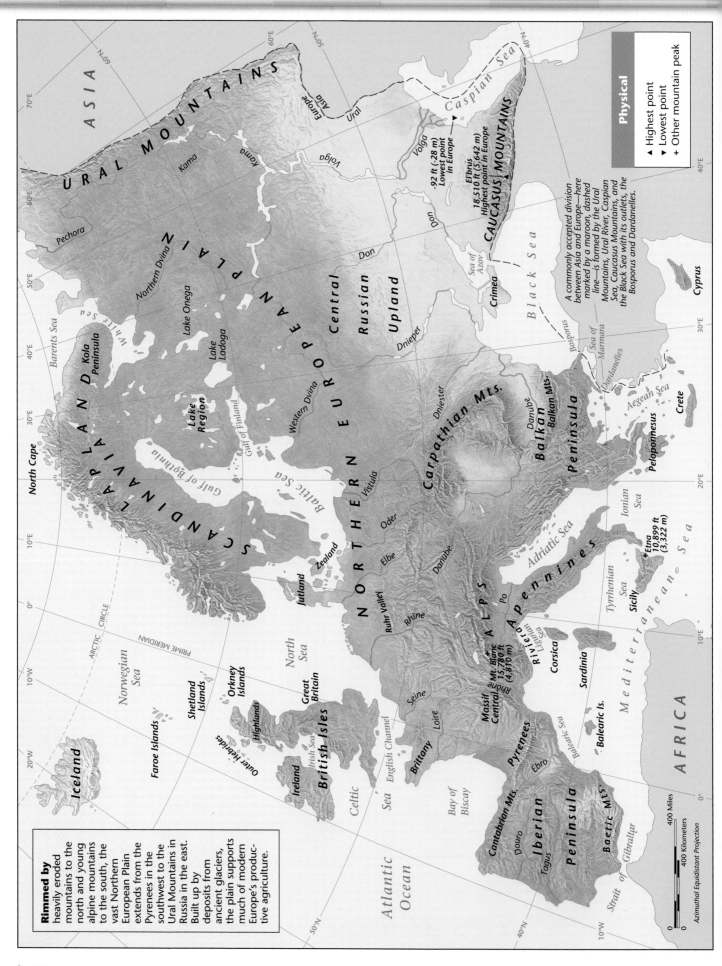

Physical
- ▲ Highest point
- ▼ Lowest point
- + Other mountain peak

A commonly accepted division between Asia and Europe—here marked by a maroon, dashed line—is formed by the Ural Mountains, Ural River, Caspian Sea, Caucasus Mountains, and the Black Sea with its outlets, the Bosporus and Dardanelles.

ASIA

URAL MOUNTAINS

Pechora

Kama

Kama

Volga

Ural

Europe

Asia

Caspian Sea

-92 ft (-28 m) Lowest point in Europe

Elbrus 18,510 ft (5,642 m) Highest point in Europe

CAUCASUS MOUNTAINS

Don

Volga

Don

Northern Dvina

Lake Onega

Lake Ladoga

Barents Sea

White Sea

Kola Peninsula

L A P L A N D

Western Dvina

Dnieper

CENTRAL RUSSIAN UPLAND

NORTHERN EUROPEAN PLAIN

Crimea

Black Sea

Bosporus

Sea of Azov

Sea of Marmara

Dardanelles

Aegean Sea

Cyprus

Crete

Lake Region

Gulf of Finland

Gulf of Bothnia

Baltic Sea

S C A N D I N A V I A

Dniester

Danube

Carpathian Mts.

Balkan Mts.

Balkan Peninsula

Peloponnesus

Ionian Sea

North Cape

Vistula

Oder

Elbe

Danube

Po

Adriatic Sea

A L P S

Apennines

Tyrrhenian Sea

Mediterranean Sea

+ Etna 10,899 ft (3,322 m)

Sicily

Zealand

Jutland

Ruhr Valley

Rhine

Mt. Blanc 15,780 ft (4,810 m)

Massif Central

Rhône

Riviera

Ligurian Sea

Corsica

Sardinia

Balearic Is.

Norwegian Sea

North Sea

Shetland Islands

Orkney Islands

Highlands

Outer Hebrides

Faroe Islands

Iceland

Great Britain

British Isles

Ireland

Irish Sea

Celtic Sea

English Channel

Seine

Loire

Brittany

Bay of Biscay

Pyrenees

Ebro

Cantabrian Mts.

Douro

Tagus

Iberian Peninsula

Baetic Mts.

Strait of Gibraltar

Balearic Sea

AFRICA

Atlantic Ocean

ARCTIC CIRCLE

PRIME MERIDIAN

Rimmed by heavily eroded mountains to the north and young alpine mountains to the south, the vast Northern European Plain extends from the Pyrenees in the southwest to the Ural Mountains in Russia in the east. Built up by deposits from ancient glaciers, the plain supports much of modern Europe's productive agriculture.

400 Miles

400 Kilometers

0

0

Azimuthal Equidistant Projection

▶82

Europe

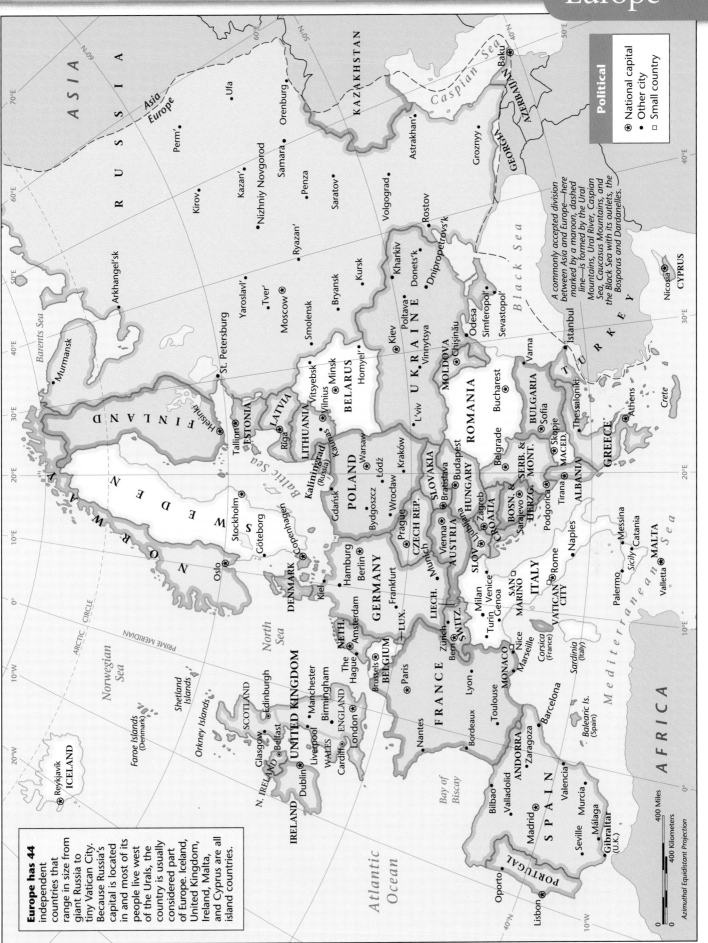

Political

⊛ National capital
• Other city
□ Small country

Europe has 44 independent countries that range in size from giant Russia to tiny Vatican City. Because Russia's capital is located in and most of its people live west of the Urals, the country is usually considered part of Europe. Iceland, United Kingdom, Ireland, Malta, and Cyprus are all island countries.

A commonly accepted division between Asia and Europe—here marked by a maroon, dashed line—is formed by the Ural Mountains, Ural River, Caspian Sea, Caucasus Mountains, and the Black Sea with its outlets, the Bosporus and Dardanelles.

Azimuthal Equidistant Projection

400 Miles

400 Kilometers

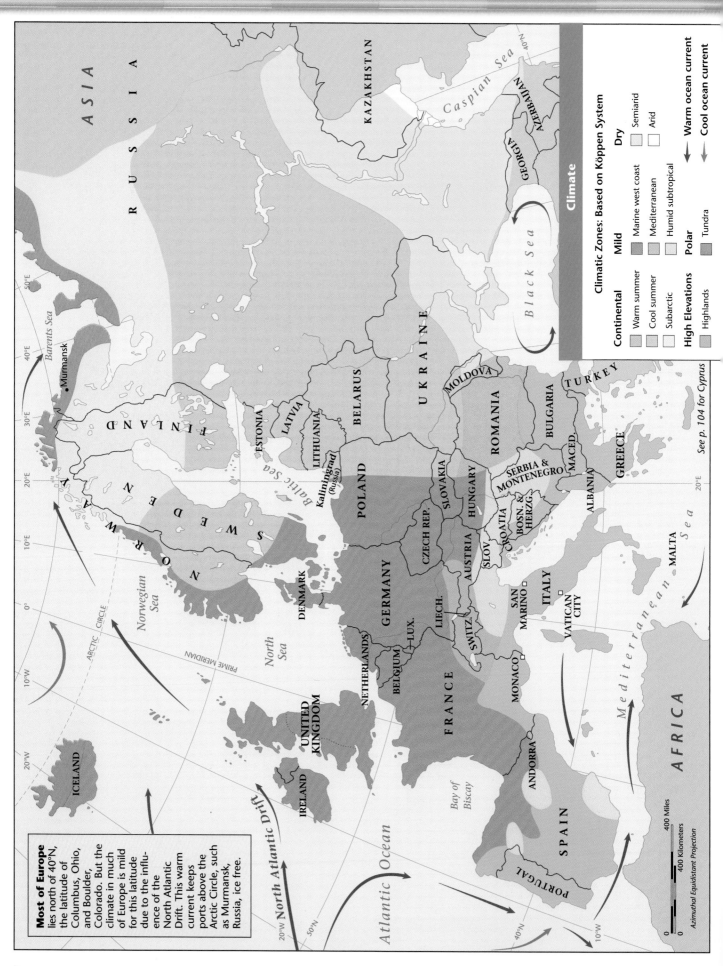

Most of Europe lies north of 40°N, the latitude of Columbus, Ohio, and Boulder, Colorado. But the climate in much of Europe is mild for this latitude due to the influence of the North Atlantic Drift. This warm current keeps ports above the Arctic Circle, such as Murmansk, Russia, ice free.

Climate

Climatic Zones: Based on Köppen System

Continental
- Warm summer
- Cool summer
- Subarctic

Mild
- Marine west coast
- Mediterranean
- Humid subtropical

Dry
- Semiarid
- Arid

Polar
- Tundra

High Elevations
- Highlands

→ Warm ocean current
→ Cool ocean current

See p. 104 for Cyprus

ASIA

RUSSIA

KAZAKHSTAN

Caspian Sea

Barents Sea

Murmansk

GEORGIA

AZERBAIJAN

FINLAND

ESTONIA

LATVIA

LITHUANIA

Kaliningrad (Russia)

BELARUS

UKRAINE

MOLDOVA

Black Sea

ROMANIA

TURKEY

BULGARIA

MACED.

GREECE

SWEDEN

Baltic Sea

POLAND

NORWAY

DENMARK

GERMANY

CZECH REP.

SLOVAKIA

HUNGARY

AUSTRIA

SLOV.

CROATIA

SERBIA & MONTENEGRO

BOSN. & HERZG.

ALBANIA

LIECH.

SWITZ.

SAN MARINO

ITALY

VATICAN CITY

Norwegian Sea

ARCTIC CIRCLE

PRIME MERIDIAN

North Sea

NETHERLANDS

BELGIUM

LUX.

FRANCE

MONACO

ANDORRA

Mediterranean Sea

MALTA

AFRICA

ICELAND

UNITED KINGDOM

IRELAND

North Atlantic Drift

Atlantic Ocean

Bay of Biscay

SPAIN

PORTUGAL

0   400 Miles
0   400 Kilometers
Azimuthal Equidistant Projection

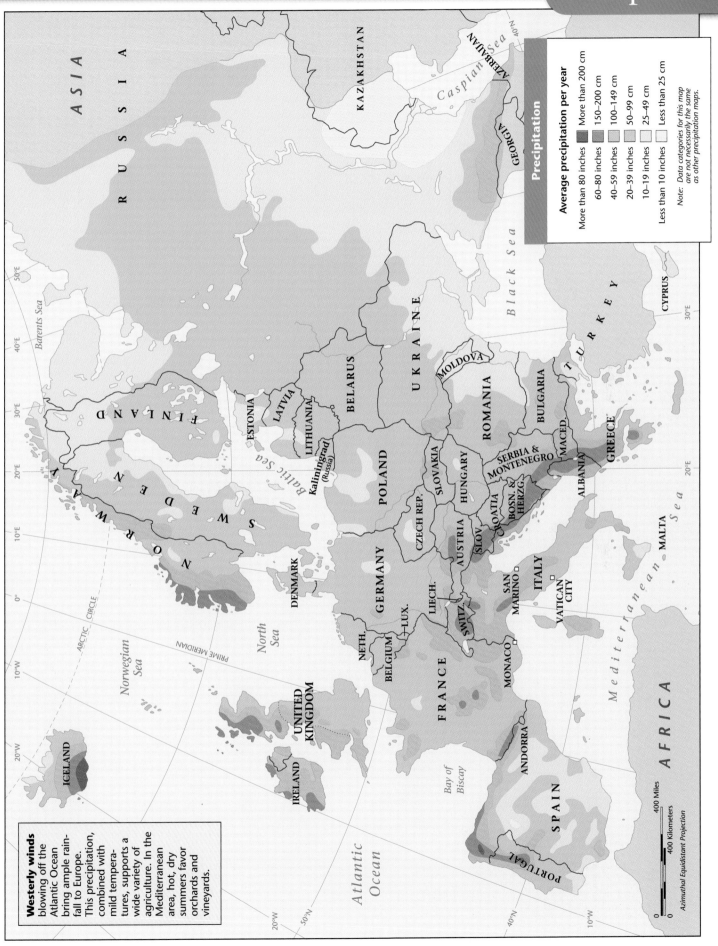

Precipitation

Average precipitation per year

More than 80 inches	More than 200 cm
60–80 inches	150–200 cm
40–59 inches	100–149 cm
20–39 inches	50–99 cm
10–19 inches	25–49 cm
Less than 10 inches	Less than 25 cm

Note: Data categories for this map are not necessarily the same as other precipitation maps.

Westerly winds blowing off the Atlantic Ocean bring ample rainfall to Europe. This precipitation, combined with mild temperatures, supports a wide variety of agriculture. In the Mediterranean area, hot, dry summers favor orchards and vineyards.

400 Miles
400 Kilometers
Azimuthal Equidistant Projection

85 ◀

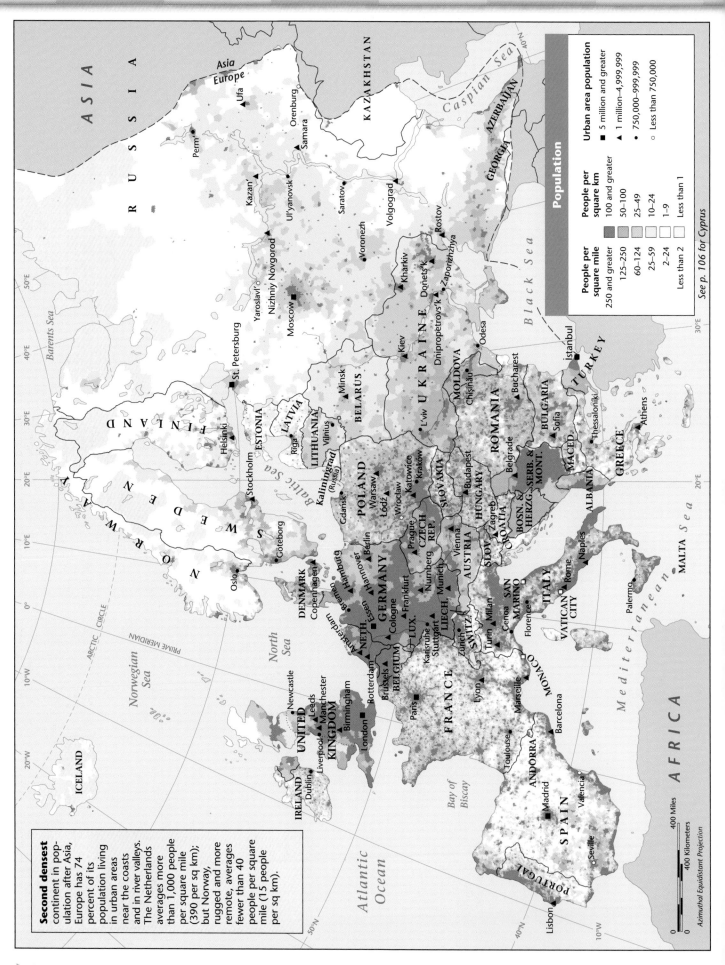

Population

Urban area population
- ■ 5 million and greater
- ▲ 1 million–4,999,999
- ● 750,000–999,999
- ○ Less than 750,000

People per square km	People per square mile
100 and greater	250 and greater
50–100	125–250
25–49	60–124
10–24	25–59
1–9	2–24
Less than 1	Less than 2

See p. 106 for Cyprus

Second densest continent in population after Asia, Europe has 74 percent of its population living in urban areas near the coasts and in river valleys. The Netherlands averages more than 1,000 people per square mile (390 per sq km); but Norway, rugged and more remote, averages fewer than 40 people per square mile (15 people per sq km).

Azimuthal Equidistant Projection

The Industrial Revolution had its beginnings in Europe, and manufacturing is still an important part of the continent's economy. Main industrial centers in the United Kingdom and in Germany's Ruhr region are located near coal deposits, reflecting a time when coal was the main source of energy. Although agriculture is important, the region is not self-sufficient in food production.

Legend (industry symbols):

- ■ Cement industry
- ◗ Chemical and pharmaceutical
- ⚒ High-tech centers
- ⊥ Pulp and paper
- ⛴ Shipbuilding and ship repair
- ◆ Textile industry

Predominant Economies

- Agriculture
- Agriculture and forestry
- Fishing
- Forestry (lumber and pulpwood)
- Hunting, fishing and forestry
- Subsistence agriculture
- Little or no economic activity
- Manufacturing
- Nomadic herding
- Stock raising on ranges

See p. 107 for Cyprus

400 Miles
400 Kilometers
Azimuthal Equidistant Projection

Labels:

ASIA
RUSSIA
KAZAKHSTAN
AZERBAIJAN
GEORGIA
Caspian Sea
Perm'
Yaroslavl'
Moscow
Volgograd
Kharkiv
Kyiv
UKRAINE
BELARUS
MOLDOVA
ROMANIA
BULGARIA
TURKEY
Black Sea
GREECE
Athens
MACED.
ALBANIA
SERB. & MONT.
BOSN. & HERZG.
CROATIA
HUNGARY
SLOVAKIA
AUSTRIA
SLOV.
ITALY
SAN MARINO
VATICAN CITY
MONACO
Mediterranean Sea
MALTA
AFRICA
ANDORRA
Barcelona
SPAIN
Madrid
PORTUGAL
Atlantic Ocean
IRELAND
UNITED KINGDOM
London
FRANCE
Paris
NETH.
BELGIUM
LUX.
GERMANY
Berlin
Hamburg
DENMARK
North Sea
LIECH.
SWITZ.
CZECH REP.
POLAND
Warsaw
Kaliningrad (Russia)
LITHUANIA
LATVIA
ESTONIA
FINLAND
SWEDEN
NORWAY
Baltic Sea
ARCTIC CIRCLE
PRIME MERIDIAN
ICELAND

20°W
20°E
40°E
50°E
40°N
40°N
10°W

87

Time Line
Key Events in the Evolution of the European Union

1950 Union of Europe's coal and steel industries was proposed by Robert Schuman of France.

1951 European Coal and Steel Community (ECSC) was established, composed of Belgium, Italy, Netherlands, Luxembourg, France, and West Germany.

1957 European Economic Community (EEC) was set up to oversee economic integration of European nations.

1965 European Community (EC) was formed from EEC and other European organizations.

1973 Denmark, Republic of Ireland, and the United Kingdom became members of the EC.

1979 European Monetary System (EMS) was initiated.

1981 Greece became a member.

1986 Spain and Portugal became members.

1989 Plan for an Economic and Monetary Union (EMU) was endorsed.

1990 Former East Germany was admitted as part of a reunited Germany.

1993 Maastricht Treaty created the European Union (EU) after ratification by member countries.

1995 Austria, Finland, and Sweden became members of the EU.

1999 Euro was introduced as an accounting currency in 11 EMU member countries.

2002 Euro began circulating, replacing national currencies in all EMU member countries.

2004 Cyprus, Czech Republic, Estonia, Hungary, Latvia, Lithuania, Malta, Poland, Slovakia, and Slovenia became members of the EU, bringing the total membership to 25.

FOCUS ON

European Union

In the years following World War II, the countries of Europe looked for ways to restore political stability to the continent while rebuilding their war-ravaged economies. The first step toward the European Union was taken in 1950 when France proposed creating common institutions to govern coal and steel production in Europe jointly. In 1951 France, West Germany, Italy, Belgium, Netherlands, and Luxembourg created the European Coal and Steel Community with the goal of bringing former adversaries together. In 1965 that organization joined with others to form the European Community (EC).

The Maastricht Treaty took effect in 1993, establishing today's European Union (EU) and paving the way for a common foreign policy and a single European currency—the euro. The treaty also laid plans for the open flow of people, products, and services among member countries. In 1995 membership rose to 15 when Austria, Sweden, and Finland joined, and in May 2004 ten more countries were added: Estonia, Latvia, Lithuania, Poland, Czech Republic, Slovakia, Hungary, Cyprus, Slovenia, and Malta. Romania, Bulgaria, Croatia, and Turkey have applied for membership.

▲ ***Main trade outlet*** *for Germany's heavily industrialized Ruhr Valley, the port of Rotterdam in the Netherlands accommodates massive supertankers and container ships.*

Web Link for information on the European Union: www.europa.eu.int

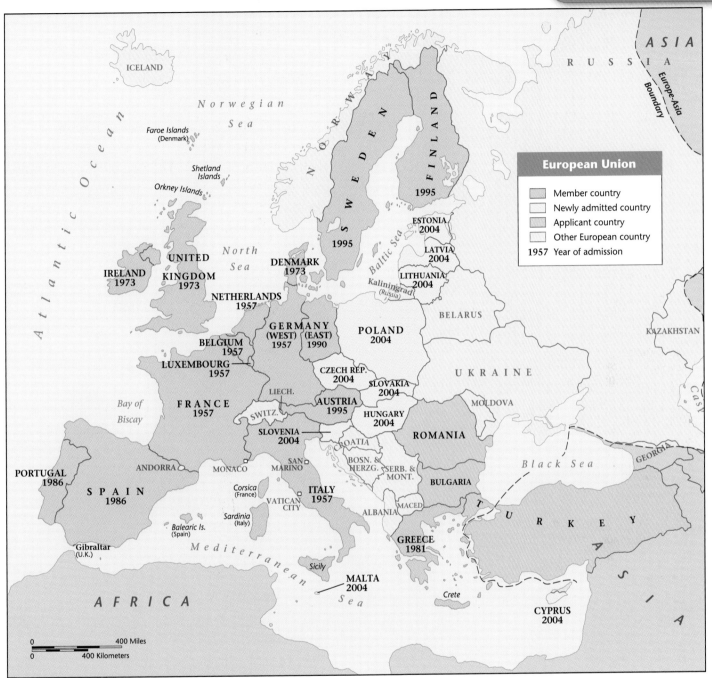

European Union

- Member country
- Newly admitted country
- Applicant country
- Other European country
- 1957   Year of admission

ICELAND

Norwegian Sea

Faroe Islands (Denmark)

Shetland Islands

Orkney Islands

Atlantic Ocean

North Sea

IRELAND 1973

UNITED KINGDOM 1973

NETHERLANDS 1957

BELGIUM 1957

LUXEMBOURG 1957

DENMARK 1973

N O R W A Y

S W E D E N 1995

FINLAND 1995

ESTONIA 2004

Baltic Sea

LATVIA 2004

LITHUANIA 2004

Kaliningrad (Russia)

BELARUS

GERMANY (WEST) 1957 (EAST) 1990

POLAND 2004

CZECH REP. 2004

SLOVAKIA 2004

UKRAINE

LIECH.

AUSTRIA 1995

HUNGARY 2004

MOLDOVA

Bay of Biscay

FRANCE 1957

SWITZ.

SLOVENIA 2004

CROATIA

ROMANIA

A S I A

R U S S I A

Europe-Asia Boundary

KAZAKHSTAN

Casp

GEORGIA

PORTUGAL 1986

ANDORRA

MONACO

SAN MARINO

BOSN. & HERZG.

SERB. & MONT.

Black Sea

S P A I N 1986

Corsica (France)

VATICAN CITY

ITALY 1957

Sardinia (Italy)

ALBANIA

MACED.

BULGARIA

T U R K E Y

Gibraltar (U.K.)

Balearic Is. (Spain)

M e d i t e r r a n e a n

Sicily

GREECE 1981

A S I A

A F R I C A

MALTA 2004

Sea

Crete

CYPRUS 2004

0   400 Miles
0   400 Kilometers

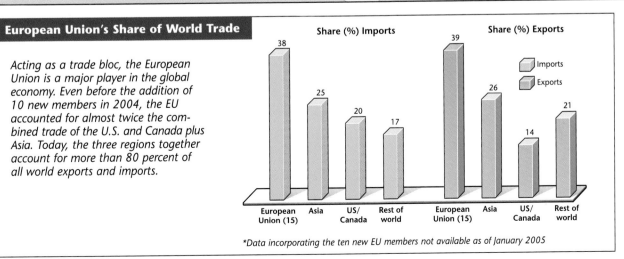

European Union's Share of World Trade

Acting as a trade bloc, the European Union is a major player in the global economy. Even before the addition of 10 new members in 2004, the EU accounted for almost twice the combined trade of the U.S. and Canada plus Asia. Today, the three regions together account for more than 80 percent of all world exports and imports.

Share (%) Imports

- European Union (15): 38
- Asia: 25
- US/Canada: 20
- Rest of world: 17

Share (%) Exports

- European Union (15): 39
- Asia: 26
- US/Canada: 14
- Rest of world: 21

Imports
Exports

*Data incorporating the ten new EU members not available as of January 2005

Africa

From space, Africa appears divided into three regions: the northern third, dominated by the vast Sahara, largest hot desert in the world; a central green band of rain forests and tropical grasslands; and more dry lands to the south. Africa itself may be dividing literally: The Great Rift Valley, which runs from the Red Sea through the volcanic Afar Triangle to the lake district in the south (see map page 99), eventually may split apart the continent.

Facts & Figures

▲ **Land area:** 11,609,000 sq mi (30,065,000 sq km)

▲ **Population:** 884,966,000

▲ **Highest point:** Kilimanjaro, Tanzania: 19,340 ft (5,895 m)

▲ **Lowest point:** Lake Assal, Djibouti: 512 ft (156 m) below sea level

▲ **Longest river:** Nile: 4,241 mi (6,825 km)

▲ **Largest Lake:** Victoria: 26,836 sq mi (69,500 sq km)

▲ **Number of independent countries:** 53

▲ **Largest country:** Sudan: 967,500 sq mi (2,505,813 sq km)

▲ **Smallest country:** Seychelles: 176 sq mi (455 sq km)

▲ **Most populous country:** Nigeria: Pop. 137,253,000

▲ **Least populous country:** Seychelles: Pop. 80,000

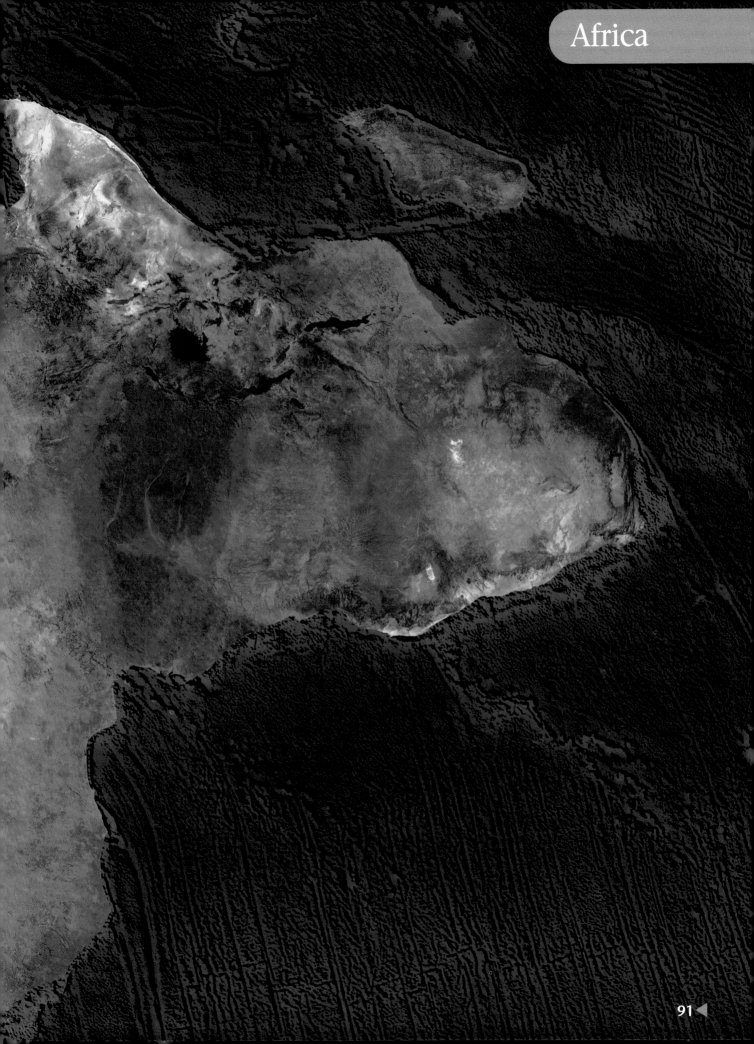

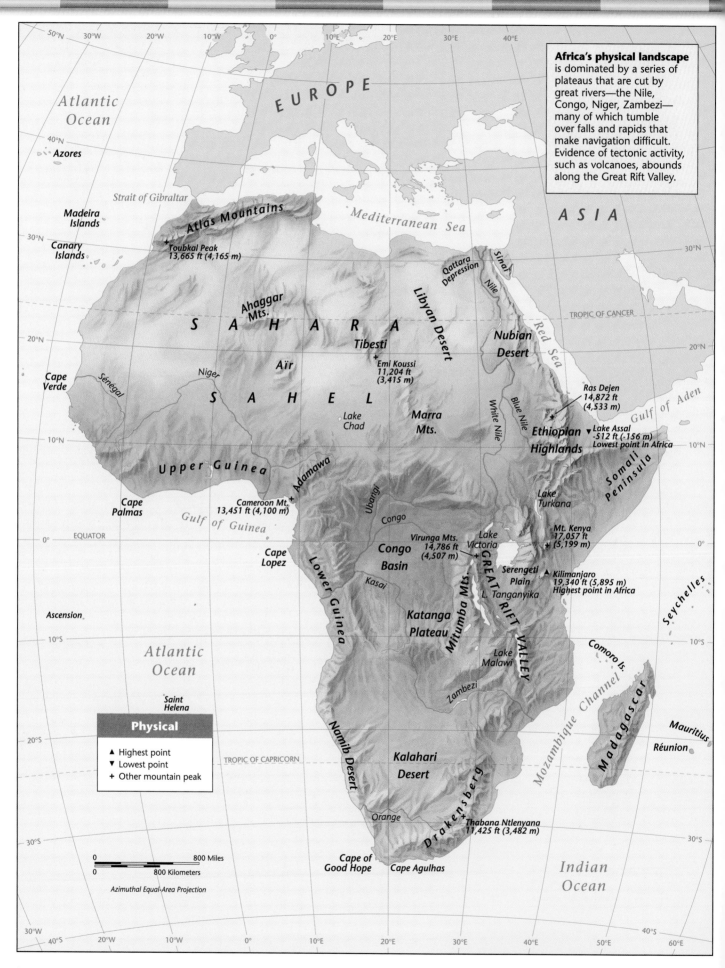

Atlantic
Ocean

EUROPE

ASIA

Azores

Madeira
Islands

Canary
Islands

Strait of Gibraltar

Atlas Mountains

+ Toubkal Peak
13,665 ft (4,165 m)

Mediterranean Sea

Qattara
Depression

Sinai

Nile

Red Sea

TROPIC OF CANCER

Ahaggar
Mts.

S A H A R A

Libyan Desert

Nubian
Desert

Cape
Verde

Sénégal

Niger

Air

S A H E L

Tibesti

+ Emi Koussi
11,204 ft
(3,415 m)

Lake
Chad

Marra
Mts.

White Nile

Blue Nile

Ethiopian
Highlands

Ras Dejen
14,872 ft
(4,533 m)
+

Gulf of Aden

Lake Assal ▼
-512 ft (-156 m)
Lowest point in Africa

Somali
Peninsula

Cape
Palmas

Gulf of Guinea

Upper Guinea

Adamawa

Cameroon Mt. +
13,451 ft (4,100 m)

Ubangi

Congo

Lake
Turkana

Mt. Kenya
17,057 ft
+ (5,199 m)

EQUATOR

Cape
Lopez

Congo
Basin

Kasai

Virunga Mts.
14,786 ft
(4,507 m)

Lake
Victoria

GREAT
RIFT
VALLEY

Serengeti
Plain

L. Tanganyika

▲ Kilimanjaro
19,340 ft (5,895 m)
Highest point in Africa

Seychelles

Ascension

Lower Guinea

Katanga
Plateau

Mitumba Mts.

Lake
Malawi

Comoro Is.

Atlantic
Ocean

Saint
Helena

Zambezi

Mozambique Channel

Madagascar

Mauritius

Réunion

Physical

▲ Highest point
▼ Lowest point
+ Other mountain peak

Namib Desert

TROPIC OF CAPRICORN

Kalahari
Desert

Drakensberg

Orange

Thabana Ntlenyana
+ 11,425 ft (3,482 m)

0   800 Miles
0   800 Kilometers

Azimuthal Equal-Area Projection

Cape of
Good Hope

Cape Agulhas

Indian
Ocean

Africa's physical landscape
is dominated by a series of
plateaus that are cut by
great rivers—the Nile,
Congo, Niger, Zambezi—
many of which tumble
over falls and rapids that
make navigation difficult.
Evidence of tectonic activity,
such as volcanoes, abounds
along the Great Rift Valley.

Africa

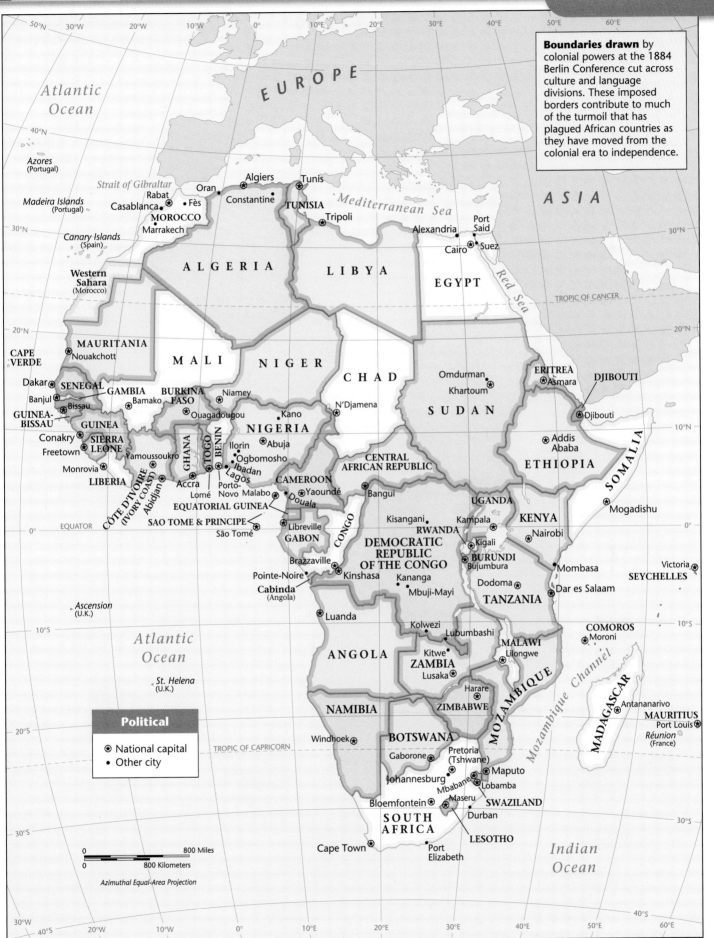

Boundaries drawn by colonial powers at the 1884 Berlin Conference cut across culture and language divisions. These imposed borders contribute to much of the turmoil that has plagued African countries as they have moved from the colonial era to independence.

EUROPE

ASIA

Atlantic Ocean

Azores (Portugal)

Madeira Islands (Portugal)

Strait of Gibraltar

Oran • Algiers • Tunis
Rabat • • Constantine • TUNISIA
Casablanca • • Fès
MOROCCO • Tripoli
Marrakech •

Canary Islands (Spain)

Mediterranean Sea

Alexandria • Port Said
Cairo • • Suez

Red Sea

Western Sahara (Morocco)

ALGERIA

LIBYA

EGYPT

TROPIC OF CANCER

CAPE VERDE

MAURITANIA
• Nouakchott

MALI

NIGER

CHAD

Omdurman •
Khartoum •

SUDAN

ERITREA
• Asmara

DJIBOUTI
• Djibouti

Dakar •
SENEGAL **GAMBIA** **BURKINA FASO**
Banjul • • Niamey
Bamako •
GUINEA-BISSAU Bissau •
GUINEA
Conakry • **SIERRA LEONE**
Freetown •
Monrovia •
LIBERIA

Ouagadougou •
• Kano
NIGERIA
Ilorin • • Abuja
Ogbomosho •
Yamoussoukro • Ibadan •
Accra • Lagos
CÔTE D'IVOIRE (IVORY COAST) Lomé Porto-Novo Malabo •
Abidjan **GHANA** **TOGO** **BENIN**

N'Djamena •

CENTRAL AFRICAN REPUBLIC

Addis Ababa •

ETHIOPIA

SOMALIA

• Mogadishu

EQUATORIAL GUINEA
SAO TOME & PRINCIPE
São Tomé •

• Yaoundé
CAMEROON
Douala •
Libreville •
GABON
CONGO

Bangui •

UGANDA
Kampala •
Kisangani •
RWANDA
Kigali •
BURUNDI
Bujumbura •

KENYA
• Nairobi

EQUATOR

Brazzaville •
Pointe-Noire •
Cabinda (Angola)

Kinshasa •
DEMOCRATIC REPUBLIC OF THE CONGO
Kananga •
Mbuji-Mayi •

Dodoma •
Dar es Salaam •
TANZANIA

Mombasa •

Victoria •
SEYCHELLES

Ascension (U.K.)

• Luanda

Kolwezi •

COMOROS
• Moroni

Atlantic Ocean

St. Helena (U.K.)

Lubumbashi •
Kitwe •
ANGOLA
ZAMBIA
Lusaka •

MALAWI
Lilongwe •

MADAGASCAR
Antananarivo •
MAURITIUS
Port Louis •
Réunion (France)

Mozambique Channel

NAMIBIA

Harare •
ZIMBABWE

MOZAMBIQUE

Windhoek •

TROPIC OF CAPRICORN

BOTSWANA

Political

⊛ National capital
• Other city

Gaborone •
Pretoria (Tshwane) •
Johannesburg •
Mbabane • Maputo •
Lobamba •
Bloemfontein • Maseru • **SWAZILAND**
LESOTHO
Durban •
SOUTH AFRICA
Cape Town • Port Elizabeth

Indian Ocean

0   800 Miles
0   800 Kilometers

Azimuthal Equal-Area Projection

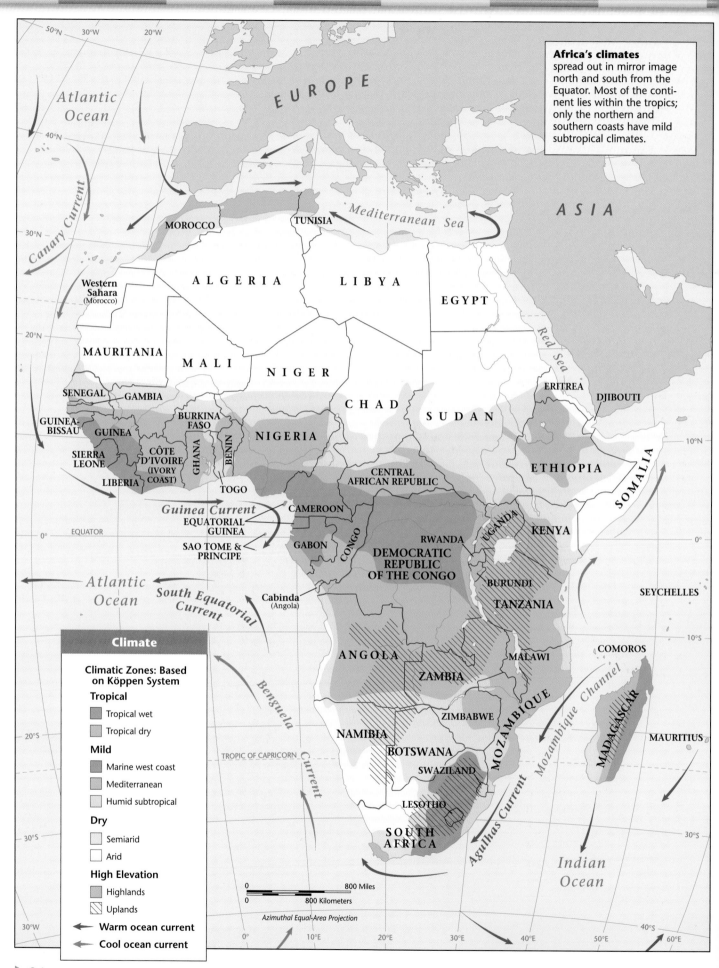

Africa's climates
spread out in mirror image north and south from the Equator. Most of the continent lies within the tropics; only the northern and southern coasts have mild subtropical climates.

EUROPE

ASIA

Atlantic Ocean

Mediterranean Sea

Canary Current

MOROCCO

TUNISIA

Western Sahara (Morocco)

ALGERIA

LIBYA

EGYPT

Red Sea

MAURITANIA

MALI

NIGER

CHAD

SUDAN

ERITREA

DJIBOUTI

SENEGAL

GAMBIA

GUINEA-BISSAU

GUINEA

BURKINA FASO

NIGERIA

CENTRAL AFRICAN REPUBLIC

ETHIOPIA

SOMALIA

SIERRA LEONE

CÔTE D'IVOIRE (IVORY COAST)

GHANA

BENIN

TOGO

LIBERIA

Guinea Current

CAMEROON

EQUATORIAL GUINEA

SAO TOME & PRINCIPE

GABON

CONGO

DEMOCRATIC REPUBLIC OF THE CONGO

RWANDA

UGANDA

KENYA

BURUNDI

TANZANIA

EQUATOR

Atlantic Ocean

South Equatorial Current

Cabinda (Angola)

SEYCHELLES

COMOROS

ANGOLA

MALAWI

ZAMBIA

MOZAMBIQUE

Mozambique Channel

MADAGASCAR

MAURITIUS

ZIMBABWE

NAMIBIA

Benguela Current

TROPIC OF CAPRICORN

BOTSWANA

SWAZILAND

Agulhas Current

LESOTHO

SOUTH AFRICA

Indian Ocean

Climate

Climatic Zones: Based on Köppen System

Tropical
- Tropical wet
- Tropical dry

Mild
- Marine west coast
- Mediterranean
- Humid subtropical

Dry
- Semiarid
- Arid

High Elevation
- Highlands
- Uplands

→ **Warm ocean current**
→ **Cool ocean current**

0   800 Miles
0   800 Kilometers

Azimuthal Equal-Area Projection

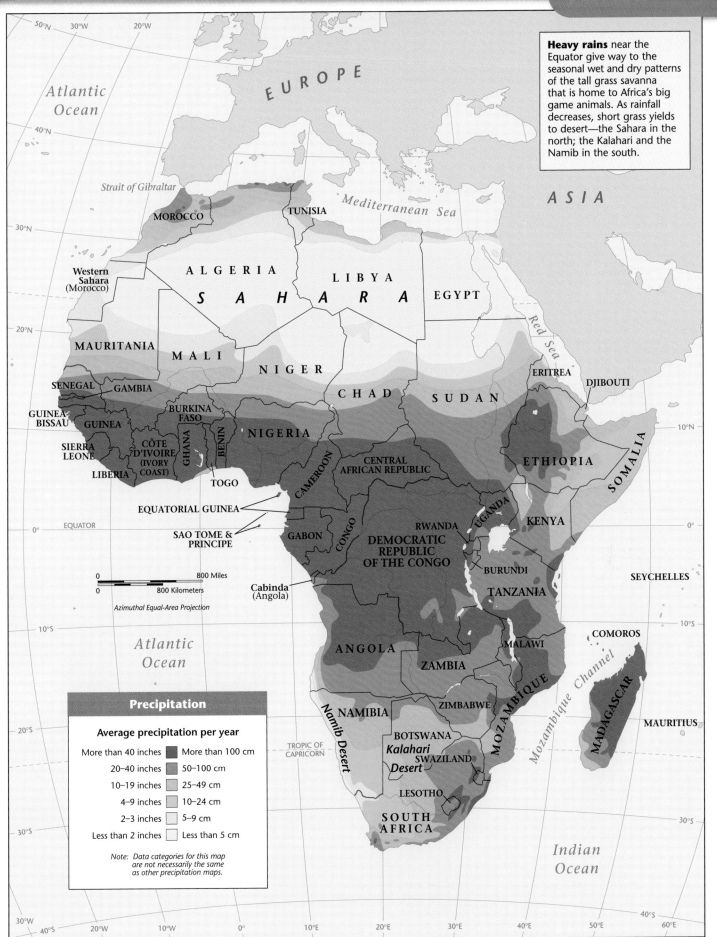

Heavy rains near the Equator give way to the seasonal wet and dry patterns of the tall grass savanna that is home to Africa's big game animals. As rainfall decreases, short grass yields to desert—the Sahara in the north; the Kalahari and the Namib in the south.

Atlantic Ocean

EUROPE

ASIA

Strait of Gibraltar

Mediterranean Sea

MOROCCO   TUNISIA

ALGERIA   LIBYA   EGYPT

S A H A R A

Western Sahara (Morocco)

Red Sea

MAURITANIA   M A L I

N I G E R   C H A D   S U D A N   ERITREA   DJIBOUTI

SENEGAL   GAMBIA
GUINEA-BISSAU   GUINEA   BURKINA FASO
SIERRA LEONE   CÔTE D'IVOIRE (IVORY COAST)   GHANA   BENIN   N I G E R I A   CAMEROON   CENTRAL AFRICAN REPUBLIC   ETHIOPIA   SOMALIA
LIBERIA   TOGO

EQUATORIAL GUINEA

SAO TOME & PRINCIPE

GABON   CONGO   DEMOCRATIC REPUBLIC OF THE CONGO   UGANDA   RWANDA   KENYA
BURUNDI

EQUATOR

Cabinda (Angola)

TANZANIA   SEYCHELLES

0   800 Miles
0   800 Kilometers
Azimuthal Equal-Area Projection

Atlantic Ocean

ANGOLA   ZAMBIA   MALAWI   COMOROS

ZIMBABWE   MOZAMBIQUE   MADAGASCAR   MAURITIUS

Namib Desert   NAMIBIA   BOTSWANA
Kalahari Desert   SWAZILAND

TROPIC OF CAPRICORN

LESOTHO

SOUTH AFRICA

Mozambique Channel

Indian Ocean

Precipitation

Average precipitation per year

More than 40 inches	More than 100 cm
20–40 inches	50–100 cm
10–19 inches	25–49 cm
4–9 inches	10–24 cm
2–3 inches	5–9 cm
Less than 2 inches	Less than 5 cm

Note: Data categories for this map are not necessarily the same as other precipitation maps.

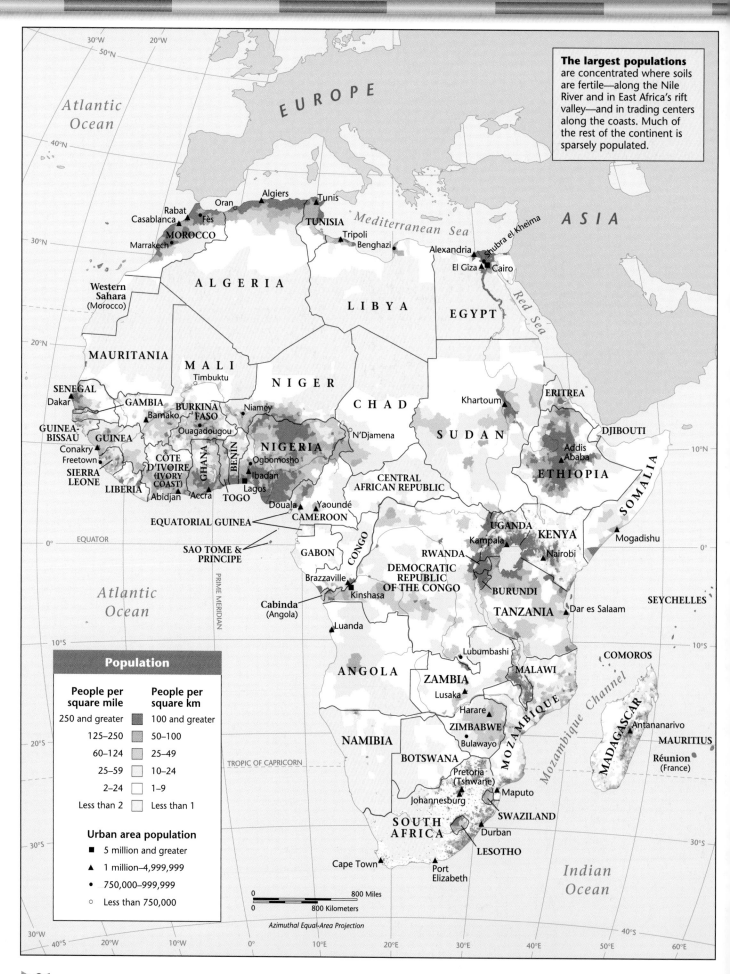

The largest populations are concentrated where soils are fertile—along the Nile River and in East Africa's rift valley—and in trading centers along the coasts. Much of the rest of the continent is sparsely populated.

EUROPE

ASIA

Atlantic Ocean

Mediterranean Sea

Red Sea

MOROCCO
Rabat
Casablanca
Fès
Oran
Algiers
Tunis
TUNISIA
Tripoli
Benghazi
Alexandria
Shubra el Kheima
El Gîza
Cairo
Marrakech

Western Sahara (Morocco)

ALGERIA

LIBYA

EGYPT

MAURITANIA

MALI
Timbuktu

NIGER

CHAD

SUDAN
Khartoum

ERITREA

DJIBOUTI

SENEGAL
Dakar
GAMBIA
BURKINA FASO
Bamako
Niamey
Ouagadougou
GUINEA-BISSAU
GUINEA
Conakry
Freetown
SIERRA LEONE
LIBERIA
CÔTE D'IVOIRE (IVORY COAST)
GHANA
BENIN
TOGO
Abidjan
Accra
Ogbomosho
Ibadan
Lagos
NIGERIA
N'Djamena
CENTRAL AFRICAN REPUBLIC
Addis Ababa
ETHIOPIA
SOMALIA

Douala
Yaoundé
CAMEROON
EQUATORIAL GUINEA
SAO TOME & PRINCIPE
GABON
CONGO
Brazzaville
Kinshasa
Cabinda (Angola)
DEMOCRATIC REPUBLIC OF THE CONGO
UGANDA
Kampala
RWANDA
BURUNDI
KENYA
Nairobi
Mogadishu

EQUATOR

Atlantic Ocean

Luanda

TANZANIA
Dar es Salaam

SEYCHELLES

Lubumbashi

ANGOLA
ZAMBIA
Lusaka
MALAWI
MOZAMBIQUE
COMOROS
Mozambique Channel
MADAGASCAR
Antananarivo
MAURITIUS
Réunion (France)

Harare
ZIMBABWE
Bulawayo

NAMIBIA
BOTSWANA
TROPIC OF CAPRICORN

Pretoria (Tshwane)
Johannesburg
Maputo
SWAZILAND
Durban
LESOTHO
SOUTH AFRICA
Cape Town
Port Elizabeth

Indian Ocean

PRIME MERIDIAN

Population

People per square mile	People per square km
250 and greater	100 and greater
125–250	50–100
60–124	25–49
25–59	10–24
2–24	1–9
Less than 2	Less than 1

Urban area population

■ 5 million and greater
▲ 1 million–4,999,999
● 750,000–999,999
○ Less than 750,000

0   800 Miles
0   800 Kilometers

Azimuthal Equal-Area Projection

Africa

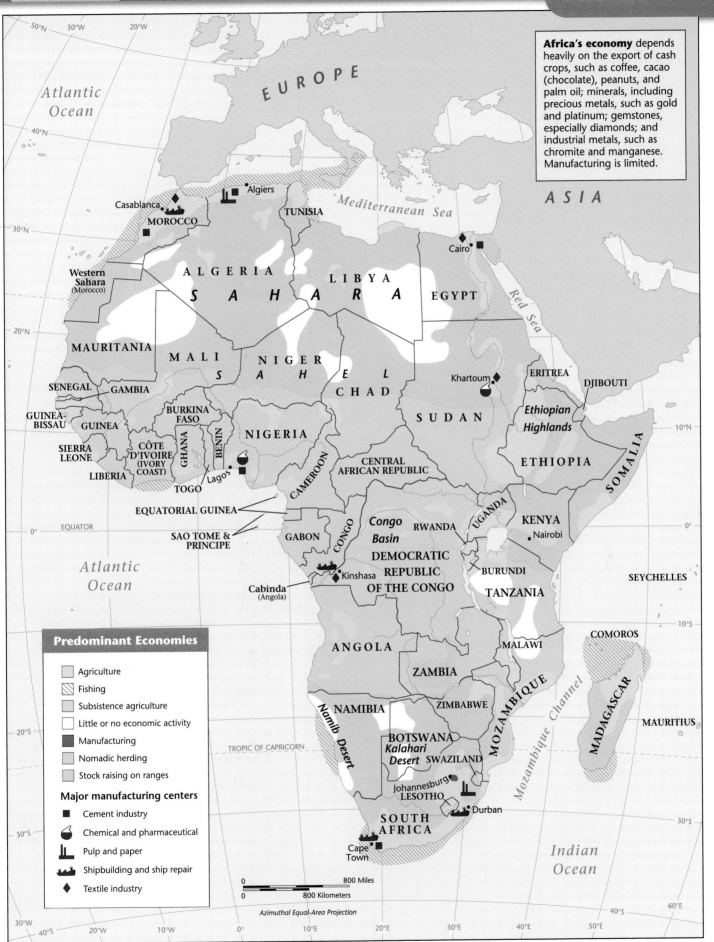

Africa's economy depends heavily on the export of cash crops, such as coffee, cacao (chocolate), peanuts, and palm oil; minerals, including precious metals, such as gold and platinum; gemstones, especially diamonds; and industrial metals, such as chromite and manganese. Manufacturing is limited.

EUROPE

Atlantic Ocean

Mediterranean Sea

ASIA

Casablanca
Algiers
MOROCCO
TUNISIA
Cairo
Western Sahara (Morocco)
ALGERIA
LIBYA
EGYPT
SAHARA
Red Sea
MAURITANIA
MALI
NIGER
SAHEL
CHAD
Khartoum
ERITREA
DJIBOUTI
SENEGAL
GAMBIA
SUDAN
Ethiopian Highlands
GUINEA-BISSAU
GUINEA
BURKINA FASO
NIGERIA
CENTRAL AFRICAN REPUBLIC
ETHIOPIA
SOMALIA
SIERRA LEONE
CÔTE D'IVOIRE (IVORY COAST)
GHANA
BENIN
LIBERIA
TOGO
Lagos
EQUATORIAL GUINEA
CAMEROON
UGANDA
KENYA
SAO TOME & PRINCIPE
GABON
CONGO
Congo Basin
RWANDA
Nairobi
EQUATOR
DEMOCRATIC REPUBLIC OF THE CONGO
Kinshasa
BURUNDI
SEYCHELLES
Cabinda (Angola)
TANZANIA
Atlantic Ocean
COMOROS
ANGOLA
MALAWI
ZAMBIA
MADAGASCAR
ZIMBABWE
MOZAMBIQUE
MAURITIUS
NAMIBIA
Namib Desert
BOTSWANA
Kalahari Desert
Mozambique Channel
TROPIC OF CAPRICORN
SWAZILAND
Johannesburg
LESOTHO
Durban
SOUTH AFRICA
Cape Town
Indian Ocean

Predominant Economies

- ☐ Agriculture
- ▨ Fishing
- ☐ Subsistence agriculture
- ☐ Little or no economic activity
- ■ Manufacturing
- ☐ Nomadic herding
- ☐ Stock raising on ranges

Major manufacturing centers

- ■ Cement industry
- ♨ Chemical and pharmaceutical
- ⊥ Pulp and paper
- ⚓ Shipbuilding and ship repair
- ◆ Textile industry

0   800 Miles
0   800 Kilometers

Azimuthal Equal-Area Projection

Great Rift Valley

More than a hundred million years ago, Gondwana, the southern part of the supercontinent Pangaea, began to break apart. Landmasses that we know today as South America, Antarctica, Australia, and the Indian subcontinent slowly moved away, propelled by tectonic forces originating deep within Earth (see map page 14). The part of Gondwana that was left behind is what we know as Africa.

The forces that tore apart Gondwana continue today, especially in East Africa where the Great Rift Valley marks the boundary of what many earth scientists believe eventually will be a new sea that will separate part of eastern and southern Africa from the rest of the continent.

30 million years before present

The Arabian Peninsula and Africa were joined as one landmass 30 million years ago.

7 million years before present

ASIA

AFRICA

Fiery-hot magma rising from within Earth caused rifting that began to push apart the land along what is now the Red Sea.

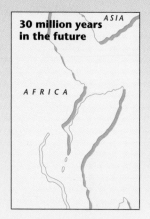

30 million years in the future

ASIA

AFRICA

Long, narrow lakes could become a single channel if rifting continues and causes the Somali Plate to break away.

▶ **Volcanic cones** *in the tiny country of Djibouti mark the area where active tectonic rifting may someday result in the formation of a new ocean.*

▼ **Colorful flamingos** *are attracted to rift valley lakes, where high evaporation rates help create alkaline waters. The birds feed on brine shrimp and various kinds of algae.*

▶ **Subsistence farmers,** *many of them women, grow staple crops of maize (corn) and beans in the fertile volcanic soils. Large commercial farms produce cash crops, such as coffee and sisal.*

Web Link for information on Great Rift Valley: http://4dw.net/geolor/EastAfrican_Rift_Valley_geolor.htm

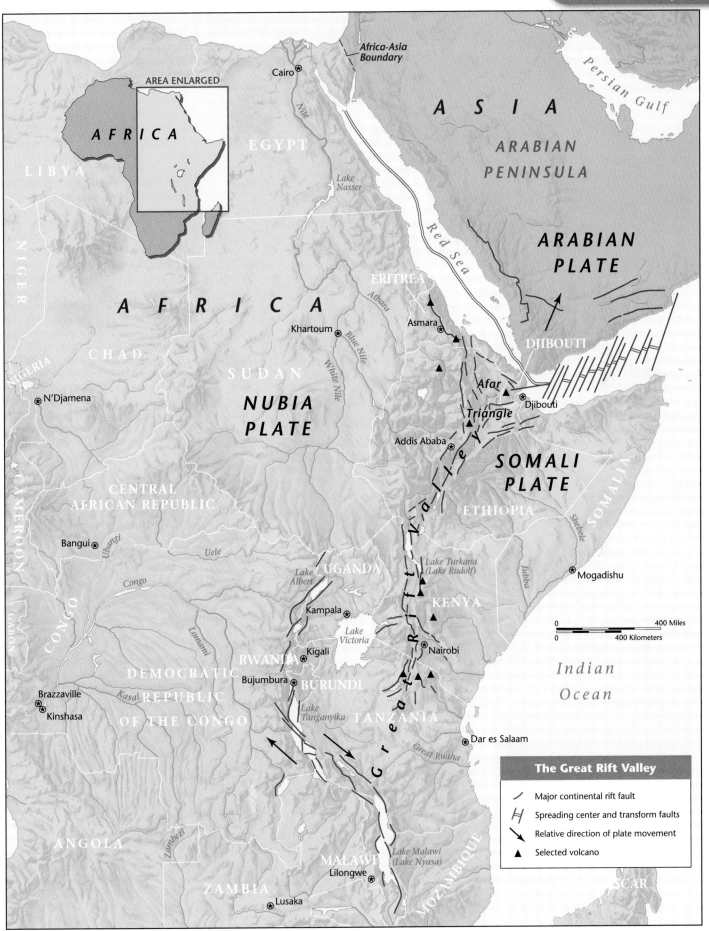

Africa
Great Rift Valley

The Great Rift Valley

- / Major continental rift fault
- H Spreading center and transform faults
- ↗ Relative direction of plate movement
- ▲ Selected volcano

Asia

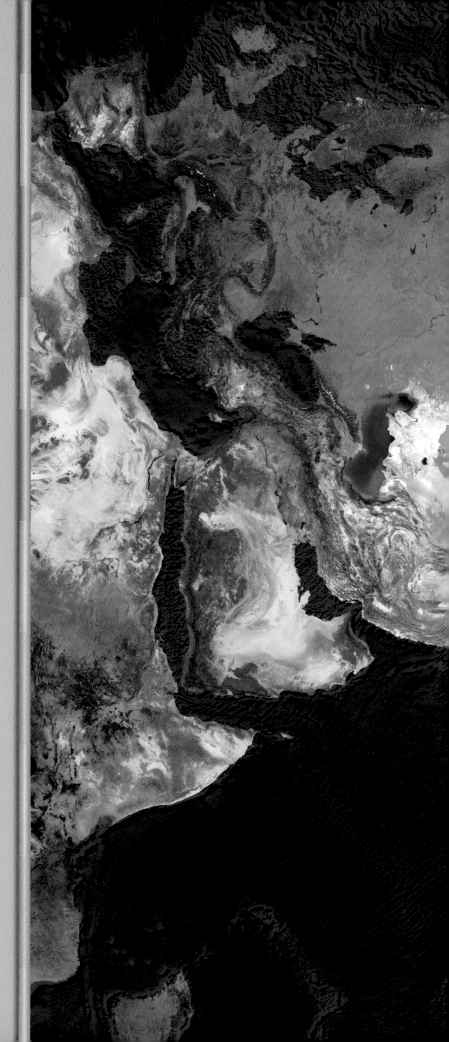

From the frozen shores of the Arctic Ocean to the equatorial islands of Indonesia, Asia stretches across 90 degrees of latitude. From the Ural Mountains to the Pacific Ocean it covers more than 150 degrees of longitude. Here, three of history's great culture hearths emerged in the valleys of the Tigris and Euphrates, the Indus, and the Yellow (Huang) Rivers. Today, Asia is home to more than 60 percent of Earth's people and some of the world's fastest growing economies.

Facts & Figures

▶ **Land area:** 17,213,300 sq mi (44,579,000 sq km)

▶ **Population:** 3,874,984,000

▶ **Highest point:** Mount Everest, China-Nepal: 29,035 ft (8,850 m)

▶ **Lowest point:** Dead Sea, Israel-Jordan: 1,365 ft (416 m) below sea level

▶ **Longest river:** Yangtze (Chang), China: 3,964 mi (6,380 km)

▶ **Largest lake entirely in Asia:** Baikal, Russia: 12,163 sq mi (31,500 sq km)

▶ **Number of independent countries:** 46 (excluding Russia)

▶ **Largest country entirely in Asia:** China: 3,705,405 sq mi (9,596,960 sq km)

▶ **Smallest country:** Maldives: 115 sq mi (298 sq km)

▶ **Most populous country:** China: Pop. 1,300,060,000

▶ **Least populous country:** Maldives: Pop. 298,000

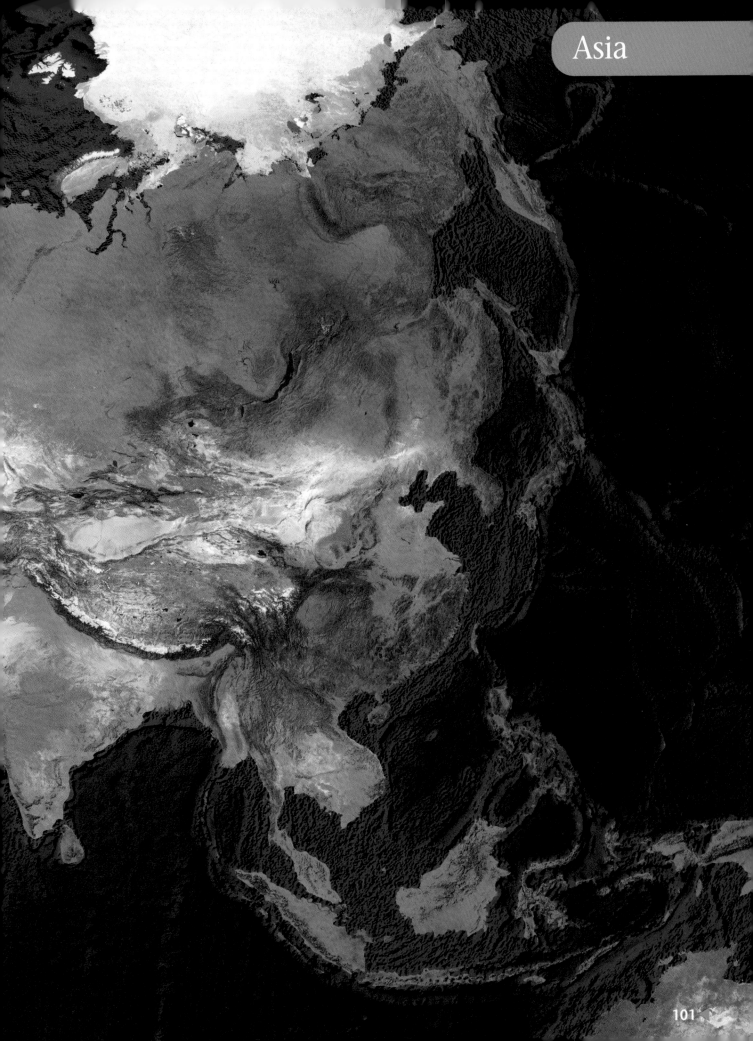

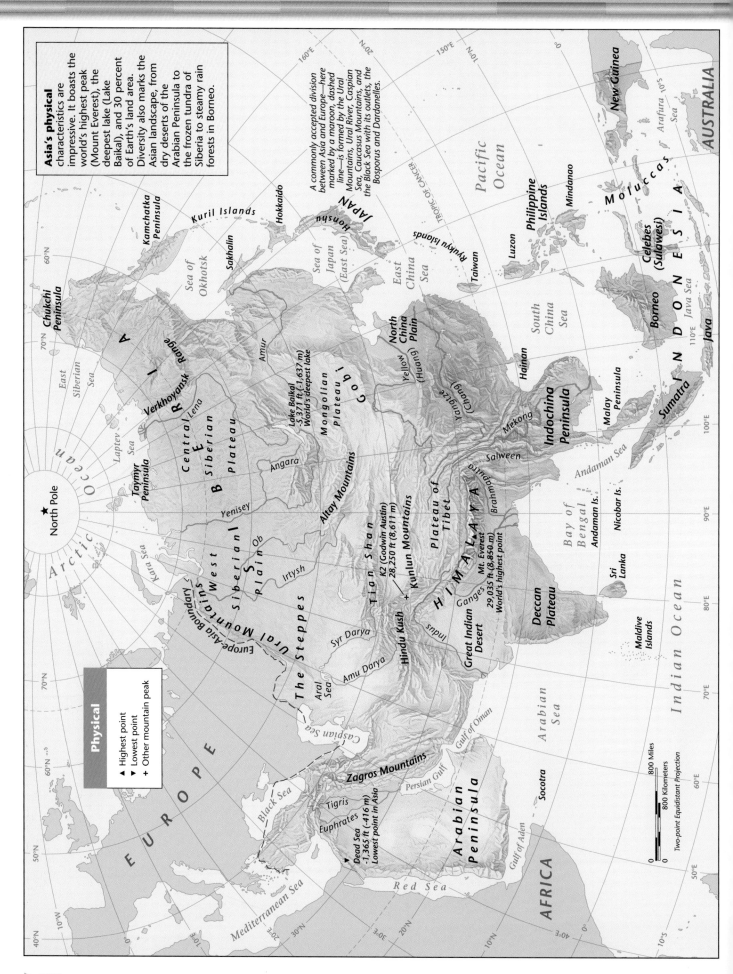

Asia's physical
characteristics are
impressive. It boasts the
world's highest peak
(Mount Everest), the
deepest lake (Lake
Baikal), and 30 percent
of Earth's land area.
Diversity also marks the
Asian landscape, from
dry deserts of the
Arabian Peninsula to
the frozen tundra of
Siberia to steamy rain
forests in Borneo.

A commonly accepted division
between Asia and Europe—here
marked by a maroon, dashed
line—is formed by the Ural
Mountains, Ural River, Caspian
Sea, Caucasus Mountains, and
the Black Sea with its outlets, the
Bosporus and Dardanelles.

Physical

▲ Highest point
▼ Lowest point
+ Other mountain peak

AUSTRALIA

New Guinea

Arafura Sea

Moluccas

Celebes (Sulawesi)

Mindanao

Philippine Islands

Luzon

Borneo

Java Sea

Java

Sumatra

INDONESIA

Malay Peninsula

Hainan

South China Sea

Taiwan

Indochina Peninsula

East China Sea

Ryukyu Islands

TROPIC OF CANCER

Pacific Ocean

Mekong

Salween

North China Plain

Yellow (Huang)

Yangtze (Chang)

JAPAN

Honshu

Hokkaido

Sea of Japan (East Sea)

Sakhalin

Kuril Islands

Kamchatka Peninsula

Sea of Okhotsk

Chukchi Peninsula

East Siberian Sea

Verkhoyansk Range

Lena

Central Siberian Plateau

Taymyr Peninsula

Laptev Sea

Yenisey

North Pole

Arctic Ocean

Kara Sea

Ob

West Siberian Plain

Irtysh

Ural Mountains

Europe-Asia Boundary

EUROPE

The Steppes

Aral Sea

Syr Darya

Amu Darya

Caspian Sea

Black Sea

Tigris

Euphrates

Zagros Mountains

Persian Gulf

Gulf of Oman

Arabian Sea

Arabian Peninsula

Socotra

Gulf of Aden

Red Sea

Mediterranean Sea

AFRICA

Dead Sea
-1,365 ft (-416 m)
Lowest point in Asia

Hindu Kush

Indus

Great Indian Desert

Ganges

Brahmaputra

Deccan Plateau

Sri Lanka

Maldive Islands

Indian Ocean

Bay of Bengal

Andaman Is.

Nicobar Is.

Andaman Sea

HIMALAYA

Mt. Everest
29,035 ft (8,850 m)
World's highest point

Plateau of Tibet

Kunlun Mountains

K2 (Godwin Austin)
28,250 ft (8,611 m)

Tian Shan

Altay Mountains

Gobi

Mongolian Plateau

Lake Baikal
-5,371 ft (-1,637 m)
World's deepest lake

Amur

Angara

A

Amu Darya

800 Miles
800 Kilometers
Two-point Equidistant Projection

10°W
0°
10°E
20°E
30°E
40°E
50°E
60°E
70°E
80°E
90°E
100°E
110°E
120°E
130°E
140°E
150°E
160°E
170°E

40°N
50°N
60°N
70°N
10°N
20°N
30°N
10°S

Asia

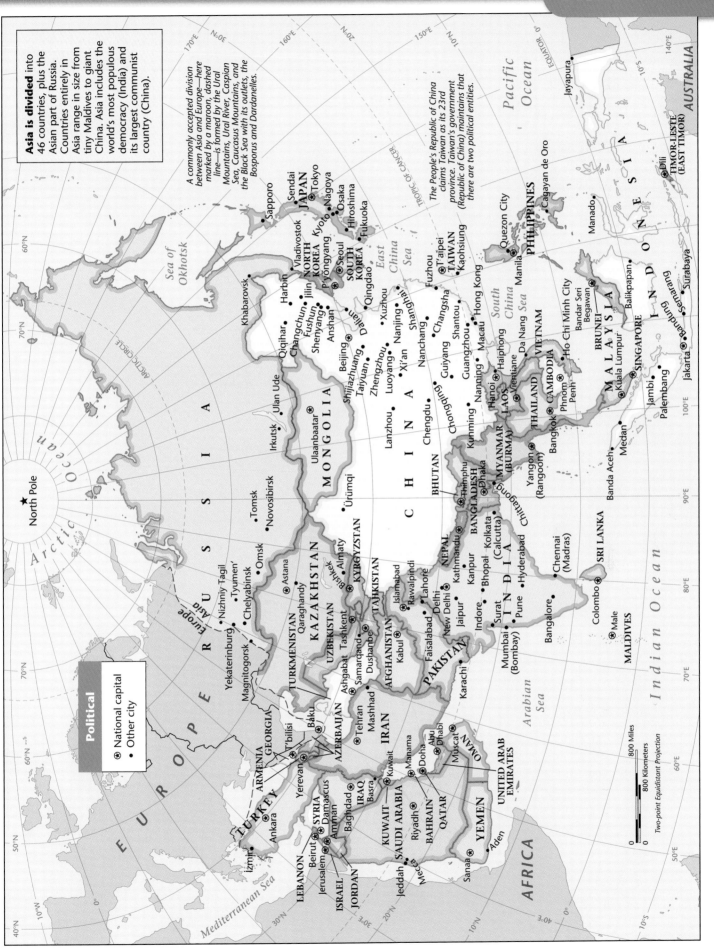

Asia is divided into 46 countries, plus the Asian part of Russia. Countries entirely in Asia range in size from tiny Maldives to giant China. Asia includes the world's most populous democracy (India) and its largest communist country (China).

A commonly accepted division between Asia and Europe—here marked by a maroon, dashed line—is formed by the Ural Mountains, Ural River, Caspian Sea, Caucasus Mountains, and the Black Sea with its outlets, the Bosporus and Dardanelles.

The People's Republic of China claims Taiwan as its 23rd province. Taiwan's government (Republic of China) maintains that there are two political entities.

Political

⊛ National capital
• Other city

Pacific Ocean

Arctic Ocean

★ North Pole

Sea of Okhotsk

RUSSIA

Sapporo
Sendai
JAPAN
Tokyo
Vladivostok
Kyoto Nagoya
NORTH KOREA Osaka
Pyongyang Hiroshima
Seoul Fukuoka
SOUTH KOREA
Qingdao
Harbin
Khabarovsk
Jilin
Changchun
Fushun
Shenyang
Anshan
Dalian
East China Sea
Fuzhou
T'aipei
TAIWAN
Kaohsiung
Qiqihar
Beijing
Shijiazhuang
Taiyuan
Xuzhou
Nanjing
Shanghai
Changsha
Shantou
Macau Hong Kong
South China Sea
Quezon City
PHILIPPINES
Cagayan de Oro
Manado
Manila
Ulan Ude
Irkutsk
MONGOLIA
Ulaanbaatar
Zhengzhou
Luoyang
Xi'an
Nanchang
Guiyang
Guangzhou
Nanning
Haiphong
Da Nang
VIETNAM
Ho Chi Minh City
Bandar Seri Begawan
BRUNEI
MALAYSIA
Kuala Lumpur
Balikpapan
I N D O N E S I A
Javapura
Dili
TIMOR-LESTE (EAST TIMOR)
AUSTRALIA
Tomsk
Novosibirsk
Ürümqi
C H I N A
Lanzhou
Chengdu
Chongqing
Kunming
MYANMAR (BURMA)
Yangon (Rangoon)
Bangkok
THAILAND
LAOS
Vientiane
CAMBODIA
Phnom Penh
SINGAPORE
Medan
Banda Aceh
Jambi
Palembang
Jakarta
Bandung
Semarang
Surabaya
Omsk
KAZAKHSTAN
Astana
Qaraghandy
Almaty
Bishkek
KYRGYZSTAN
BHUTAN
Thimphu
BANGLADESH
Dhaka
Chittagong
NEPAL
Kathmandu
Nizhniy Tagil
Tyumen'
Chelyabinsk
Yekaterinburg
Magnitogorsk
Europe Asia
Qaraghandy
UZBEKISTAN
Tashkent
Samarqand
TAJIKISTAN
Dushanbe
Islamabad
Rawalpindi
Lahore
Faisalabad
PAKISTAN
Delhi
New Delhi
Jaipur
Kanpur
Indore
Bhopal
Surat
I N D I A
Pune
Hyderabad
Bangalore
Chennai (Madras)
SRI LANKA
Colombo
Male
MALDIVES
Kolkata (Calcutta)
Mumbai (Bombay)
TURKMENISTAN
Ashgabat
AFGHANISTAN
Kabul
Mashhad
Indian Ocean
Baku
AZERBAIJAN
T'bilisi
GEORGIA
ARMENIA
Yerevan
Tehran
IRAN
ARCTIC CIRCLE
Karachi
Arabian Sea
Abu Dhabi
OMAN
Muscat
UNITED ARAB EMIRATES
TURKEY
Ankara
Izmir
LEBANON
Beirut
Damascus
SYRIA
Amman
Baghdad
IRAQ
Basra
JORDAN
ISRAEL
Jerusalem
Jeddah
Mecca
SAUDI ARABIA
Riyadh
KUWAIT
Kuwait
Manama
BAHRAIN
Doha
QATAR
YEMEN
Sanaa
Aden
AFRICA
Mediterranean Sea

800 Miles
800 Kilometers
Two-point Equidistant Projection

40°N 50°N 60°N 70°N
30°N 40°N 50°N 60°N 70°N
10°W 0° 10°E 20°E 30°E 40°E 50°E 60°E 70°E 80°E 90°E 100°E 110°E 120°E 130°E 140°E 150°E 160°E 170°E
TROPIC OF CANCER
EQUATOR 0°
10°S

103

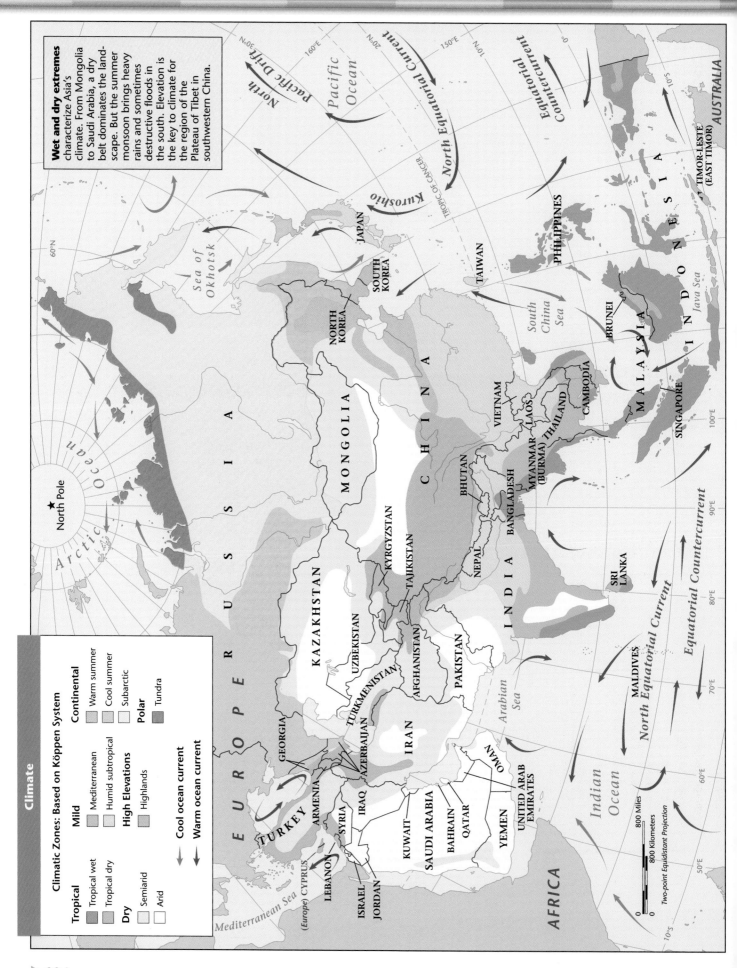

Climate

Climatic Zones: Based on Köppen System

Tropical
- Tropical wet
- Tropical dry

Dry
- Semiarid
- Arid

Mild
- Mediterranean
- Humid subtropical

High Elevations
- Highlands

Continental
- Warm summer
- Cool summer
- Subarctic

Polar
- Tundra

→ Cool ocean current
→ Warm ocean current

Wet and dry extremes characterize Asia's climate. From Mongolia to Saudi Arabia, a dry belt dominates the landscape. But the summer monsoon brings heavy rains and sometimes destructive floods in the south. Elevation is the key to climate for the region of the Plateau of Tibet in southwestern China.

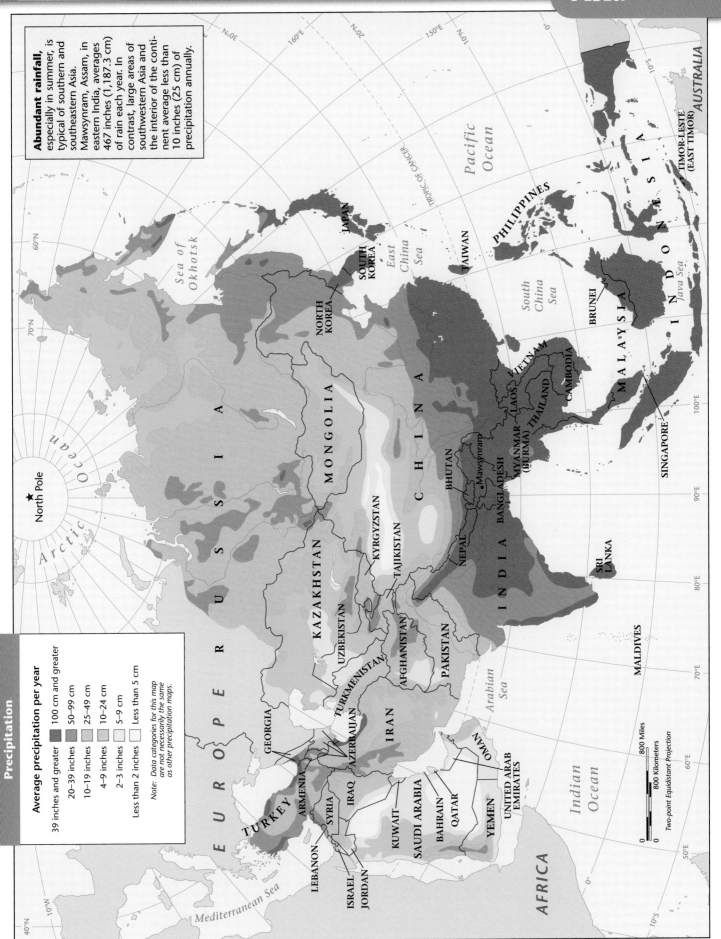

Abundant rainfall, especially in summer, is typical of southern and southeastern Asia. Mawsynram, Assam, in eastern India, averages 467 inches (1,187.3 cm) of rain each year. In contrast, large areas of southwestern Asia and the interior of the continent average less than 10 inches (25 cm) of precipitation annually.

Precipitation

Average precipitation per year

	100 cm and greater
39 inches and greater	
	50–99 cm
20–39 inches	
	25–49 cm
10–19 inches	
	10–24 cm
4–9 inches	
	5–9 cm
2–3 inches	
	Less than 5 cm
Less than 2 inches	

Note: Data categories for this map are not necessarily the same as other precipitation maps.

800 Miles

800 Kilometers

Two-point Equidistant Projection

North Pole

Arctic Ocean

R U S S I A

Sea of Okhotsk

E U R O P E

MONGOLIA

KAZAKHSTAN

C H I N A

JAPAN

NORTH KOREA

SOUTH KOREA

East China Sea

TAIWAN

Pacific Ocean

PHILIPPINES

South China Sea

UZBEKISTAN

KYRGYZSTAN

TAJIKISTAN

TURKMENISTAN

AFGHANISTAN

PAKISTAN

BHUTAN

NEPAL

BANGLADESH

I N D I A

MYANMAR (BURMA)

LAOS

VIETNAM

THAILAND

CAMBODIA

Mawsynram

M A L A Y S I A

BRUNEI

I N D O N E S I A

SINGAPORE

Java Sea

AUSTRALIA

TIMOR-LESTE (EAST TIMOR)

SRI LANKA

MALDIVES

Arabian Sea

Indian Ocean

GEORGIA

ARMENIA

AZERBAIJAN

IRAN

TURKEY

LEBANON

ISRAEL

JORDAN

SYRIA

IRAQ

KUWAIT

SAUDI ARABIA

BAHRAIN

QATAR

UNITED ARAB EMIRATES

OMAN

YEMEN

AFRICA

Mediterranean Sea

TROPIC OF CANCER

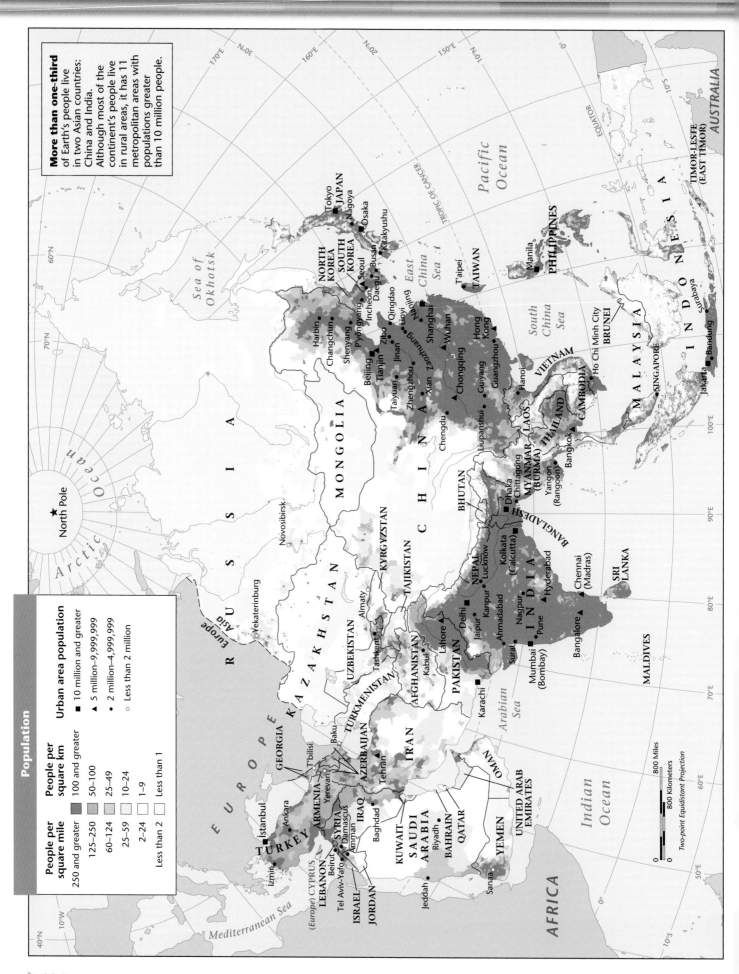

Population

People per square mile
- 250 and greater
- 125–250
- 60–124
- 25–59
- 2–24
- Less than 2

People per square km
- 100 and greater
- 50–100
- 25–49
- 10–24
- 1–9
- Less than 1

Urban area population
- ■ 10 million and greater
- ▲ 5 million–9,999,999
- ● 2 million–4,999,999
- ○ Less than 2 million

More than one-third of Earth's people live in two Asian countries: China and India. Although most of the continent's people live in rural areas, it has 11 metropolitan areas with populations greater than 10 million people.

Asia

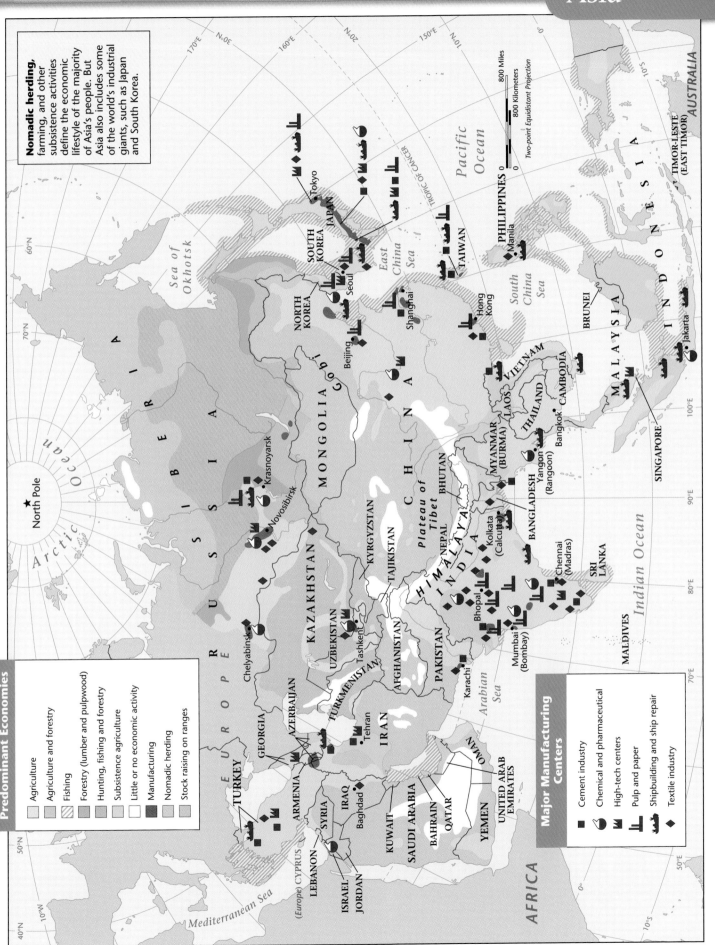

Nomadic herding, farming, and other subsistence activities define the economic lifestyle of the majority of Asia's people. But Asia also includes some of the world's industrial giants, such as Japan and South Korea.

Predominant Economies

- Agriculture
- Agriculture and forestry
- Fishing
- Forestry (lumber and pulpwood)
- Hunting, fishing and forestry
- Subsistence agriculture
- Little or no economic activity
- Manufacturing
- Nomadic herding
- Stock raising on ranges

Major Manufacturing Centers

- ■ Cement industry
- ◖ Chemical and pharmaceutical
- ⚒ High-tech centers
- ⊥ Pulp and paper
- ⚓ Shipbuilding and ship repair
- ◆ Textile industry

800 Miles
800 Kilometers
Two-point Equidistant Projection

Pacific Ocean
TROPIC OF CANCER
Sea of Okhotsk
East China Sea
South China Sea
Indian Ocean
Arabian Sea
Mediterranean Sea
Arctic Ocean
North Pole

SIBERIA
RUSSIA
MONGOLIA
Gobi
CHINA
Plateau of Tibet
HIMALAYA
INDIA
KAZAKHSTAN
UZBEKISTAN
KYRGYZSTAN
TAJIKISTAN
TURKMENISTAN
AFGHANISTAN
PAKISTAN
NEPAL
BHUTAN
BANGLADESH
MYANMAR (BURMA)
LAOS
THAILAND
VIETNAM
CAMBODIA
MALAYSIA
SINGAPORE
INDONESIA
BRUNEI
PHILIPPINES
TAIWAN
SOUTH KOREA
NORTH KOREA
JAPAN
SRI LANKA
MALDIVES
TIMOR-LESTE (EAST TIMOR)
AUSTRALIA

EUROPE
TURKEY
GEORGIA
ARMENIA
AZERBAIJAN
SYRIA
IRAQ
IRAN
LEBANON
(Europe) CYPRUS
ISRAEL
JORDAN
SAUDI ARABIA
KUWAIT
BAHRAIN
QATAR
UNITED ARAB EMIRATES
OMAN
YEMEN
AFRICA

Tokyo
Seoul
Beijing
Shanghai
Hong Kong
Manila
Jakarta
Yangon (Rangoon)
Bangkok
Kolkata (Calcutta)
Chennai (Madras)
Bhopal
Mumbai (Bombay)
Karachi
Tehran
Baghdad
Tashkent
Krasnoyarsk
Novosibirsk
Chelyabinsk

World Heritage Sites

In 1972, the United Nations Educational, Scientific and Cultural Organization (UNESCO) adopted a treaty, signed by more than 150 countries, dedicated to the preservation of cultural and natural sites of "outstanding universal value" that are "testimonies to an enduring past." These sites are designated as World Heritage Sites because they are part of the universal heritage of people everywhere.

Since much of human history is rooted in Asia, the continent is home to many of the best known World Heritage Sites, including the Taj Mahal, in India, and the temple complex at Angkor in Cambodia. Some of the world's endangered and vulnerable animals, such as the tiger and the komodo dragon, are native to Asia, and their habitats also are preserved as World Heritage Sites.

In July 2004, the World Heritage List included 788 sites in 134 countries. Among these, 163 sites are in Asian countries, including five in the part of Russia that lies east of the Ural Mountains.

▲ **Cappadocia,** a centuries-old complex of caves, dwellings, and Christian churches carved into ancient volcanic rock in central Turkey, is an example of a mixed World Heritage Site.

World Heritage Sites

These sites are chosen for their universal value. Cultural sites reflect unusual human ingenuity or represent the traditions or values of an established culture or civilization. Natural sites are often examples of important geological processes or the habitats of endangered species. A few sites are selected because they combine cultural and natural characteristics.

Natural
Cultural
Mixed

	Australia/Oceania	U.S./Canada	Africa	Latin America	Asia	Europe
Natural	14	20	34	27	25	34
Cultural	5	13	64	78	132	319
Mixed	2	0	3	3	6	9

▲ **Angkor Wat,** which is part of a cultural site in Cambodia, honors the Hindu god Vishnu. Nearby temples at Angkor Thom are Buddhist.

Web Link for information on World Heritage Sites: http://whc.unesco.org/

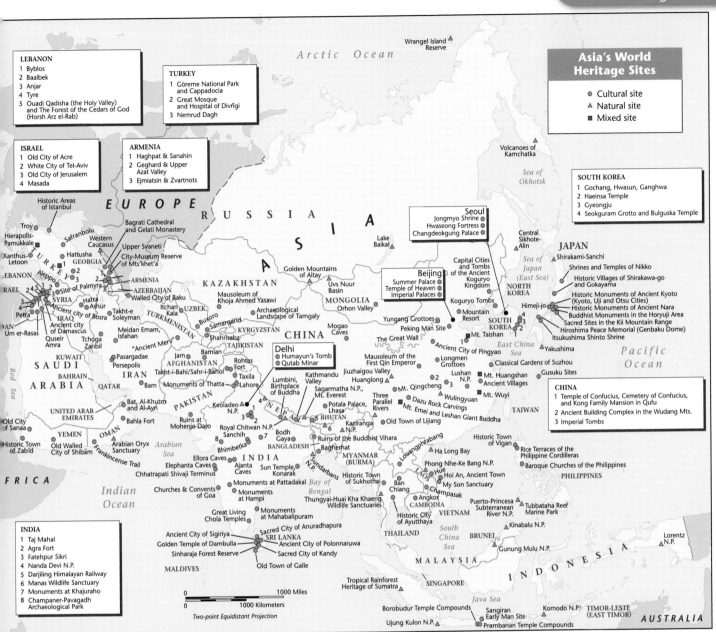

Asia's World Heritage Sites

- ● Cultural site
- ▲ Natural site
- ■ Mixed site

LEBANON
1. Byblos
2. Baalbek
3. Anjar
4. Tyre
5. Ouadi Qadisha (the Holy Valley) and The Forest of the Cedars of God (Horsh Arz el-Rab)

TURKEY
1. Göreme National Park and Cappadocia
2. Great Mosque and Hospital of Divriği
3. Nemrud Dagh

ISRAEL
1. Old City of Acre
2. White City of Tel-Aviv
3. Old City of Jerusalem
4. Masada

ARMENIA
1. Haghpat & Sanahin
2. Geghard & Upper Azat Valley
3. Ejmiatsin & Zvartnots

SOUTH KOREA
1. Gochang, Hwasun, Ganghwa
2. Haeinsa Temple
3. Gyeongju
4. Seokguram Grotto and Bulguska Temple

CHINA
1. Temple of Confucius, Cemetery of Confucius, and Kong Family Mansion in Qufu
2. Ancient Building Complex in the Wudang Mts.
3. Imperial Tombs

INDIA
1. Taj Mahal
2. Agra Fort
3. Fatehpur Sikri
4. Nanda Devi N.P.
5. Darjiling Himalayan Railway
6. Manas Wildlife Sanctuary
7. Monuments at Khajuraho
8. Champaner-Pavagadh Archaeological Park

Map labels: Arctic Ocean; Wrangel Island Reserve; EUROPE; RUSSIA; ASIA; Sea of Okhotsk; Volcanoes of Kamchatka; Historic Areas of Istanbul; Troy; Hierapolis-Pamukkale; Xanthus-Letoon; TURKEY; Safranbolu; Hattusha; Western Caucasus; Bagrati Cathedral and Gelati Monastery; Upper Svaneti; City-Museum Reserve of Mts'khet'a; GEORGIA; ARMENIA; AZERBAIJAN; Walled City of Baku; Lake Baikal; Golden Mountains of Altay; Uvs Nuur Basin; KAZAKHSTAN; Mausoleum of Khoja Ahmed Yasawi; Archaeological Landscape of Tamgaly; MONGOLIA; Orhon Valley; Aleppo; Site of Palmyra; SYRIA; Ancient city of Bosra; Hatra; Ashur; IRAQ; Ancient city of Damascus; Itchan Kala; UZBEK.; Buxoro; Samarqand; Shahrisabz; TURKMENISTAN; KYRGYZSTAN; TAJIKISTAN; CHINA; "Ancient Merv"; Meidan Emam, Isfahan; Tchoga Zanbil; Queiser Amra; Um er-Rasas; Petra; IRAEL; LEBANON; KUWAIT; SAUDI ARABIA; BAHRAIN; QATAR; UNITED ARAB EMIRATES; IRAN; Pasargadae; Persepolis; Bam; Takht-e Soleyman; Jam; Bamian; AFGHANISTAN; Takht-i-Bahi/Sahr-i-Bahol; Rohtas Fort; Delhi; Humayun's Tomb; Qutab Minar; Taxila; Lahore; Monuments of Thatta; PAKISTAN; Kathmandu Valley; Lumbini, Birthplace of Buddha; Sagarmatha N.P., Mt. Everest; Potala Palace, Lhasa; NEPAL; BHUTAN; Mausoleum of the First Qin Emperor; Jiuzhaigou Valley; Huanglong; Three Parallel Rivers; Mt. Qingcheng; Dazu Rock Carvings; Wulingyuan; Mt. Emei and Leshan Giant Buddha; Mt. Wuyi; Old Town of Lijiang; Ancient City of Pingyao; Longmen Grottoes; Lushan N.P.; Mt. Huangshan; Ancient Villages; Classical Gardens of Suzhou; Gusuku Sites; Yungang Grottoes; Peking Man Site; The Great Wall; Mogao Caves; Mountain Resort; Capital Cities and Tombs of the Ancient Koguryo Kingdom; Koguryo Tombs; Mt. Taishan; Beijing; Summer Palace; Temple of Heaven; Imperial Palaces; Seoul; Jongmyo Shrine; Hwaseong Fortress; Changdeokgung Palace; NORTH KOREA; SOUTH KOREA; Central Sikhote-Alin; JAPAN; Shirakami-Sanchi; Shrines and Temples of Nikko; Historic Villages of Shirakawa-go and Gokayama; Historic Monuments of Ancient Kyoto (Kyoto, Uji and Otsu Cities); Historic Monuments of Ancient Nara; Buddhist Monuments in the Horyuji Area; Sacred Sites in the Kii Mountain Range; Hiroshima Peace Memorial (Genbaku Dome); Itsukushima Shinto Shrine; Himeji-jo; Yakushima; Sea of Japan (East Sea); East China Sea; Pacific Ocean; TAIWAN; OMAN; YEMEN; Old City of Sanaa; Historic Town of Zabid; Old Walled City of Shibam; Frankincense Trail; Arabian Oryx Sanctuary; Bat, Al-Khutm and Al-Ayn; Bahla Fort; Ruins at Mohenjo Daro; Royal Chitwan N.P.; Sanchih; Keoladeo N.P.; Bodh Gaya; Kaziranga N.P.; Ruins of the Buddhist Vihara; Baghreat; Sundarbans; Historic Town of Vigan; Rice Terraces of the Philippine Cordilleras; Baroque Churches of the Philippines; PHILIPPINES; Ha Long Bay; Phong Nhe-Ke Bang N.P.; Hue; Hoi An, Ancient Town; My Son Sanctuary; Champasak; Louangphrabang; LAOS; Ban Chiang; Historic Town of Sukhothai; Thungyai-Huai Kha Khaeng Wildlife Sanctuaries; Historic City of Ayutthaya; THAILAND; MYANMAR (BURMA); Angkor; CAMBODIA; VIETNAM; Puerto-Princesa Subterranean River N.P.; Tubbataha Reef Marine Park; Kinabalu N.P.; Gunung Mulu N.P.; South China Sea; BRUNEI; MALAYSIA; SINGAPORE; INDONESIA; TIMOR-LESTE (EAST TIMOR); AUSTRALIA; Lorentz N.P.; Java Sea; Komodo N.P.; Sangiran Early Man Site; Ujung Kulon N.P.; Borobudur Temple Compounds; Prambanan Temple Compounds; Tropical Rainforest Heritage of Sumatra; Ellora Caves; Elephanta Caves; Ajanta Caves; Sun Temple, Konarak; Chhatrapati Shivaji Terminus; Churches & Convents of Goa; Monuments at Pattadakal; Monuments at Hampi; Great Living Chola Temples; Monuments at Mahabalipuram; Bhimbetka; INDIA; Bay of Bengal; BANGLADESH; Sacred City of Anuradhapura; Ancient City of Sigiriya; Golden Temple of Dambulla; Sinharaja Forest Reserve; Ancient City of Polonnaruwa; Sacred City of Kandy; Old Town of Galle; SRI LANKA; MALDIVES; Arabian Sea; Indian Ocean; AFRICA; Red Sea; Historic Town of Zabid; Old City of Sanaa

1000 Miles / 1000 Kilometers
Two-point Equidistant Projection

▲ **The Taj Mahal,** *a cultural site in India, is an outstanding example of Muslim architecture in a country most often associated with Hinduism.*

▲ **Tubbataha Reef Marine Park,** *a natural site in the Philippines, is habitat for birds, sea turtles, and fish.*

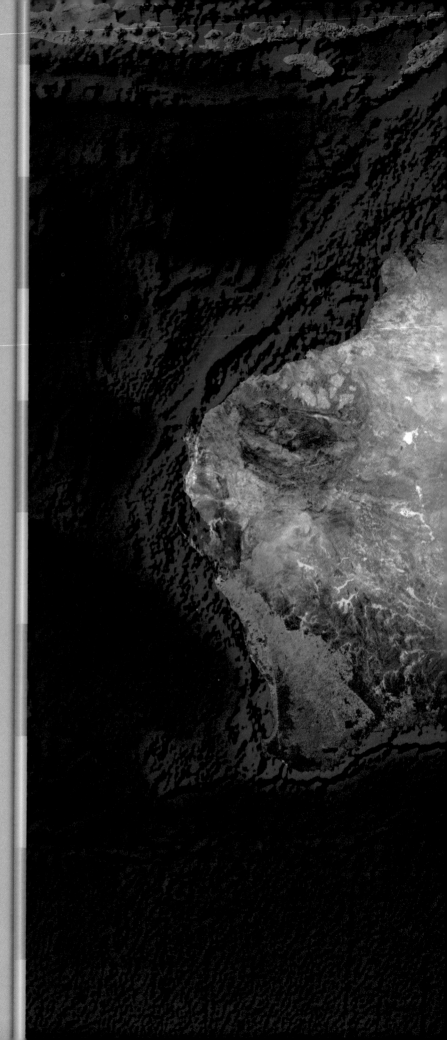

Australia & Oceania

Smallest of Earth's great landmasses, Australia is the only one that is both a continent and a country. It is part of the greater region of Oceania, which includes New Zealand, the eastern part of New Guinea, and hundreds of smaller islands scattered across the Pacific Ocean. Although Hawai'i is politically part of the United States, geographically and culturally it is part of Oceania.

Facts & Figures

▶ **Land area:** 3,278,062 sq mi (8,490,180 sq km)

▶ **Population:** 32,822,000

▶ **Highest point:** Mount Wilhelm, Papua New Guinea: 14,793 ft (4,509 m)

▶ **Lowest point:** Lake Eyre, Australia: 52 ft (16 m) below sea level

▶ **Longest river:** Murray-Darling, Australia: 2,094 mi (3,370 km)

▶ **Largest lake:** Lake Eyre, Australia: 3,430 sq mi (8,884 sq km)

▶ **Number of independent countries:** 14

▶ **Largest country:** Australia: 2,969,906 sq mi (7,692,024 sq km)

▶ **Smallest country:** Nauru: 8 sq mi (21 sq km)

▶ **Most populous country:** Australia: Pop. 20,125,000

▶ **Least populous country:** Tuvalu: Pop. 9,000

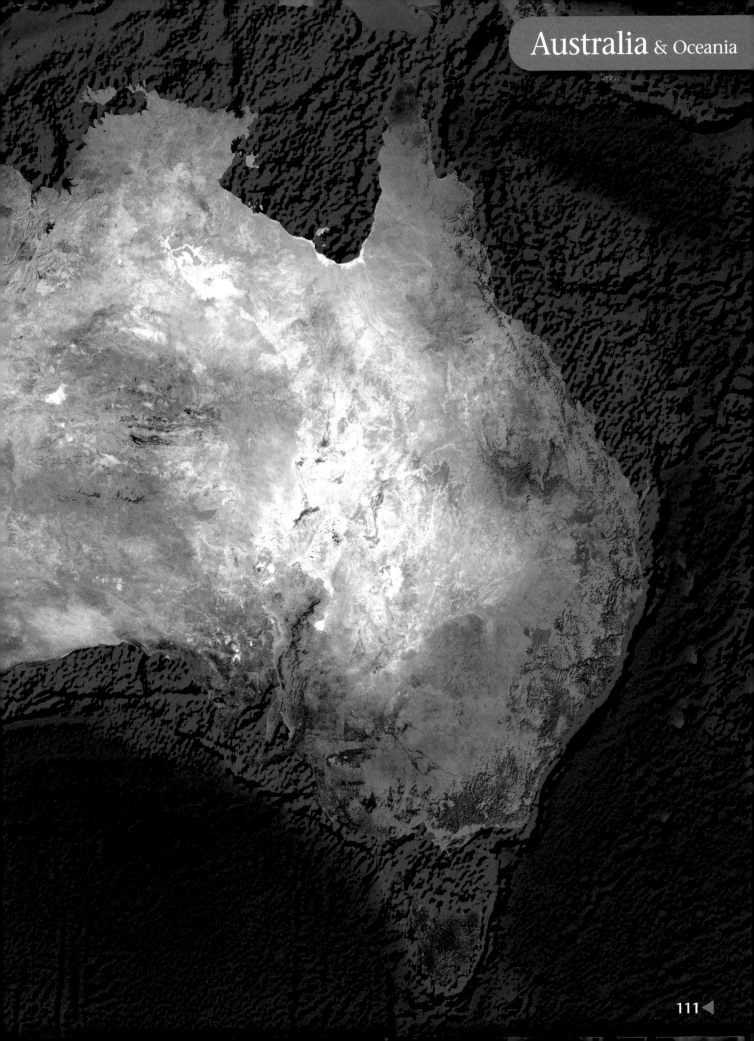

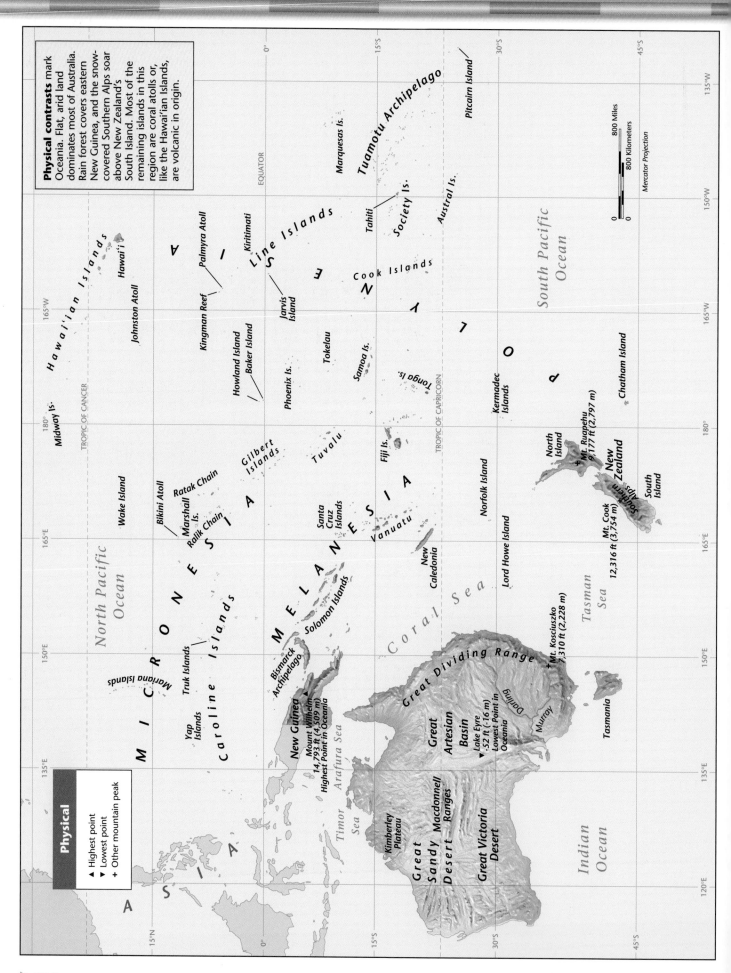

Physical contrasts mark Oceania. Flat, arid land dominates most of Australia. Rain forest covers eastern New Guinea, and the snow-covered Southern Alps soar above New Zealand's South Island. Most of the remaining islands in this region are coral atolls or, like the Hawai'ian Islands, are volcanic in origin.

Physical

▲ Highest point
▼ Lowest point
+ Other mountain peak

800 Miles
800 Kilometers
Mercator Projection

EQUATOR

0°
15°S
30°S
45°S
135°W
150°W
165°W
180°
165°E
150°E
135°E
120°E
0°
15°N
15°S
30°S
45°S
135°E
165°E
180°
165°W
150°W

TROPIC OF CANCER
TROPIC OF CAPRICORN

North Pacific Ocean
South Pacific Ocean
Indian Ocean
Arafura Sea
Timor Sea
Coral Sea
Tasman Sea

Hawaiian Islands
Hawai'i
Midway Is.
Johnston Atoll
Palmyra Atoll
Kingman Reef
Kiritimati
Line Islands
Marquesas Is.
Tuamotu Archipelago
Pitcairn Island
Tahiti
Society Is.
Austral Is.
Cook Islands
POLYNESIA
Jarvis Island
Howland Island
Baker Island
Phoenix Is.
Tokelau
Samoa Is.
Tonga Is.
Kermadec Islands
Chatham Island
Wake Island
Bikini Atoll
Ratak Chain
Marshall Is.
Ralik Chain
Gilbert Islands
Tuvalu
Fiji Is.
Norfolk Island
Lord Howe Island
MICRONESIA
Mariana Islands
Yap Islands
Truk Islands
Caroline Islands
MELANESIA
Bismarck Archipelago
Solomon Islands
Santa Cruz Islands
Vanuatu
New Caledonia
New Guinea
▲ Mount Wilhelm
14,793 ft (4,509 m)
Highest Point in Oceania

North Island
New Zealand
+ Mt. Ruapehu
9,177 ft (2,797 m)
South Island
Southern Alps
▲ Mt. Cook
12,316 ft (3,754 m)

Great Dividing Range
+ Mt. Kosciuszko
7,310 ft (2,228 m)
Great Artesian Basin
▼ Lake Eyre
-52 ft (-16 m)
Lowest Point in Oceania
Darling
Murray
Tasmania
Great Sandy Desert
Kimberley Plateau
Macdonnell Ranges
Great Victoria Desert

ASIA

Australia & Oceania

Oceania is made up of more than two dozen countries and dependencies. In the early years of the 20th century, most of the islands were under the control of the United Kingdom, France, or the United States. Independence has been a slow and sometimes difficult process.

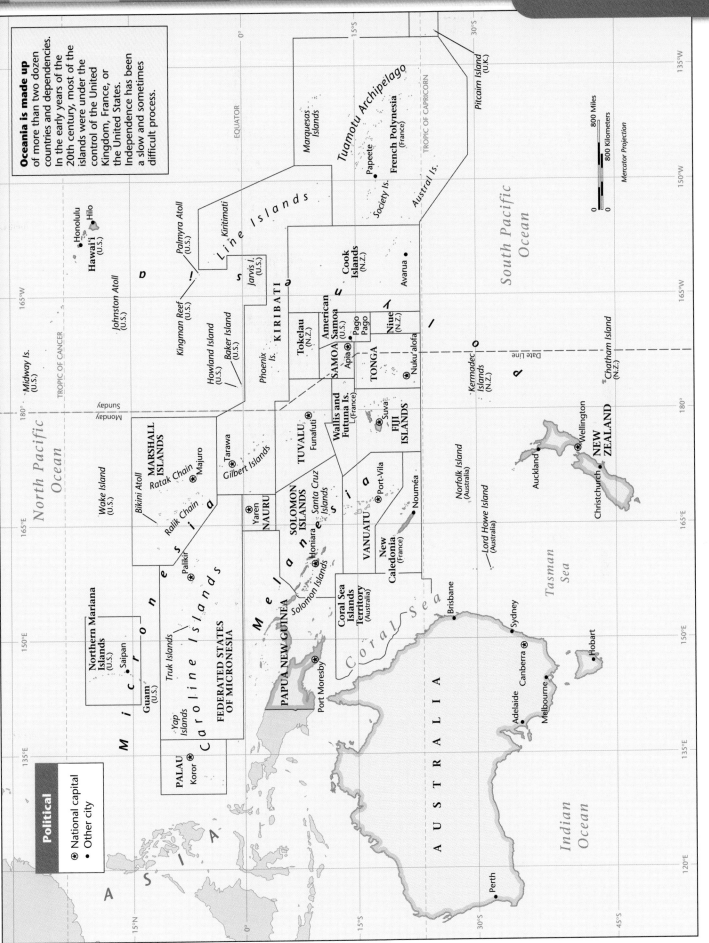

Political
⊗ National capital
• Other city

North Pacific Ocean

South Pacific Ocean

Indian Ocean

Tasman Sea

Coral Sea

EQUATOR

TROPIC OF CANCER

TROPIC OF CAPRICORN

Date Line

Mercator Projection

800 Miles
800 Kilometers

Monday
Sunday

Midway Is. (U.S.)

Wake Island (U.S.)

Honolulu • Hilo
Hawai'i (U.S.)

Johnston Atoll (U.S.)

Line Islands
Kiritimati

Palmyra Atoll (U.S.)

Kingman Reef (U.S.)

Jarvis I. (U.S.)

Howland Island (U.S.)
Baker Island (U.S.)

Marquesas Islands

Tuamotu Archipelago

Papeete • **French Polynesia** (France)

Society Is.

Austral Is.

Pitcairn Island (U.K.)

Cook Islands (N.Z.)
Avarua •

Phoenix Is.

KIRIBATI

American Samoa (U.S.)
Tokelau (N.Z.)
Pago Pago

Niue (N.Z.)

SAMOA ⊗ Apia
Nuku'alofa ⊗
TONGA

Kermadec Islands (N.Z.)

TUVALU ⊗ Funafuti

Wallis and Futuna Is. (France)

Suva ⊗
FIJI ISLANDS

Chatham Island (N.Z.)

Northern Mariana Islands (U.S.)
• Saipan

Truk Islands

Guam (U.S.)

Yap Islands

PALAU
Koror ⊗

Caroline Islands

FEDERATED STATES OF MICRONESIA
Palikir ⊗

Micronesia

MARSHALL ISLANDS
Ratak Chain
Majuro ⊗
Bikini Atoll
Ralik Chain

Tarawa •
Gilbert Islands

Yaren ⊗
NAURU

SOLOMON ISLANDS
Honiara ⊗
Solomon Islands
Santa Cruz Islands

Melanesia

VANUATU
• Port-Vila

New Caledonia (France)
Nouméa •

Norfolk Island (Australia)

Lord Howe Island (Australia)

NEW ZEALAND
Wellington ⊗
Auckland •
Christchurch •

PAPUA NEW GUINEA
Port Moresby •

Coral Sea Islands Territory (Australia)

AUSTRALIA

Brisbane •
Sydney •
Adelaide • Canberra ⊗
Melbourne •
Hobart •
Perth •

ASIA

0°

15°S

30°S

45°S

15°N

135°E 150°E 165°E 180° 165°W 150°W 135°W 120°E

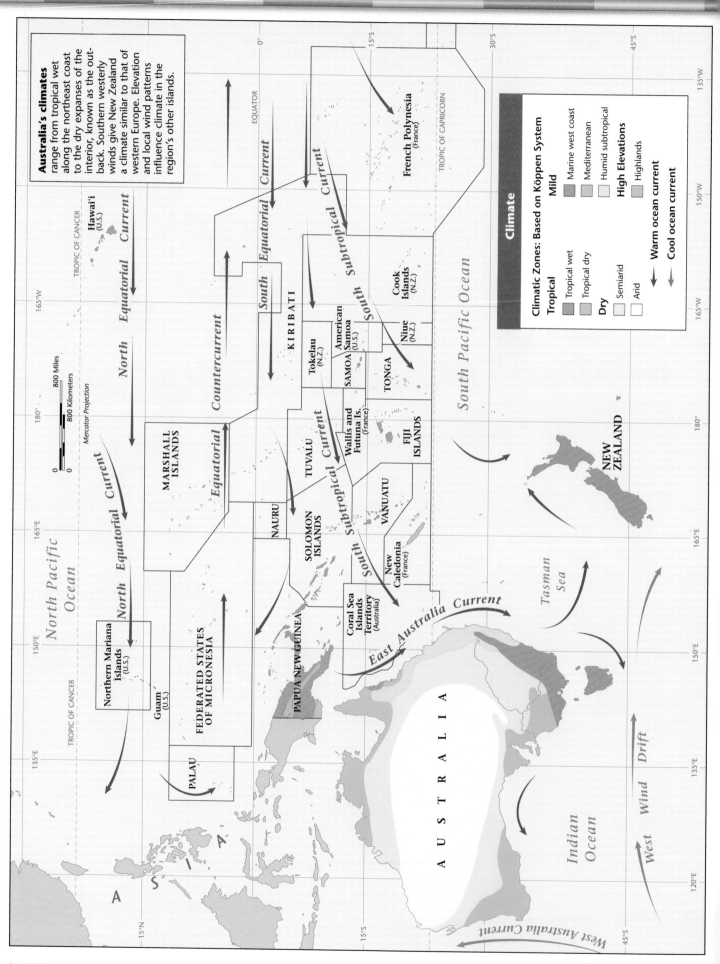

Australia's climates range from tropical wet along the northeast coast to the dry expanses of the interior, known as the outback. Southern westerly winds give New Zealand a climate similar to that of western Europe. Elevation and local wind patterns influence climate in the region's other islands.

Mercator Projection

800 Miles
800 Kilometers

Climate

Climatic Zones: Based on Köppen System

Tropical
- Tropical wet
- Tropical dry

Dry
- Semiarid
- Arid

Mild
- Marine west coast
- Mediterranean
- Humid subtropical

High Elevations
- Highlands

→ Warm ocean current
→ Cool ocean current

North Pacific Ocean

North Equatorial Current

North Equatorial Current

North Equatorial Current

Equatorial Countercurrent

South Equatorial Current

South Equatorial Current

South Subtropical Current

South Subtropical Current

South Subtropical Current

Equatorial Current

East Australia Current

Tasman Sea

South Pacific Ocean

Indian Ocean

West Wind Drift

West Australia Current

A S I A

AUSTRALIA

NEW ZEALAND

Hawai'i (U.S.)

French Polynesia (France)

Cook Islands (N.Z.)

Niue (N.Z.)

KIRIBATI

Tokelau (N.Z.)

American Samoa (U.S.)

SAMOA

TONGA

Wallis and Futuna Is. (France)

FIJI ISLANDS

TUVALU

VANUATU

New Caledonia (France)

Coral Sea Islands Territory (Australia)

NAURU

SOLOMON ISLANDS

PAPUA NEW GUINEA

MARSHALL ISLANDS

FEDERATED STATES OF MICRONESIA

Northern Mariana Islands (U.S.)

Guam (U.S.)

PALAU

EQUATOR

TROPIC OF CANCER

TROPIC OF CANCER

TROPIC OF CAPRICORN

0°

15°S

30°S

45°S

15°N

165°W

180°

165°E

150°E

135°E

120°E

135°W

150°W

165°W

180°

165°E

150°E

135°E

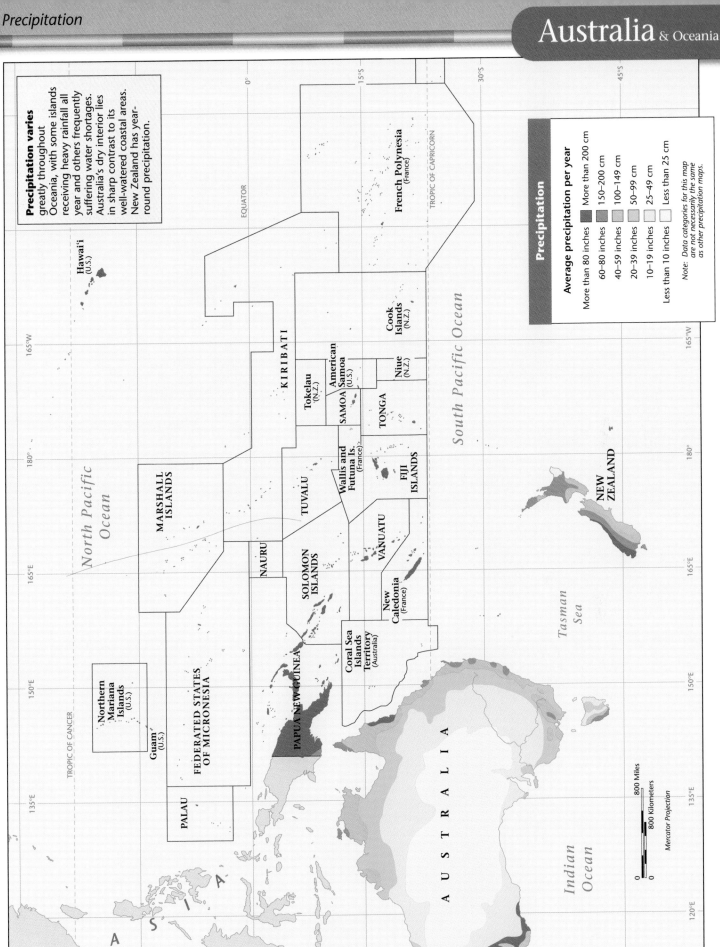

Precipitation varies greatly throughout Oceania, with some islands receiving heavy rainfall all year and others frequently suffering water shortages. Australia's dry interior lies in sharp contrast to its well-watered coastal areas. New Zealand has year-round precipitation.

Hawai'i (U.S.)

North Pacific Ocean

MARSHALL ISLANDS

NAURU

SOLOMON ISLANDS

TUVALU

KIRIBATI

Tokelau (N.Z.)

American Samoa (U.S.)

SAMOA

Niue (N.Z.)

Cook Islands (N.Z.)

French Polynesia (France)

TROPIC OF CAPRICORN

South Pacific Ocean

Wallis and Futuna Is. (France)

TONGA

FIJI ISLANDS

VANUATU

New Caledonia (France)

Coral Sea Islands Territory (Australia)

NEW ZEALAND

Tasman Sea

PAPUA NEW GUINEA

Northern Mariana Islands (U.S.)

Guam (U.S.)

FEDERATED STATES OF MICRONESIA

PALAU

TROPIC OF CANCER

A S I A

A U S T R A L I A

Indian Ocean

EQUATOR

Precipitation

Average precipitation per year

More than 80 inches — More than 200 cm
60–80 inches — 150–200 cm
40–59 inches — 100–149 cm
20–39 inches — 50–99 cm
10–19 inches — 25–49 cm
Less than 10 inches — Less than 25 cm

Note: Data categories for this map are not necessarily the same as other precipitation maps.

800 Miles
800 Kilometers
0
0

Mercator Projection

115

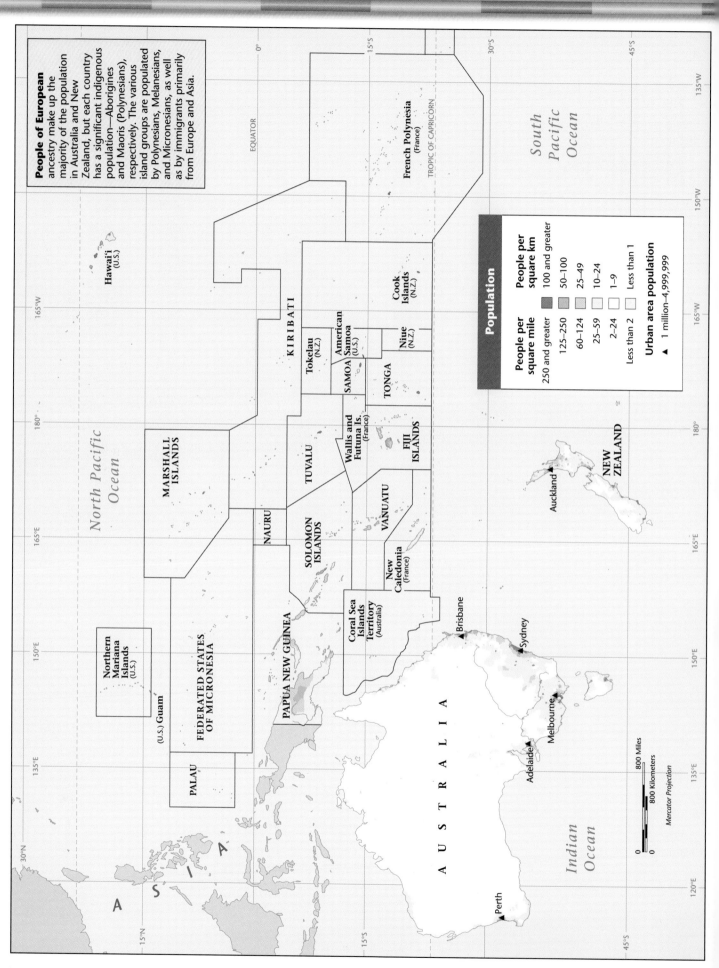

People of European ancestry make up the majority of the population in Australia and New Zealand, but each country has a significant indigenous population—Aborigines and Maoris (Polynesians), respectively. The various island groups are populated by Polynesians, Melanesians, and Micronesians, as well as by immigrants primarily from Europe and Asia.

Population

People per square mile

- 250 and greater
- 125–250
- 60–124
- 25–59
- 2–24
- Less than 2

People per square km

- 100 and greater
- 50–100
- 25–49
- 10–24
- 1–9
- Less than 1

Urban area population

- ▲ 1 million–4,999,999

North Pacific Ocean

South Pacific Ocean

Indian Ocean

Hawai'i (U.S.)

Northern Mariana Islands (U.S.)

Guam (U.S.)

PALAU

FEDERATED STATES OF MICRONESIA

MARSHALL ISLANDS

NAURU

KIRIBATI

Tokelau (N.Z.)

American Samoa (U.S.)

SAMOA

TUVALU

Wallis and Futuna Is. (France)

TONGA

Niue (N.Z.)

Cook Islands (N.Z.)

French Polynesia (France)

FIJI ISLANDS

VANUATU

SOLOMON ISLANDS

New Caledonia (France)

PAPUA NEW GUINEA

Coral Sea Islands Territory (Australia)

A S I A

AUSTRALIA

Perth

Adelaide

Melbourne

Sydney

Brisbane

NEW ZEALAND

Auckland

EQUATOR

TROPIC OF CAPRICORN

Mercator Projection

0   800 Miles
0   800 Kilometers

Australia & Oceania

Primary economic products make up much of the market in Oceania. New Zealand and Australia account for almost two-thirds of world wool exports and more than one-fifth of beef exports. Plantation agriculture, fishing, tourism, or mining form the economic base in most of the small island countries. For example, New Caledonia is a leading exporter of nickel, and Fiji exports sugar and gold.

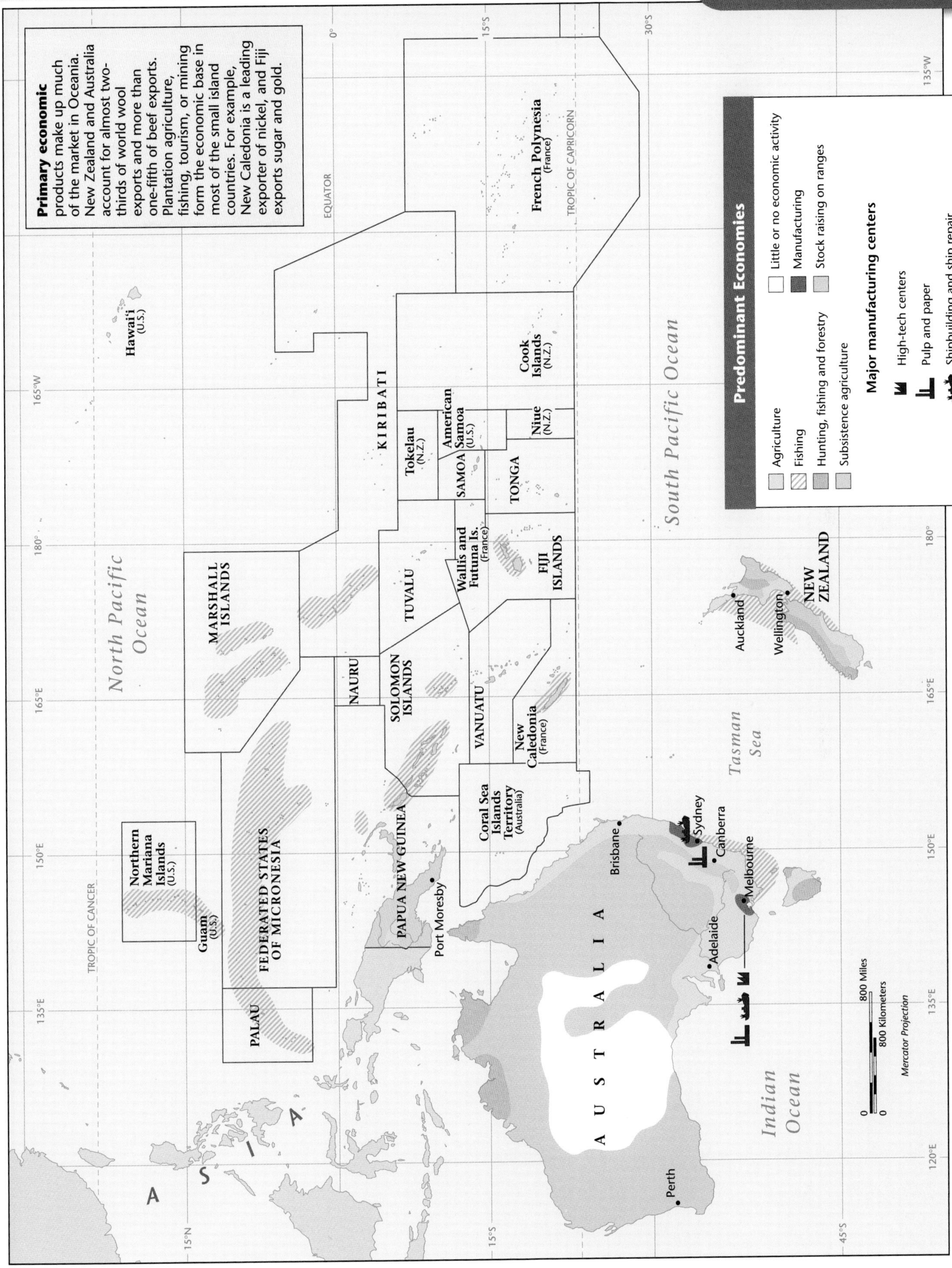

Predominant Economies

Agriculture

Fishing

Hunting, fishing and forestry

Subsistence agriculture

Little or no economic activity

Manufacturing

Stock raising on ranges

Major manufacturing centers

High-tech centers

Pulp and paper

Shipbuilding and ship repair

Hawai'i (U.S.)

KIRIBATI

French Polynesia (France)

Cook Islands (N.Z.)

Tokelau (N.Z.)

American Samoa (U.S.)

Niue (N.Z.)

SAMOA

TONGA

Wallis and Futuna Is. (France)

FIJI ISLANDS

MARSHALL ISLANDS

TUVALU

NAURU

SOLOMON ISLANDS

VANUATU

New Caledonia (France)

Northern Mariana Islands (U.S.)

Guam (U.S.)

FEDERATED STATES OF MICRONESIA

PALAU

PAPUA NEW GUINEA

Port Moresby

Coral Sea Islands Territory (Australia)

North Pacific Ocean

South Pacific Ocean

NEW ZEALAND

Auckland

Wellington

Tasman Sea

AUSTRALIA

Brisbane

Sydney

Canberra

Melbourne

Adelaide

Perth

Indian Ocean

800 Miles

800 Kilometers

Mercator Projection

ASIA

EQUATOR

TROPIC OF CANCER

TROPIC OF CAPRICORN

117

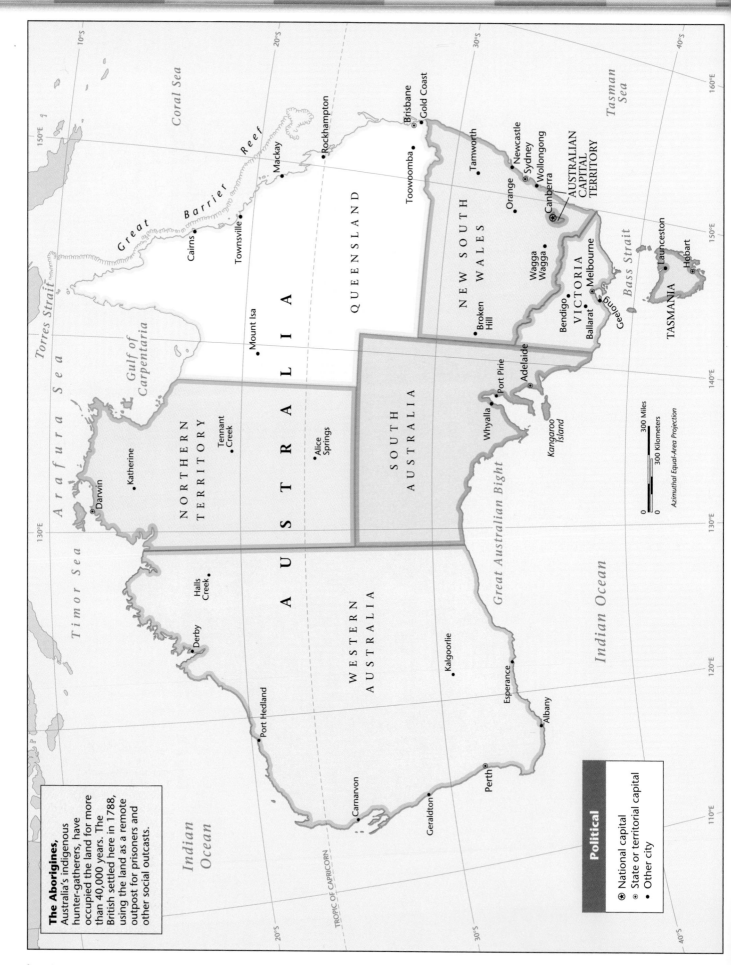

The Aborigines, Australia's indigenous hunter-gatherers, have occupied the land for more than 40,000 years. The British settled here in 1788, using the land as a remote outpost for prisoners and other social outcasts.

Indian Ocean

Timor Sea

Arafura Sea

Torres Strait

Coral Sea

Gulf of Carpentaria

Great Barrier Reef

Darwin

Katherine

Halls Creek

Derby

Port Hedland

Carnarvon

Geraldton

Perth

Kalgoorlie

Esperance

Albany

WESTERN AUSTRALIA

NORTHERN TERRITORY

Tennant Creek

Alice Springs

A U S T R A L I A

Mount Isa

SOUTH AUSTRALIA

Whyalla

Port Pirie

Adelaide

Kangaroo Island

Great Australian Bight

Indian Ocean

TROPIC OF CAPRICORN

QUEENSLAND

Cairns

Townsville

Mackay

Rockhampton

Toowoomba

Brisbane

Gold Coast

NEW SOUTH WALES

Tamworth

Newcastle

Orange

Sydney

Wollongong

Canberra

AUSTRALIAN CAPITAL TERRITORY

Broken Hill

Wagga Wagga

VICTORIA

Bendigo

Ballarat

Melbourne

Geelong

Tasman Sea

Bass Strait

TASMANIA

Launceston

Hobart

Political

⊛ National capital
⊚ State or territorial capital
• Other city

300 Miles

300 Kilometers

Azimuthal Equal-Area Projection

Political

⊗ National capital
• Other city

35°S

170°E · 175°E · 35°S

Kaitaia
Kerikeri
Whangarei

Tasman Sea

Great Barrier Island

Takapuna
Waitemata
Auckland
Manukau

North Island

Hamilton · Mount Maùnganui
Tauranga
Whakatane
Rotorua

Taupo · Gisborne

New Plymouth

Raetihi

Napier
Hastings
Wanganui

40°S · 40°S

Feilding
Palmerston North
Porirua
Levin
Masterton
Nelson
Upper Hutt
Lower Hutt
Picton
Blenheim
Wellington

Cook Strait

0 — 150 Miles
0 — 150 Kilometers
Azimuthal Equal-Area Projection

Westport

Molesworth

Kaikoura

Greymouth
Hokitika
Parnassus
Arthur's Pass

Pacific Ocean

Fox Glacier
Franz Josef Glacier
Christchurch · Lyttelton
Ashburton

Haast

Timaru

Canterbury Bight

Milford Sound
Wanaka

Oamaru

45°S

South Island

Dunedin
Gore
Balclutha
Invercargill

Foveaux Strait

Stewart Island

Two large islands
and several smaller ones make up New Zealand. The country averages 39 people per square mile (15 people per sq km), but most of the population lives in urban areas. The economy relies on primary activities, such as raising sheep, dairying, and forestry. Wellington, Christchurch, and other place-names reflect a strong British influence.

165°E · 170°E · 175°E

Great Barrier Reef

Stretching like intricate necklaces along the edges of landmasses in the warm ocean waters of the tropics, coral reefs form one of nature's most complex ecosystems. Corals are tiny marine animals that thrive in shallow coastal waters of the tropics. One type of coral, called a "hard coral," produces a limestone skeleton. When the tiny animal dies, its stonelike skeleton is left behind. The accumulation of millions of these skeletons over thousands of years has produced the large reef formations found in many coastal waters of the tropics.

Most coral reefs are formed between 30 degrees N and 30 degrees S latitude in waters with a temperature between 70 and 85 degrees Fahrenheit (21 and 29 degrees Celsius). It is estimated that Earth's coral reefs cover 110,000 square miles (284,300 sq km). Coral reefs are important because they form a habitat for marine animals such as fish, sea turtles, lobsters, and starfish. They also protect fragile coastlines from damaging ocean waves and may be a source of medicines.

The largest coral reef in the world, the Great Barrier Reef, lies off the northeast coast of Australia (see large map). This reef, which is made up of more than 400 different types of coral and home to more than 1,500 species of fish, is a popular tourist destination. People visit to snorkel and dive along the reef and view the great diversity of marine life living among the corals.

▼ *An anemone fish* is specially adapted to live among the venomous tentacles of one of the reef's sea anemones.

▲ *Brilliantly colored corals* and the fish that live among them attract divers and snorkelers to the Great Barrier Reef every year.

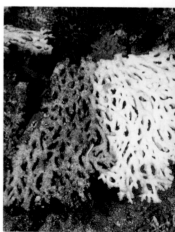

▲ *Corals are at risk* due to environmental hazards, such as storms and changes in water temperature and salinity as well as pollution and other human-related factors.

Web Link for information on coral reefs: http://www.coralreef.noaa.gov/

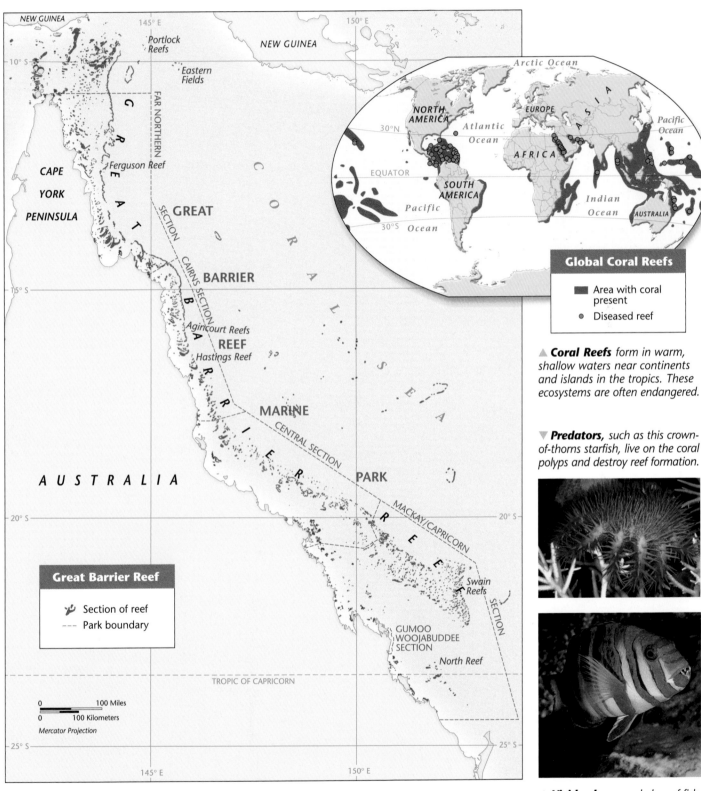

NEW GUINEA

145° E   150° E

Portlock Reefs   NEW GUINEA

10° S

Eastern Fields

CAPE

Ferguson Reef

GREAT

YORK

FAR NORTHERN SECTION

CORAL

PENINSULA

G R E A T   B A R R I E R

15° S   BARRIER

CAIRNS SECTION

Agincourt Reefs   REEF

Hastings Reef   S E A

MARINE

CENTRAL SECTION

AUSTRALIA   PARK

R E E F   MACKAY/CAPRICORN

20° S   20° S

Swain Reefs

SECTION

Great Barrier Reef

🦑 Section of reef

--- Park boundary

GUMOO WOOJABUDDEE SECTION

North Reef

TROPIC OF CAPRICORN

0   100 Miles
0   100 Kilometers
Mercator Projection

25° S   25° S

145° E   150° E

Global Coral Reefs (inset world map)

Arctic Ocean

NORTH AMERICA   EUROPE   A S I A   Pacific Ocean

30°N   Atlantic Ocean   AFRICA

EQUATOR

SOUTH AMERICA   Indian Ocean   AUSTRALIA

Pacific Ocean

30°S

Global Coral Reefs

■ Area with coral present

● Diseased reef

▲ **Coral Reefs** form in warm, shallow waters near continents and islands in the tropics. These ecosystems are often endangered.

▼ **Predators,** such as this crown-of-thorns starfish, live on the coral polyps and destroy reef formation.

▲ **Vivid colors** may help reef fish recognize others of their species. The colors of this harlequin fish darken with age.

▲ **The Great Barrier Reef** stretches along the northeast coast of Australia for 1,429 miles (2,300 km), from the tip of the Cape York Peninsula to just north of Brisbane in the state of Queensland.

Antarctica

About 180 million years ago Antarctica broke away from the ancient supercontinent Gondwana. Slowly the continent drifted to its present location at the southernmost point on Earth. Approximately 98 percent of the continent lies under permanent ice sheets that are nearly 3 miles (5 km) thick in places. It is estimated that if all of Antarctica's ice were to melt, the global ocean level would rise more than 200 feet (60 m).

Facts & Figures

▶ **Land area:** 5,100,400 sq mi (13,209,000 sq km)

▶ **Population:** no permanent residents

▶ **Highest point:** Vinson Massif: 16,067 ft (4,897 m)

▶ **Lowest point:** Bentley Subglacial Trench: 8,366 ft (2,550 m) below sea level

▶ **Number of independent countries:** 0

▶ **Number of countries claiming land:** 7

▶ **Number of countries operating year-round research stations:** 19

▶ **Number of year-round research stations:** 46

▶ **Coldest place:** Plateau Station; average annual temperature: -70°F (-56.7°C)

▶ **Average precipitation on the polar plateau:** less than 2 in (5 cm) per year

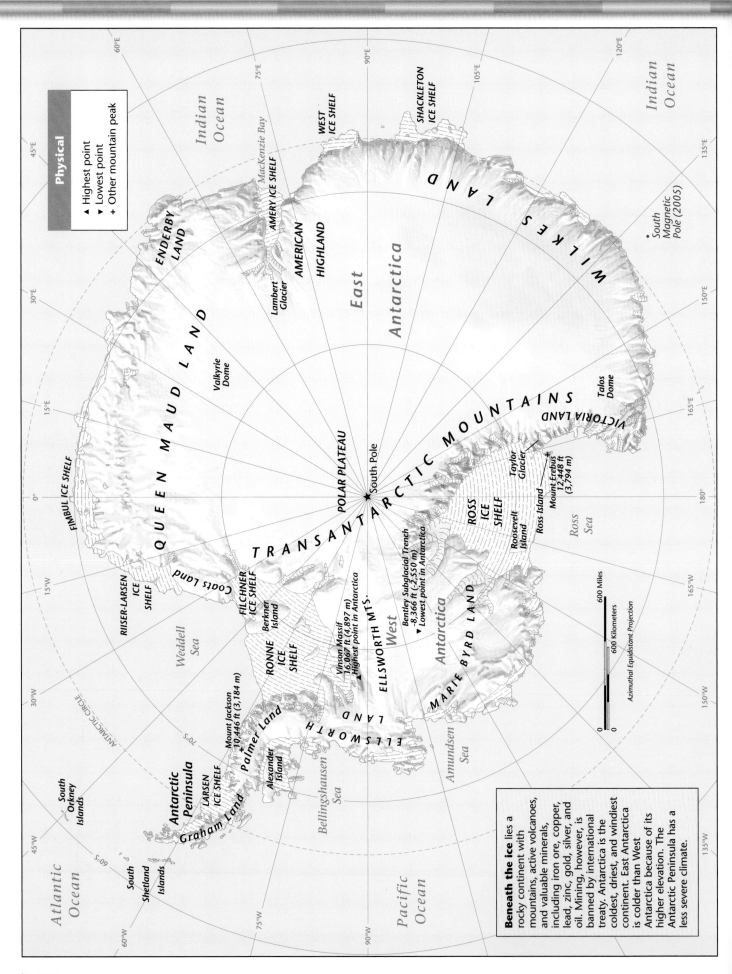

Physical

▲ Highest point
▼ Lowest point
+ Other mountain peak

Indian Ocean

Atlantic Ocean

Pacific Ocean

Indian Ocean

ENDERBY LAND

QUEEN MAUD LAND

WILKES LAND

East Antarctica

AMERICAN HIGHLAND

MacKenzie Bay

AMERY ICE SHELF

WEST ICE SHELF

SHACKLETON ICE SHELF

Lambert Glacier

South Magnetic Pole (2005)

Valkyrie Dome

Talos Dome

VICTORIA LAND

POLAR PLATEAU

TRANSANTARCTIC MOUNTAINS

South Pole

FIMBUL ICE SHELF

RIISER-LARSEN ICE SHELF

Coats Land

FILCHNER ICE SHELF

Berkner Island

RONNE ICE SHELF

Vinson Massif 16,067 ft (4,897 m) ▲ Highest point in Antarctica

ELLSWORTH MTS.

West Antarctica

Bentley Subglacial Trench -8,366 ft (-2,550 m) ▼ Lowest point in Antarctica

MARIE BYRD LAND

ELLSWORTH LAND

Taylor Glacier

Mount Erebus 12,448 ft (3,794 m)

Ross Island

Roosevelt Island

ROSS ICE SHELF

Ross Sea

Weddell Sea

Antarctic Peninsula

Mount Jackson 10,446 ft (3,184 m) +

Palmer Land

Alexander Island

LARSEN ICE SHELF

Graham Land

Bellingshausen Sea

Amundsen Sea

South Orkney Islands

South Shetland Islands

ANTARCTIC CIRCLE

600 Miles

600 Kilometers

Azimuthal Equidistant Projection

Beneath the ice lies a rocky continent with mountains, active volcanoes, and valuable minerals, including iron ore, copper, lead, zinc, gold, silver, and oil. Mining, however, is banned by international treaty. Antarctica is the coldest, driest, and windiest continent. East Antarctica is colder than West Antarctica because of its higher elevation. The Antarctic Peninsula has a less severe climate.

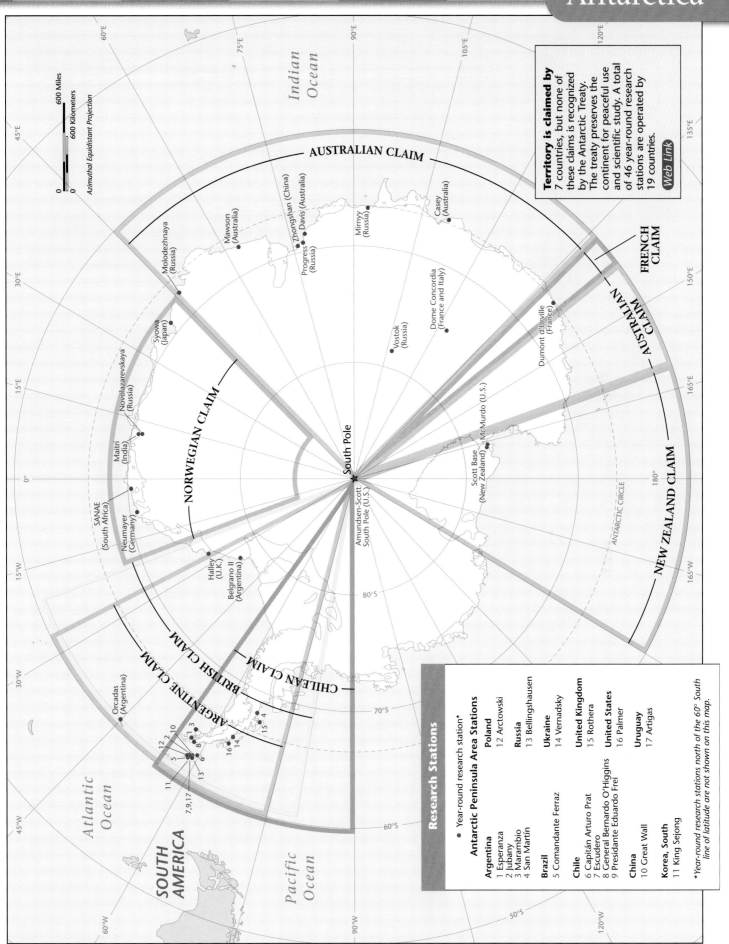

Territory is claimed by 7 countries, but none of these claims is recognized by the Antarctic Treaty. The treaty preserves the continent for peaceful use and scientific study. A total of 46 year-round research stations are operated by 19 countries.

Web Link

600 Miles
600 Kilometers
Azimuthal Equidistant Projection

AUSTRALIAN CLAIM

FRENCH CLAIM

AUSTRALIAN CLAIM

NEW ZEALAND CLAIM

NORWEGIAN CLAIM

CHILEAN CLAIM

BRITISH CLAIM

ARGENTINE CLAIM

South Pole

Amundsen–Scott South Pole (U.S.)

ANTARCTIC CIRCLE

Indian Ocean

Atlantic Ocean

Pacific Ocean

SOUTH AMERICA

Mawson (Australia)
Zhongshan (China)
Davis (Australia)
Progress (Russia)
Mirnyy (Russia)
Casey (Australia)
Molodezhnaya (Russia)
Syowa (Japan)
Novolazarevskaya (Russia)
Maitri (India)
SANAE (South Africa)
Neumayer (Germany)
Halley (U.K.)
Belgrano II (Argentina)
Orcadas (Argentina)
Dome Concordia (France and Italy)
Vostok (Russia)
Dumont d'Urville (France)
McMurdo (U.S.)
Scott Base (New Zealand)

Research Stations

• Year-round research station*

Antarctic Peninsula Area Stations

Argentina
1 Esperanza
2 Jubany
3 Marambio
4 San Martín

Brazil
5 Comandante Ferraz

Chile
6 Capitán Arturo Prat
7 Escudero
8 General Bernardo O'Higgins
9 Presidante Eduardo Frei

China
10 Great Wall

Korea, South
11 King Sejong

Poland
12 Arctowski

Russia
13 Bellingshausen

Ukraine
14 Vernadsky

United Kingdom
15 Rothera

United States
16 Palmer

Uruguay
17 Artigas

Year-round research stations north of the 60° South line of latitude are not shown on this map.

The flags and fact boxes below represent the world's 192 independent countries—those with national governments that are recognized as having the highest legal authority over the land and people within their boundaries. The flags shown are national flags recognized by the United Nations. Area figures include land and surface areas for inland bodies of water. Population figures are for the year 2004 as provided by the Population Reference Bureau of the United States. The languages listed are either the ones most commonly spoken within a country or official languages of a country.

NORTH AMERICA

Antigua and Barbuda
Area: 171 sq mi (442 sq km)
Population: 76,000
Capital: St. John's
Languages: English (official), local dialects

Bahamas
Area: 5,382 sq mi (13,939 sq km)
Population: 317,000
Capital: Nassau
Languages: English (official), Creole

Barbados
Area: 166 sq mi (430 sq km)
Population: 256,000
Capital: Bridgetown
Language: English

Belize
Area: 8,867 sq mi (22,965 sq km)
Population: 276,000
Capital: Belmopan
Languages: English (official), Spanish, Mayan, Garifuna, Creole

Canada
Area: 3,855,101 sq mi (9,984,670 sq km)
Population: 31,892,000
Capital: Ottawa
Languages: English, French (both official)

Costa Rica
Area: 19,730 sq mi (51,100 sq km)
Population: 4,220,000
Capital: San José
Languages: Spanish (official), English

Cuba
Area: 42,803 sq mi (110,860 sq km)
Population: 11,267,000
Capital: Havana
Language: Spanish

Dominica
Area: 290 sq mi (751 sq km)
Population: 69,000
Capital: Roseau
Languages: English (official), French patois

Dominican Republic
Area: 18,704 sq mi (48,442 sq km)
Population: 8,820,000
Capital: Santo Domingo
Language: Spanish

El Salvador
Area: 8,124 sq mi (21,041 sq km)
Population: 6,706,000
Capital: San Salvador
Languages: Spanish, Nahua

Grenada
Area: 133 sq mi (344 sq km)
Population: 106,000
Capital: St. George's
Languages: English (official), French patois

Guatemala
Area: 42,042 sq mi (108,889 sq km)
Population: 12,661,000
Capital: Guatemala City
Languages: Spanish, Amerindian languages

Haiti
Area: 10,714 sq mi (27,750 sq km)
Population: 8,106,000
Capital: Port-au-Prince
Languages: French, Creole (both official)

Honduras
Area: 43,433 sq mi (112,492 sq km)
Population: 7,028,000
Capital: Tegucigalpa
Languages: Spanish, Amerindian dialects

Jamaica
Area: 4,244 sq mi (10,991 sq km)
Population: 2,643,000
Capital: Kingston
Languages: English, English patois

Mexico
Area: 758,449 sq mi (1,964,375 sq km)
Population: 106,204,000
Capital: Mexico City
Languages: Spanish, Mayan, Nahuatl, other indigenous languages

Nicaragua
Area: 50,193 sq mi (130,000 sq km)
Population: 5,626,000
Capital: Managua
Languages: Spanish (official), English, indigenous languages

Panama
Area: 29,157 sq mi (75,517 sq km)
Population: 3,172,000
Capital: Panama City
Languages: Spanish (official), English

St. Kitts and Nevis
Area: 104 sq mi (269 sq km)
Population: 47,000
Capital: Basseterre
Language: English

St. Lucia
Area: 238 sq mi (616 sq km)
Population: 164,000
Capital: Castries
Languages: English (official), French patois

St. Vincent and the Grenadines
Area: 150 sq mi (389 sq km)
Population: 110,000
Capital: Kingstown
Languages: English, French patois

Trinidad and Tobago
Area: 1,980 sq mi (5,128 sq km)
Population: 1,315,000
Capital: Port-of-Spain
Languages: English (official), Hindi, French, Spanish

United States
Area: 3,794,083 sq mi (9,826,630 sq km)
Population: 293,633,000
Capital: Washington, D.C.
Languages: English, Spanish

SOUTH AMERICA

Argentina
Area: 1,073,518 sq mi
(2,780,400 sq km)
Population: 37,880,000
Capital: Buenos Aires
Languages: Spanish
(official), English, Italian,
German, French

Bolivia
Area: 424,164 sq mi
(1,098,581 sq km)
Population: 8,766,000
Capitals: La Paz, Sucre
Languages: Spanish,
Quechua, Aymara (all official)

Brazil
Area: 3,300,169 sq mi
(8,547,403 sq km)
Population: 179,091,000
Capital: Brasília
Languages: Portuguese
(official), Spanish, English,
French

Chile
Area: 291,930 sq mi
(756,096 sq km)
Population: 15,988,000
Capital: Santiago
Language: Spanish

Colombia
Area: 440,831 sq mi
(1,141,748 sq km)
Population: 45,325,000
Capital: Bogotá
Language: Spanish

Ecuador
Area: 109,483 sq mi
(283,560 sq km)
Population: 13,402,000
Capital: Quito
Languages: Spanish
(official), Quechua

Guyana
Area: 83,000 sq mi
(214,969 sq km)
Population: 767,000
Capital: Georgetown
Languages: English,
Amerindian dialects,
Creole, Hindi, Urdu

Paraguay
Area: 157,048 sq mi
(406,752 sq km)
Population: 6,018,000
Capital: Asunción
Languages: Spanish, Guaraní
(both official)

Peru
Area: 496,224 sq mi
(1,285,216 sq km)
Population: 27,547,000
Capital: Lima
Languages: Spanish,
Quechua (both official),
Aymara

Suriname
Area: 63,037 sq mi
(163,265 sq km)
Population: 449,000
Capital: Paramaribo
Languages: Dutch (official),
English, Sranang Tongo
(Taki-Taki), Hindustani,
Javanese

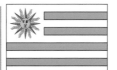

Uruguay
Area: 68,037 sq mi
(176,215 sq km)
Population: 3,399,000
Capital: Montevideo
Languages: Spanish,
Portunol, Brazilero

Venezuela
Area: 352,144 sq mi
(912,050 sq km)
Population: 26,170,000
Capital: Caracas
Language: Spanish (official)

EUROPE

Albania
Area: 11,100 sq mi
(28,748 sq km)
Population: 3,232,000
Capital: Tirana
Languages: Albanian, Greek

Andorra
Area: 181 sq mi
(468 sq km)
Population: 69,000
Capital: Andorra la Vella
Languages: Catalan
(official), French, Castilian

Austria
Area: 32,378 sq mi
(83,858 sq km)
Population: 8,106,000
Capital: Vienna
Language: German

Belarus
Area: 80,153 sq mi
(207,595 sq km)
Population: 9,800,000
Capital: Minsk
Languages: Belarusian,
Russian

Belgium
Area: 11,787 sq mi
(30,528 sq km)
Population: 10,417,000
Capital: Brussels
Languages: Flemish
(Dutch), French, German
(all official)

Bosnia and
Herzegovina
Area: 19,741 sq mi
(51,129 sq km)
Population: 3,889,000
Capital: Sarajevo
Languages: Croatian,
Serbian, Bosnian

Bulgaria
Area: 42,855 sq mi
(110,994 sq km)
Population: 7,778,000
Capital: Sofia
Language: Bulgarian

Croatia
Area: 21,831 sq mi
(56,542 sq km)
Population: 4,433,000
Capital: Zagreb
Language: Croatian

Cyprus
Area: 3,572 sq mi
(9,251 sq km)
Population: 948,000
Capital: Nicosia
Languages: Greek, Turkish,
English

Czech Republic
Area: 30,450 sq mi
(78,866 sq km)
Population: 10,201,000
Capital: Prague
Language: Czech

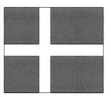

Denmark
Area: 16,640 sq mi
(43,098 sq km)
Population: 5,403,000
Capital: Copenhagen
Languages: Danish,
Faroese, Greenlandic

Estonia
Area: 17,462 sq mi
(45,227 sq km)
Population: 1,349,000
Capital: Tallinn
Languages: Estonian
(official), Russian, Ukrainian

Finland
Area: 130,558 sq mi
(338,145 sq km)
Population: 5,222,000
Capital: Helsinki
Languages: Finnish,
Swedish (both official)

France
Area: 210,026 sq mi
(543,965 sq km)
Population: 60,033,000
Capital: Paris
Language: French

Germany
Area: 137,847 sq mi
(357,022 sq km)
Population: 82,558,000
Capital: Berlin
Language: German

Greece
Area: 50,949 sq mi
(131,957 sq km)
Population: 11,000,000
Capital: Athens
Language: Greek

Hungary
Area: 35,919 sq mi
(93,030 sq km)
Population: 10,077,000
Capital: Budapest
Language: Hungarian

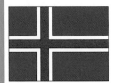

Iceland
Area: 39,769 sq mi
(103,000 sq km)
Population: 292,000
Capital: Reykjavík
Languages: Icelandic,
English, Nordic languages,
German

Ireland
Area: 27,133 sq mi
(70,273 sq km)
Population: 4,057,000
Capital: Dublin
Languages: English, Irish
(Gaelic)

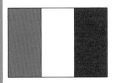

Italy
Area: 116,345 sq mi
(301,333 sq km)
Population: 57,816,000
Capital: Rome
Languages: Italian,
German, French, Slovene

Latvia
Area: 24,938 sq mi
(64,589 sq km)
Population: 2,313,000
Capital: Riga
Languages: Latvian (official),
Lithuanian, Russian

Liechtenstein
Area: 62 sq mi
(160 sq km)
Population: 34,000
Capital: Vaduz
Languages: German
(official), Alemannic dialect

Lithuania
Area: 25,212 sq mi
(65,300 sq km)
Population: 3,436,000
Capital: Vilnius
Languages: Lithuanian
(official), Polish, Russian

Luxembourg
Area: 998 sq mi
(2,586 sq km)
Population: 453,000
Capital: Luxembourg
Languages: Luxembourgish
(official), German, French

Macedonia
Area: 9,928 sq mi
(25,713 sq km)
Population: 2,038,000
Capital: Skopje
Languages: Macedonian,
Albanian

Malta
Area: 122 sq mi
(316 sq km)
Population: 399,000
Capital: Valletta
Languages: Maltese,
English (both official)

Moldova
Area: 13,050 sq mi
(33,800 sq km)
Population: 4,203,000
Capital: Chişinău
Languages: Moldovan
(official), Russian, Gagauz

Monaco
Area: 0.75 sq mi
(1.95 sq km)
Population: 33,000
Capital: Monaco
Languages: French (official),
English, Italian, Monegasque

Netherlands
Area: 16,034 sq mi
(41,528 sq km)
Population: 16,286,000
Capital: Amsterdam
Languages: Dutch, Frisian
(both official)

Norway
Area: 125,004 sq mi
(323,758 sq km)
Population: 4,590,000
Capital: Oslo
Language: Norwegian
(official)

Poland
Area: 120,728 sq mi
(312,685 sq km)
Population: 38,175,000
Capital: Warsaw
Language: Polish

Portugal
Area: 35,655 sq mi
(92,345 sq km)
Population: 10,466,000
Capital: Lisbon
Languages: Portuguese,
Mirandese (both official)

Romania
Area: 92,043 sq mi
(238,391 sq km)
Population: 21,672,000
Capital: Bucharest
Languages: Romanian
(official), Hungarian,
German

Russia
Area: 6,592,850 sq mi
(17,075,400 sq km)
Population: 144,115,000
Capital: Moscow
Language: Russian

San Marino
Area: 24 sq mi
(61 sq km)
Population: 29,000
Capital: San Marino
Language: Italian

Serbia and
Montenegro
Area: 39,450 sq mi
(102,173 sq km)
Population: 10,705,000
Capitals: Belgrade,
Podgorica
Languages: Serbian,
Albanian

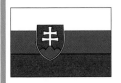

Slovakia
Area: 18,932 sq mi
(49,035 km)
Population: 5,380,000
Capital: Bratislava
Languages: Slovak (official),
Hungarian

Slovenia
Area: 7,827 sq mi
(20,273 sq km)
Population: 1,997,000
Capital: Ljubljana
Languages: Slovenian,
Serbo-Croatian

Spain
Area: 195,363 sq mi
(505,988 sq km)
Population: 42,525,000
Capital: Madrid
Languages: Castilian
Spanish, Catalan, Galician,
Basque

Sweden
Area: 173,732 sq mi
(449,964 sq km)
Population: 8,996,000
Capital: Stockholm
Language: Swedish

Switzerland
Area: 15,940 sq mi
(41,284 sq km)
Population: 7,404,000
Capital: Bern
Languages: German,
French, Italian, Romansch
(all official)

Ukraine
Area: 233,090 sq mi
(603,700 sq km)
Population: 47,432,000
Capital: Kiev
Languages: Ukrainian,
Russian, Romanian, Polish,
Hungarian

United Kingdom
Area: 93,788 sq mi
(242,910 sq km)
Population: 59,675,000
Capital: London
Languages: English, Welsh,
Scottish form of Gaelic

Vatican City
Area: 0.2 sq mi
(0.4 sq km)
Population: 1,000
Languages: Italian, Latin,
French

AFRICA

Algeria
Area: 919,595 sq mi
(2,381,741 sq km)
Population: 32,323,000
Capital: Algiers
Languages: Arabic (official),
French, Berber dialects

Angola
Area: 481,354 sq mi
(1,246,700 sq km)
Population: 13,294,000
Capital: Luanda
Languages: Portuguese
(official), Bantu

Benin
Area: 43,484 sq mi
(112,622 sq km)
Population: 7,250,000
Capital: Porto-Novo,
Languages: French (official),
Fon, Yoruba, other indige-
nous languages

Botswana
Area: 224,607 sq mi
(581,730 sq km)
Population: 1,684,000
Capital: Gaborone
Languages: English (official),
Setswana

Burkina Faso
Area: 105,869 sq mi
(274,200 sq km)
Population: 13,575,000
Capital: Ouagadougou
Languages: French (official),
indigenous languages

Burundi
Area: 10,747 sq mi
(27,834 sq km)
Population: 6,231,000
Capital: Bujumbura
Languages: Kirundi, French
(both official), Swahili

Cameroon
Area: 183,569 sq mi
(475,442 sq km)
Population: 16,064,000
Capital: Yaoundé
Languages: French, English
(both official), 24 major
African language groups

Cape Verde
Area: 1,558 sq mi
(4,036 sq km)
Population: 467,000
Capital: Praia
Languages: Portuguese,
Crioulo

Central African
Republic
Area: 240,535 sq mi
(622,984 sq km)
Population: 3,742,000
Capital: Bangui
Languages: French (official),
Sangho, Arabic, indigenous
languages

Chad
Area: 495,755 sq mi
(1,284,000 sq km)
Population: 9,539,000
Capital: N'Djamena
Languages: French, Arabic
(both official), Sara, more
than 120 other languages
and dialects

Comoros
Area: 719 sq mi
(1,862 sq km)
Population: 652,000
Capital: Moroni
Languages: Arabic, French
(both official), Shikomoro

Congo
Area: 132,047 sq mi
(342,000 sq km)
Population: 3,818,000
Capital: Brazzaville
Languages: French (official),
Lingala, Monokutuba, many
local languages and dialects

Congo, Democratic
Republic of the
Area: 905,365 sq mi
(2,344,885 sq km)
Population: 58,318,000
Capital: Kinshasa
Languages: French (official),
Lingala, Kingwana, Kikongo,
Tshiluba

Côte d'Ivoire
Area: 124,503 sq mi
(322,462 sq km)
Population: 16,897,000
Capitals: Abidjan,
Yamoussoukro
Languages: French (official),
Dioula, 60 native dialects

Djibouti
Area: 8,958 sq mi
(23,200 sq km)
Population: 712,000
Capital: Djibouti
Languages: French, Arabic
(both official), Somali, Afar

Egypt
Area: 386,874 sq mi
(1,002,000 sq km)
Population: 73,390,000
Capital: Cairo
Languages: Arabic (official),
English, French

Equatorial Guinea
Area: 10,831 sq mi
(28,051 sq km)
Population: 507,000
Capital: Malabo
Languages: Spanish,
French (both official), pidgin
English, Fang, Bubi, Ibo

Eritrea
Area: 46,774 sq mi
(121,144 sq km)
Population: 4,447,000
Capital: Asmara
Languages: Afar, Arabic,
Tigre, Kunama, Tigrinya

Ethiopia
Area: 437,600 sq mi
(1,133,380 sq km)
Population: 72,420,000
Capital: Addis Ababa
Languages: Amharic,
Tigrinya, Orominga,
Guaraginga, Somali, Arabic

Gabon
Area: 103,347 sq mi
(267,667 sq km)
Population: 1,351,000
Capital: Libreville
Languages: French, Fang,
Myene, Bateke, Bapounou/
Eschira, Bandjabi

Gambia
Area: 4,361 sq mi
(11,295 sq km)
Population: 1,547,000
Capital: Banjul
Languages: English (official),
Mandinka, Wolof, Fula

Ghana
Area: 92,100 sq mi
(238,537 sq km)
Population: 21,377,000
Capital: Accra
Languages: English (official),
African languages (including
Akan, Moshi-Dagomba,
Ewe, and Ga)

Guinea
Area: 94,926 sq mi
(245,857 sq km)
Population: 9,246,000
Capital: Conakry
Languages: French (official),
indigenous languages

Guinea-Bissau
Area: 13,948 sq mi
(36,125 sq km)
Population: 1,538,000
Capital: Bissau
Languages: Portuguese
(official), Crioulo, indigenous
languages

Kenya
Area: 224,081 sq mi
(580,367 sq km)
Population: 32,420,000
Capital: Nairobi
Languages: English,
Kiswahili (both official),
indigenous languages

Lesotho
Area: 11,720 sq mi
(30,355 sq km)
Population: 1,808,000
Capital: Maseru
Languages: Sesotho,
English (official), Zulu, Xhosa

Liberia
Area: 43,000 sq mi
(111,370 sq km)
Population: 3,487,000
Capital: Monrovia
Languages: English (official),
20 ethnic group languages

Libya
Area: 679,362 sq mi
(1,759,540 sq km)
Population: 5,632,000
Capital: Tripoli
Languages: Arabic, Italian,
English

Madagascar
Area: 226,658 sq mi
(587,041 sq km)
Population: 17,502,000
Capital: Antananarivo
Languages: French,
Malagasy (both official)

Malawi
Area: 45,747 sq mi
(118,484 sq km)
Population: 11,938,000
Capital: Lilongwe
Languages: English,
Chichewa (both official)

Mali
Area: 478,841 sq mi
(1,240,192 sq km)
Population: 13,409,000
Capital: Bamako
Languages: French,
Bambara (both official),
numerous African languages

Mauritania
Area: 397,955 sq mi
(1,030,700 sq km)
Population: 2,980,000
Capital: Nouakchott
Languages: Hassaniya Arabic
(official), Pulaar, Soninke,
Wolof (official), French

Mauritius
Area: 788 sq mi
(2,040 sq km)
Population: 1,235,000
Capital: Port Louis
Languages: English (official),
Creole, French (official),
Hindi, Urdu, Hakka, Bhojpuri

Morocco
Area: 274,461 sq mi
(710,850 sq km)
Population: 30,575,000
Capital: Rabat
Languages: Arabic (official),
Berber dialects, French

Mozambique
Area: 308,642 sq mi
(799,380 sq km)
Population: 19,182,000
Capital: Maputo
Languages: Portuguese
(official), indigenous dialects

Namibia
Area: 318,261 sq mi
(824,292 sq km)
Population: 1,911,000
Capital: Windhoek
Languages: English
(official), Afrikaans, German,
indigenous languages

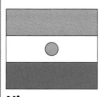

Niger
Area: 489,191 sq mi
(1,267,000 sq km)
Population: 12,415,000
Capital: Niamey
Languages: French (official),
Hausa, Djerma

Nigeria
Area: 356,669 sq mi
(923,768 sq km)
Population: 137,253,000
Capital: Abuja
Languages: English (official),
Hausa, Yoruba, Igbo, Fulani

Rwanda
Area: 10,169 sq mi
(26,338 sq km)
Population: 8,427,000
Capital: Kigali
Languages: Kinyarwanda,
French, English (all official),
Kiswahili (Swahili)

Sao Tome and Principe
Area: 386 sq mi
(1,001 sq km)
Population: 165,000
Capital: São Tomé
Language: Portuguese
(official)

Senegal
Area: 75,955 sq mi
(196,722 sq km)
Population: 10,852,000
Capital: Dakar
Languages: French (official),
Wolof, Pulaar, Diola, Jola,
Mandinka

Seychelles
Area: 176 sq mi
(455 sq km)
Population: 80,000
Capital: Victoria
Languages: English, French
(both official), Creole

Sierra Leone
Area: 27,699 sq mi
(71,740 sq km)
Population: 5,168,000
Capital: Freetown
Languages: English (official),
Mende, Temne, Krio

Somalia
Area: 246,201 sq mi
(637,657 sq km)
Population: 8,305,000
Capital: Mogadishu
Languages: Somali (official),
Arabic, Italian, English

South Africa
Area: 470,693 sq mi
(1,219,090 sq km)
Population: 46,906,000
Capitals: Pretoria (Tshwane),
Cape Town, Bloemfontein
Languages: Afrikaans, English,
Ndebele, Pedi, Sotho, Swazi,
Tsonga, Tswana, Venda,
Xhosa, Zulu (all official)

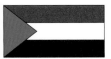

Sudan
Area: 967,500 sq mi
(2,505,813 sq km)
Population: 39,148,000
Capital: Khartoum
Languages: Arabic (official),
Nubian, Ta Bedawie, many
local dialects

Swaziland
Area: 6,704 sq mi
(17,363 sq km)
Population: 1,169,000
Capitals: Mbabane, Lobamba
Languages: English, siSwati
(both official)

Tanzania
Area: 364,900 sq mi
(945,087 sq km)
Population: 36,106,000
Capitals: Dar es Salaam,
Dodoma
Languages: Kiswahili
(Swahili), English (both
official), Arabic, many local
languages

Togo
Area: 21,925 sq mi
(56,785 sq km)
Population: 5,557,000
Capital: Lomé
Languages: French (official),
Ewe, Mina, Kabye, Dagomba

Tunisia
Area: 63,170 sq mi
(163,610 sq km)
Population: 10,002,000
Capital: Tunis
Languages: Arabic (official),
French

Uganda
Area: 93,104 sq mi
(241,139 sq km)
Population: 26,083,000
Capital: Kampala
Languages: English (offi-
cial), Ganda or Luganda,
many local languages

Zambia
Area: 290,586 sq mi
(752,614 sq km)
Population: 10,920,000
Capital: Lusaka
Languages: English (official),
indigenous languages

Zimbabwe
Area: 150,872 sq mi
(390,757 sq km)
Population: 12,672,000
Capital: Harare
Languages: English (official),
Shona, Sindebele

ASIA

Afghanistan
Area: 251,773 sq mi
(652,090 sq km)
Population: 28,514,000
Capital: Kabul
Languages: Pashtu,
Afghan Persian (Dari),
Uzbek, Turkman, 30 minor
languages

Armenia
Area: 11,484 sq mi
(29,743 sq km)
Population: 3,206,000
Capital: Yerevan
Languages: Armenian,
Russian

Azerbaijan
Area: 33,436 sq mi
(86,600 sq km)
Population: 8,295,000
Capital: Baku
Languages: Azerbaijani
(Azeri), Russian, Armenian

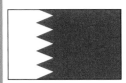

Bahrain
Area: 277 sq mi
(717 sq km)
Population: 723,000
Capital: Manama
Languages: Arabic,
English, Farsi, Urdu

Bangladesh
Area: 56,977 sq mi
(147,570 sq km)
Population: 141,340,000
Capital: Dhaka
Languages: Bangla
(Bengali) (official), English

Bhutan
Area: 17,954 sq mi
(46,500 sq km)
Population: 967,000
Capital: Thimphu
Languages: Dzongkha
(official), Tibetan, Nepali
dialects

Brunei
Area: 2,226 sq mi
(5,765 sq km)
Population: 370,000
Capital: Bandar Seri
Begawan
Languages: Malay (official),
English, Chinese

Cambodia
Area: 69,898 sq mi
(181,035 sq km)
Population: 13,107,000
Capital: Phnom Penh
Languages: Khmer (official),
French, English

China
Area: 3,705,405 sq mi
(9,596,960 sq km)
Population: 1,300,060,000
Capital: Beijing
Languages: Chinese
(Mandarin), Cantonese,
other dialects and minority
languages

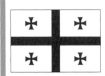

East Timor
(Timor-Leste)
Area: 5,640 sq mi
(14,609 sq km)
Population: 820,000
Capital: Dili
Languages: Tetum, Portu-
guese, Bahasa Indonesian

Georgia
Area: 26,911 sq mi
(69,700 sq km)
Population: 4,526,000
Capital: T'bilisi
Languages: Georgian,
Russian, Armenian, Azeri

India
Area: 1,269,221 sq mi
(3,287,270 sq km)
Population: 1,086,640,000
Capital: New Delhi
Languages: Hindi, English,
14 other official languages

Indonesia
Area: 742,308 sq mi
(1,922,570 sq km)
Population: 218,746,000
Capital: Jakarta
Languages: Bahasa
Indonesian, English, Dutch,
Javanese and other local
dialects

Iran
Area: 636,296 sq mi
(1,648,000 sq km)
Population: 67,433,000
Capital: Tehran
Languages: Persian, Turkic,
Kurdish, various local dialects

Iraq
Area: 168,754 sq mi
(437,072 sq km)
Population: 25,856,000
Capital: Baghdad
Languages: Arabic,
Kurdish (official in Kurdish
regions), Assyrian, Armenian

Israel
Area: 8,550 sq mi
(22,145 sq km)
Population: 6,807,000
Capital: Jerusalem
Languages: Hebrew,
Arabic, English

Japan
Area: 145,902 sq mi
(377,887 sq km)
Population: 127,635,000
Capital: Tokyo
Language: Japanese

Jordan
Area: 34,495 sq mi
(89,342 sq km)
Population: 5,635,000
Capital: Amman
Languages: Arabic, English
understood

Kazakhstan
Area: 1,049,155 sq mi
(2,717,300 sq km)
Population: 14,998,000
Capital: Astana
Languages: Kazakh,
Russian (both official)

Korea, North
Area: 46,540 sq mi
(120,538 sq km)
Population: 22,776,000
Capital: Pyongyang
Language: Korean

Korea, South
Area: 38,321 sq mi
(99,250 sq km)
Population: 48,199,000
Capital: Seoul
Languages: Korean;
English widely taught

Kuwait
Area: 6,880 sq mi
(17,818 sq km)
Population: 2,493,000
Capital: Kuwait City
Languages: Arabic (official),
English

Kyrgyzstan
Area: 77,182 sq mi
(199,900 sq km)
Population: 5,064,000
Capital: Bishkek
Languages: Kyrgyz,
Russian (both official)

Laos
Area: 91,429 sq mi
(236,800 sq km)
Population: 5,787,000
Capital: Vientiane
Languages: Lao (official),
French, English, various
ethnic languages

Lebanon
Area: 4,036 sq mi
(10,452 sq km)
Population: 4,502,000
Capital: Beirut
Languages: Arabic (official),
French, English, Armenian

Malaysia
Area: 127,355 sq mi
(329,847 sq km)
Population: 25,581,000
Capital: Kuala Lumpur
Languages: Bahasa Melayu
(official), English, Chinese
dialects, other regional
dialects and indigenous
languages

Maldives
Area: 115 sq mi
(298 sq km)
Population: 298,000
Capital: Male
Languages: Maldivian
Dhivehi, English

Mongolia
Area: 603,909 sq mi
(1,564,116 sq km)
Population: 2,519,000
Capital: Ulaanbaatar
Languages: Khalkha
Mongol, Turkic, Russian

Myanmar
Area: 261,218 sq mi
(676,552 sq km)
Population: 50,101,000
Capital: Yangon (Rangoon)
Languages: Burmese,
minority ethnic languages

Nepal
Area: 56,827 sq mi
(147,181 sq km)
Population: 24,746,000
Capital: Kathmandu
Languages: Nepali (offi-
cial), English, many other
languages and dialects

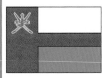

Oman
Area: 119,500 sq mi
(309,500 sq km)
Population: 2,662,000
Capital: Muscat
Languages: Arabic (official),
English, Baluchi, Urdu,
Indian dialects

Pakistan
Area: 307,374 sq mi
(796,095 sq km)
Population: 159,196,000
Capital: Islamabad
Languages: Punjabi,
Sindhi, Siraiki, Pashtu,
Urdu, English

Philippines
Area: 115,831 sq mi
(300,000 sq km)
Population: 83,661,000
Capital: Manila
Languages: Filipino,
English (both official),
8 major dialects

Qatar
Area: 4,448 sq mi
(11,521 sq km)
Population: 743,000
Capital: Doha
Languages: Arabic (official),
English

Saudi Arabia
Area: 756,985 sq mi
(1,960,582 sq km)
Population: 25,131,000
Capital: Riyadh
Language: Arabic

Singapore
Area: 255 sq mi
(660 sq km)
Population: 4,199,000
Capital: Singapore
Languages: Chinese,
Malay, Tamil, English
(all official)

Sri Lanka
Area: 25,299 sq mi
(65,525 sq km)
Population: 19,569,000
Capital: Colombo
Languages: Sinhala
(official), Tamil, English

Syria
Area: 71,498 sq mi
(185,180 sq km)
Population: 17,954,000
Capital: Damascus
Languages: Arabic (official),
Kurdish, Armenian,
Aramaic, Circassian

Tajikistan
Area: 55,251 sq mi
(143,100 sq km)
Population: 6,615,000
Capital: Dushanbe
Languages: Tajik (official),
Russian

Thailand
Area: 198,115 sq mi
(513,115 sq km)
Population: 63,763,000
Capital: Bangkok
Languages: Thai, English,
ethnic and regional dialects

Turkey
Area: 300,948 sq mi
(779,452 sq km)
Population: 71,300,000
Capital: Ankara
Languages: Turkish (official),
Kurdish, Arabic, Armenian,
Greek

Turkmenistan
Area: 188,456 sq mi
(488,100 sq km)
Population: 5,719,000
Capital: Ashgabat
Languages: Turkmen,
Russian, Uzbek

United Arab Emirates
Area: 30,000 sq mi
(77,700 sq km)
Population: 4,193,000
Capital: Abu Dhabi
Languages: Arabic (official),
Persian, English, Hindi, Urdu

Uzbekistan
Area: 172,742 sq mi
(447,400 sq km)
Population: 26,359,000
Capital: Tashkent
Languages: Uzbek,
Russian, Tajik

Vietnam
Area: 127,844 sq mi
(331,114 sq km)
Population: 81,465,000
Capital: Hanoi
Languages: Vietnamese (offi-
cial), English, French, Chinese,
Khmer, tribal languages

Yemen
Area: 207,286 sq mi
(536,869 sq km)
Population: 20,025,000
Capital: Sanaa
Language: Arabic

AUSTRALIA & OCEANIA

Australia
Area: 2,969,906 sq mi
(7,692,024 sq km)
Population: 20,125,000
Capital: Canberra
Languages: English,
indigenous languages

Fiji Islands
Area: 7,095 sq mi
(18,376 sq km)
Population: 845,000
Capital: Suva
Languages: English (official),
Fijian, Hindustani

Kiribati
Area: 313 sq mi
(811 sq km)
Population: 90,000
Capital: Tarawa
Languages: English (official),
I-Kiribati

Marshall Islands
Area: 70 sq mi
(181 sq km)
Population: 57,000
Capital: Majuro
Languages: English, local
dialects, Japanese

Micronesia
Population: 271 sq mi
(702 sq km)
Population: 108,000
Capital: Palikir
Languages: English (official),
Trukese, Pohnpeian,
Yapese, Kosraean

Nauru
Area: 8 sq mi
(21 sq km)
Population: 12,000
Capital: Yaren
Languages: Nauruan
(official), English

New Zealand
Area: 104,454 sq mi
(270,534 sq km)
Population: 4,071,000
Capital: Wellington
Languages: English, Maori
(both official)

Palau
Area: 189 sq mi
(489 sq km)
Population: 21,000
Capital: Koror
Languages: English, Palaun,
Japanese, Sonsoralese,
Tobi, Angaur

Papua New Guinea
Area: 178,703 sq mi
(462,840 sq km)
Population: 5,680,000
Capital: Port Moresby
Languages: 715 indigenous
languages

Samoa
Area: 1,093 sq mi
(2,831 sq km)
Population: 183,000
Capital: Apia
Languages: Samoan
(Polynesian), English

Solomon Islands
Area: 10,954 sq mi
(28,370 sq km)
Population: 460,000
Capital: Honiara
Languages: Melanesian
pidgin, 120 indigenous
languages, English

Tonga
Area: 289 sq mi
(748 sq km)
Population: 102,000
Capital: Nuku'alofa
Languages: Tongan,
English

Tuvalu
Area: 10 sq mi
(26 sq km)
Population: 9,000
Capital: Funafuti
Languages: Tuvaluan,
English

Vanuatu
Area: 4,707 sq mi
(12,190 sq km)
Population: 216,000
Capital: Port-Vila
Languages: English,
French, pidgin (Bislama)
(all official)

Web Link

Glossary

Note: Terms defined within the main body of the atlas text are not listed below.

Alkaline describes soil or natural body of water that has a high salt content; most often found in dry areas where soluble salts have not been washed away or where evaporation rates are high (p. 98)

Arid climate type of dry climate in which annual precipitation is often less than 10 inches (25 cm); experiences great daily variations in day-night temperatures (pp. 18–19)

Asylum a place where a person can go to find safety; to offer asylum means to offer protection in a safe country to people who fear being persecuted or who have been persecuted in their own country. (pp. 46–47)

Bandwidth in computers, the rate at which information can be transmitted along a communications line or device (p. 48)

Bathymetry measurement of depth at various places in the ocean or other body of water (p. 11)

Boreal forest *see northern coniferous forest*

Boundary line established by people to separate one political or mapped area from another; physical features, such as mountains and rivers, or latitude and longitude lines sometimes act as boundaries (p. 10)

Breadbasket a geographic region that is a principal source of grain (p. 64)

Brine solution containing a much higher concentration of salt than seawater (p. 98)

Canadian Shield region containing the oldest rock in North America; areas are exposed in much of eastern Canada and some bordering U.S. regions (pp. 56, 62)

Coastal plain any comparatively level land of low elevation that borders the ocean (p. 64)

Continental climate midlatitude climate zone occurring on large landmasses in the Northern Hemisphere and characterized by great variations of temperature, both seasonally and between day and night; **continental cool summer** climates are influenced by nearby colder subarctic climates; **continental warm summer** climates are influenced by nearby mild or dry climates (pp. 18–19)

Coordinated Universal Time (UTC) the basis for the current worldwide system of civil (versus military) time determined by highly precise atomic clocks; also known as Universal Time; formerly known as Greenwich Mean Time. (p. 53)

Culture hearth center from which major cultural traditions spread and are adopted by people in a wide geographic area (p. 100)

Cybercafe a café that has a collection of computers that customers can use to access the Internet (p. 50)

Degraded forest a forested area severely damaged by overharvesting, repeated fires, overgrazing, poor management practices, or other abuse that delays or prevents forest regrowth (p. 24)

Desert and dry shrub vegetation region with either hot or cold temperatures that annually receives 10 inches (25 cm) or less of precipitation (pp. 22–23)

Ecosystem term for classifying Earth's natural communities according to how all things in an environment, such as a forest or a coral reef, interact with each other (p. 10)

Fault break in Earth's crust along which movement up, down, or sideways occurs (pp. 14–15)

Flooded grassland wetland dominated by grasses and covered by water (pp. 22–23)

Fossil fuel a fuel, such as coal, petroleum, and natural gas, derived from the remains of ancient plants and animals (p. 42)

Geothermal energy heat energy generated within Earth (p. 43)

Gigabit the equivalent of roughly one billion information bits; a bit, which is short for "binary digit," is the smallest unit of information on a computer (p. 48)

Glacier large, slow-moving mass of ice that forms over time from snow (p. 54)

Global warming a theory about the increase of Earth's average global temperature due to a buildup of so-called greenhouse gases, such as carbon dioxide and methane, released by human activities (p. 25)

Globalization the purposeful spread of activities, technology, goods, and values throughout the world through the expansion of global links, such as trade, media, and the Internet (p. 48)

Gondwana name given to the southern part of the supercontinent Pangaea; made up of what we now call Africa, South America, Australia, Antarctica, and India (pp. 14, 98)

Greenwich Mean Time see *Coordinated Universal Time*

Groundwater water, primarily from rain or melted snow, that collects beneath Earth's surface, in saturated soil or in underground reservoirs, or aquifers, and that supplies springs and wells (p. 41)

Hemisphere one-half of the globe; the Equator divides Earth into Northern and Southern Hemispheres; the prime meridian and the 180 degree meridian divide it into Eastern and Western Hemispheres (p. 5)

Highland/upland climate region associated with mountains or plateaus that varies depending on elevation, latitude, continental location, and exposure to sun and wind; in general, temperature decreases and precipitation increases with elevation (pp. 18–19)

Host country the country where a refugee first goes to find asylum (p. 46)

Hot spot in geology, an extremely hot region beneath the lithosphere that tends to stay relatively stationary while plates of Earth's outer crust move over it; environmentally, an ecological trouble spot (pp. 15, 24)

Human rights basic universal civil, political, economic, social, and cultural rights of individuals based on the concept of personal dignity and value (p. 45)

Humid subtropical climate region characterized by hot summers, mild to cool winters, and year-round precipitation that is heaviest in summer; generally located on the southeastern margins of continents (pp. 18–19)

Ice cap climate one of two kinds of polar climate; summer temperatures rarely rise above freezing and what little precipitation occurs is mostly in the form of snow (pp. 18–19)

Indigenous native to or occurring naturally in a specific area or environment (p. 116)

Infiltration process that occurs in the water, or hydrologic, cycle when gravity causes surface water to seep down through the soil (p. 40)

Internally displaced person (IDP) a person who has fled his or her home to escape armed conflict, generalized violence, human rights abuses, or natural or man-made disasters; unlike a refugee, such a person has not crossed an international border but remains in his or her own country. (pp. 46, 47)

Internet a network of computers facilitating electronic communication across the globe by way of the World Wide Web (pp. 32, 36, 37, 48)

Internet host central computer in a network (p. 48)

Landform physical feature shaped by uplifting, weathering, and erosion; mountains, plateaus, hills, and plains are the four major types (p. 20)

Language family group of languages that share a common ancestry (pp. 32–33)

Latin America cultural region generally considered to include Mexico, Central America, South America, and the West Indies; Portuguese and Spanish are the principal languages (pp. 30–31)

Llanos extensive, mostly treeless grasslands in the Orinoco River basin of northern South America (p. 72)

Lowlands fairly level land at a lower elevation than surrounding areas (p. 12)

Mangrove vegetation tropical trees and shrubs with dense root systems that grow in tidal mud flats and extend coastlines by trapping soil (pp. 22–23)

Marine west coast type of mild climate common on the west coasts of continents in midlatitude regions; characterized by small variations in annual temperature range and wet, foggy winters (pp. 18–19)

Marginal land land that has little value for growing crops or for commercial or residential development (p. 24)

Median age midpoint of a population's age; half the population is older than this age; half is younger (p. 29)

Mediterranean climate type of mild climate common on the west coasts of continents, named for the dominant climate

along the Mediterranean coast; characterized by mild, rainy winters and hot, dry summers (pp. 18–19)

Mediterranean shrub low-growing, mostly small-leaved evergreen vegetation, such as chaparral, that thrives in Mediterranean climate regions (pp. 22–23)

Melanesia one of three major island groups that make up Oceania; includes the Fiji Islands, New Guinea, Vanuatu, the Solomon Islands, and New Caledonia (pp. 112–113)

Melanesian indigenous to Melanesia (p. 116)

Microclimate climate of a very limited area that varies from the overall climate of the surrounding region (p. 20)

Micronesia one of three major island groups that make up Oceania; made up of some 2,000 mostly coral islands, including Guam, Kiribati, the Mariana Islands, Palau, and the Federated States of Micronesia (pp. 112–113)

Micronesian indigenous to Micronesia (p. 116)

Monsoon seasonal change in the direction of the prevailing winds, which causes wet and dry seasons in some tropical areas (p. 104)

Mountain grassland vegetation region characterized by clumps of long grass that grow beyond the limit of forests at high elevations (pp. 22–23)

Nonrenewable resources elements of the natural environment, such as metals, minerals, and fossil fuels, that form within Earth by geological

processes over millions of years and thus cannot readily be replaced (pp. 42–43)

Northern coniferous forest vegetation region composed primarily of cone-bearing, needle-leafed or scale-leafed evergreen trees that grow in regions with long winters and moderate to high annual precipitation; also called boreal forest or taiga (pp. 22–23)

Oceania name for the widely scattered islands of Polynesia, Micronesia, and Melanesia; often includes Australia and New Zealand (pp. 110–121)

Pampas temperate grassland primarily in Argentina between the Andes and the Atlantic Ocean; one of the richest agricultural regions in the world (pp. 70, 72)

Patagonia cool, windy, arid plateau region primarily in southern Argentina between the Andes and the Atlantic Ocean (p. 72)

Plain large area of relatively flat land; one of the four major kinds of landforms (p. 16)

Plate tectonics study of the interaction of slabs of Earth's crust as molten rock within Earth causes them to slowly move across the surface (pp. 14–15)

Plateau large, relatively flat area that rises above the surrounding landscape; one of the four major kinds of landforms (pp. 16–17)

Polar climates climates that occur at very high latitudes; generally too cold to support tree growth; include tundra and ice cap (pp. 18–19)

Polynesia one of three major regions in Oceania made up mostly of volcanic and coral islands, including the Hawaiʻian and the Society Islands, Samoa, and French Polynesia (pp. 112–113)

Polynesian indigenous to Polynesia (p. 116)

Predominant economy main type of work that most people do to meet their wants and needs in a particular country (pp. 36–37, 61, 77, 87, 97, 107, 117)

Province land governed as a political or administrative unit of a country or empire; Canadian provinces, like U.S. states, have substantial powers of self-government (p. 63)

Rain forest see *Tropical moist broadleaf forest*

Renewable fresh water water that is replenished naturally, but the supply of which can be endangered by overuse and pollution (p. 40)

River basin area drained by a single river and its tributaries (p. 72)

Rural pertaining to the countryside, where most of the economic activity centers on agriculture-related work (pp. 30–31)

Sahel in Africa the semi-arid region of short, tropical grassland that lies between the dry Sahara and the humid savanna and that is prone to frequent droughts (p. 92)

Savanna tropical tall grassland with scattered low trees (pp. 22–23)

Selva Portuguese word referring to tropical rain forests, especially in the Amazon Basin (p. 78)

Semiarid dry climate region that experiences great daily variation in day-night temperatures; receives enough rainfall to support grasslands (pp. 18–19)

Silt mineral particles that are larger than grains of clay but smaller than grains of sand (p. 79)

Sisal tropical plant with leaves made up of strong fibers that are used to make rope (p. 98)

Stateless people those who have no recognized country (p. 46)

Steppe Slavic word referring to relatively flat, mostly treeless, temperate grasslands that stretch across much of central Europe and central Asia (p. 102)

Subarctic climate region characterized by short, cool, sometimes freezing summers and long, bitter-cold winters; most precipitation falls in summer (pp. 18–19)

Subcontinent large landmass such as India that, although part of a continent, is considered a separate feature either geographically or politically (p. 98)

Subtropical climate region between tropical and continental climates characterized by distinct seasons but with milder temperatures than continental climates (pp. 18–19)

Suburb a residential area on the outskirts of a town or city (p. 30)

Sunbelt area of rapid population and economic growth south of the 37th parallel in the United States; its mild climate is attractive to retirees and a general absence of labor unions has drawn manufacturing to the region. (p. 60)

Taiga see Northern coniferous forest

Temperate broadleaf forest vegetation region with distinct seasons and dependable rainfall; predominant species include oak, maple, and beech, all of which lose their leaves in the cold season (pp. 22–23)

Temperate coniferous forest vegetation region that has mild winters with heavy precipitation; made up of mostly evergreen, needleleaf trees that bear seeds in cones (pp. 22–23)

Temperate grassland vegetation region where grasses are dominant and the climate is characterized by hot summers, cold winters, and moderate rainfall (pp. 22–23)

Territory land under the jurisdiction of a country but that is not a state or a province (p. 57)

Tropical coniferous forest vegetation region that occurs in a cooler climate than tropical rain forests; has distinct wet and dry seasons; made up of mostly evergreen trees with seed-bearing cones (pp. 22–23)

Tropical dry climate region characterized by year-round high temperatures and sufficient precipitation to support savannas (pp. 18–19)

Tropical dry forest vegetation region that has distinct wet and dry seasons and a cooler climate than tropical moist forests; has shorter trees than rain forests and many shed their leaves in the dry season (pp. 22–23)

Tropical grassland and savanna vegetation region characterized by scattered individual trees; occurs in warm or hot climates with annual rainfall of 20 to 50 inches (50–130 cm) (pp. 22–23)

Tropical moist broadleaf forest vegetation region occurring mostly in a belt between the Tropic of Cancer and the Tropic of Capricorn in areas that have at least 80 inches (200 cm) of rain annually and an average annual temperature of 80°F (20°C) (pp. 22–23)

Tropical wet climate region characterized by year-round warm temperatures and rainfall ranging from 60 to 150 inches (150–400 cm) annually (pp. 18–19)

Troposphere region of Earth's atmosphere closest to the surface; where weather occurs (p. 5)

Tundra vegetation region at high latitudes and high elevations characterized by cold temperatures, low vegetation, and a short growing season (pp. 22–23)

Tundra climate region with one or more months of temperatures slightly above freezing when the ground is free of snow (pp. 18–19)

Universalizing religion one that attempts to appeal to all people rather than to just those in a particular region or place (p. 34)

Upland climate see Highland/upland climate

Urban pertaining to a town or city, where most of the economic activity is not based on agriculture (pp. 30–31)

Urban agglomeration a group of several cities and/or towns and their suburbs (p. 31)

West Bank area bordering the west bank of the Jordan River that, according to a 1993 peace agreement between Israelis and Palestinians, has limited Palestinian autonomy; its future is subject to ongoing negotiations between these groups. (pp. 44, 47)

World Wide Web (www) a system of Internet servers that uses HTTP to transfer specially formatted documents that can be viewed on a computer using a Web browser; although many people think of the World Wide Web and the Internet as the same thing, the Web is actually only part of the Internet. (p. 48)

Web Sites (Web Link)

Activities and lessons using maps: http://www.nationalgeographic.com/xpeditions/

Antarctica: http://www.nsf.gov/div/index.jsp?div=ANT

Cultural Diffusion: http://www.geog.okstate.edu/users/lightfoot/lfoot.htm

Earth's Climates: http://www.worldclimate.com

Earth's Geologic History:

    Earthquakes: http://earthquake.usgs.gov/

    Tsunamis: http://www.noaa.gov/tsunamis.html

    Volcanoes: http://www.geo.mtu.edu/volcanoes/

Earth's Vegetation: http://www.earthobservatory.nasa.gov/Library/LandCover/

Environmental Hot Spots: http://earthtrends.wri.org/index.cfm

    Quiz for students: http://www.myfootprint.org/

Flags of the world: http://www.fotw.us/flags/index.html

Globalization: http://www.globalisationguide.org/

Map Projections: http://www.colorado.edu/geography/gcraft/notes/mapproj/mapproj.html

Political World: http://www.cia.gov/cia/publications/factbook/index.html

Predominant World Economies: http://www.wto.org/english/res_e/statis_e/statis_e.htm

Reading Maps: http://geodepot.statcan.ca/Diss/Reference/Tutorial/RM_tut1_e.cfm

Time Zones: http://tycho.usno.navy.mil/tzones.html

Types of Maps: http://erg.usgs.gov/isb/pubs/MapProjections/projections.html

World Cities: http://www.un.org/esa/population/publications/wup2003/WUP2003Report.pdf

World Conflicts: http://www.cnn.com/interactive/maps/world/fullpage.global.conflict/world.index.html

World Energy: http://www.bp.com/worldenergy/

World Food: http://www.cgiar.org/impact/research/index.html

World Languages: http://www.ethnologue.com/web.asp

    Interactive for students: http://www.ipl.org/div/kidspace/hello/

World Population: http://www.census.gov/ipc/www/idbnew.html

World Refugees: http://www.unrefugees.org

World Religions: http://www.adherents.com/

World Water: http://water.usgs.gov/

Thematic Index

Boldface indicates illustrations

A

Afghanistan
  refugees 46, **47**
Agriculture **38**, 38–39
  slash-and-burn 7
    8, **79**
  subsistence **36, 98**
  water use **40, 41**
al Qaeda 44
Alaska (state), U.S. 68
Amazon rain forest
    78–79, **79**
  map 78–79
Amazon (river),
    Brazil 79
Angkor Wat,
    Cambodia **108**
Anglesey, Wales
  sign **33**
Angola
  refugees 46
Antarctica
  map 27
Arabian Peninsula,
    Asia **98**
Arctic regions
  map 26
Austria 88

B

Belgium 88
Bosnia and
    Herzegovina 44
Brazil
  Amazon rain forest
    78–79
  British Columbia
    (province),
    Canada 68
Buddhism **35**
Bulgaria 88
Burundi
  refugees 46

C

California (state),
    U.S. **43**, 68
  beach **24**
Cambodia **108**
Canada 68
Cellular phones 49, **49**
Central America **40**
Chad
  refugee camp **47**

Chechnya (republic),
    Russia **45**
China
  cellular phones **49**
Chinatown, U.S.
    New York, **50**
Cities 30–31
Ciudad Juarez,
    Mexico **48**
Climate 18
  controls 20–21
  graphs 18, **18–19**
  map 18–19
  zones 18–19
Columbia (river),
    British Columbia-
    Washington **36**
Conflicts 44
  map 44–45
Congo, Democratic
    Republic of the
    refugees 46
Continents 13
Corals and coral reefs
    120, **120, 121**
  map 25, 121
Corn 38, **38**
  map 38–39
Cultures 32, 34
  diffusion 50
Cyprus 88
Czech Republic 26, 88

D

Date line 53
Deforestation 24
Denmark 88
Desert shrub **22**
Djibouti
  volcanoes **98**
Dominican Republic 68

E

Earth **4–5**
  atmosphere 5, **5**
  climate map 18–19
  cross section **16–17**
  geologic history
    14–15
  plate tectonics map
    14–15
  rotation 5, **5**
  satellite map 16–17
  vegetation map
    22–23
Earthquakes 68
  map 14–15, 69
Economies 36

Elevation 20
Energy resources
  hydroelectric **41**
  map 42–43
Environmental hot
    spots
  maps 24–25
Estonia 88
Europe 88–89
  maps 82–87
European Union (EU)
    88–89
  map 89

F

Factories **48**
Farming **38**, 38–39
  slash-and-burn
    78, **79**
  subsistence **36, 98**
  water use **40, 41**
Fertilizer use 39
  map 39
Fiji 52
Finland 88
Fishing **36**
  map 25
Flags and facts
    126–133
Flamingos **98**
Floods **68**
Food 38
  map 38–39
Forests
  map 24–25
  temperate **22**
  tropical **23**, 78–79
France 88

G

Germany 26, 88
Global warming
  map 25
Globalization 48
Globes 10, **10**
Gondwana 14, 98
Grasslands **23**
Great Barrier Reef,
    Australia 120, **120**
  map 121
Great Rift Valley,
    Africa 98–99
  map 99
Greece 88
Groznya, Chechnya,
    Russia **45**
Guatemala 68

H

Hinduism **34**
Human impact
  map 24

Hungary 88
Hurricanes 68, map 69

I

Iceland
  geothermal power
    plant **43**
Illinois (state), U.S. 68
India 45
Indo-European
  language family
    32, 33
Indonesia 44
Internet **37**
  map 48–49
Iowa (state), U.S. 68
Iraq
  refugees 46
Ireland 88
Irrigation **40**
Israel **44**
Italy 88
  population
    pyramid 29

J

Jammu and Kashmir,
    India 45
Japan
  fishing **36**
JASON Project **37**
Jerusalem **34**

K

Kansas (state), U.S. 68
Kenya **51**
Kolkata, India **24, 33**
Köppen, Wladimir 18
Kurdistan, Iraq **46**

L

Landslides **24**
Languages 32–33
  map 32–33
Latitude 8, 20
Latvia 88
Liberia
  refugees 46
Lithuania 88
Logging **36**
Longitude 8
Louisiana (state),
    U.S. 68

M

Maastricht Treaty 88
Manama, Bahrain **51**
Mangroves **23**
Maps
  cartograms 10, **11**
  choropleth 10, **10**

  physical 10, **10**
  political 10, **11**
  projections 6–7, **6–7**
  reading 8–9
  satellite 11, **11**,
    16–17
  scale 8, **8**
  symbols 9, **9**
  thematic **10**, 10–11
  types 10
Maquiladoras **48**
Mariana Trench,
    North Pacific
    Ocean 12
Masai people **51**
Mauritania
  desert sand **25**
Mecca, Saudi Arabia
  Grand Mosque **35**
Mexico 68
Mid-Atlantic Ridge,
    Atlantic Ocean 12
Middle East 44
Minerals **79**
  map 42
Mississippi (river), U.S.
  floods 68, **68**
Missouri (state),
    U.S. 68
Moscow, Russia
  restaurant **32**
Muslims **35**
Myanmar 44

N

Natural hazards 68–69
  map 14–15
Natural resources 78
  energy 42–43
  water 40–41
Nebraska (state), U.S.
    68
Netherlands 88
New York,
    New York 30, **44**
Nigeria
  population
    pyramid 29
North America
  natural hazards
    68–69
  map 69
North Pole 26
Nuclear power
    plants **43**

O

Ocean currents 21
  map 18–19
Ocean floor
  map 12
Oil resources 42–43

Staff for this book

Acknowledgments: We are grateful for the assistance of Richard W. Bullington, Jan D. Morris, Karla H. Tucker, and Alfred L. Zebarth of NG Maps; the National Geographic Image Collection; and Jo H. Tunstall, Robert W. Witt, and Lyle Rosbotham, NG Book Division

Illustrations Credits: Abbreviations for terms appearing below: (t) top; (b) bottom; (l) left; (r) right; (c) center; NGS: National Geographic Staff

Locator globes on pages 2–3 and in chapter openers created by Theophilus Britt Griswold

Graphs created by Stuart Armstrong

Continent chapter openers: NASA/JPL/California Institute of Technology/Advanced Very High Resolution Radiometer Project/Cartographic Applications Group

Front cover: NOAA satellite mosaic prepared for National Geographic Television by NASA/ JPL, color enhanced by Alfred L. Zebarth; background art digitally created by Slim Films; photos top to bottom: Ed George, NGS; Ed George, NGS; NOAA; George Grall, NGS

Back cover: (top) Radu Sigheti/Reuters/CORBIS; (bottom) CORBIS

About The Earth
4 (art) © NGS; 4–5 (t) Shusei Nagaska; (b) Earth Satellite Corporation; 5 (bl) Robert Hynes; 6–7 (art) Shusei Nagaska; 10 (l) Vlad Kharitonov NGS; 11 (t–b) NASA/GISS, NOAA/NESDIS/NGDC, NASA/GSFC, University of Miami; 14–15 (t) NASA/JPL/CalTech/CAG, (b) Christopher R. Scotese/PALEOMAP Project, U. of TX, Arlington; 16–17 (t) NOAA/NESDIS/NGDC; 22, (l–r), Des & Jen Bartlett; Raymond Gehman; Cosmo Condina /Getty Images; Walter M. Edwards; 23, (l–r), Tom Bean/Getty Images; Steve Jackson; Tim Laman; Medford Taylor/NGS Image Collection; 24, (l–r), Jeremy Horner/CORBIS; Joseph Sohm; ChromoSohm, Inc./CORBIS; Priit J. Vesilind/ NGS Image Collection; 25, Steve McCurry; 28, Stuart Franklin; 32, Les Stone/CORBIS SYGMA; 33, (l–r), Jeremy Horner/CORBIS; Ric Ergenbright/CORBIS; 34, (l–r), Annie Griffiths Belt/CORBIS; Lindsay Hebberd/CORBIS; 35, (l–r), Reuters/CORBIS; CORBIS; 36, (l–r), Martin Rogers; James P. Blair; Phil Schermeister; 37, (l–r), James L. Stanfield; Mark Thiessen, NGP; 38, (l–r), Steven L. Raymer; Sisse Brimberg; Steve St. John; 40, (l–r), Steve Winter; Annie Griffiths Belt; 41, (l–r), Herve Collart/CORBIS; Jim Brandenburg; 43, (tl), James A. Sugar/BLACK STAR; (c), Marc Moritsch; (b), Bob Krist; (r), Patrick Bennett/Getty Images; 44, (l–r), Spencer Platt/Getty Images; Antoine Gyori/Emmanuel Razavi/France Reportage/CORBIS; 45, (l–r), Ismail Danish/Reuters/ CORBIS; Malcolm Linton/Liaison/Getty Images; 46, Patrick Barth/ Stringer/Getty Images; 47, (l–r), AFP/Stringer/Getty Images; Radu Sigheti/Reuters/CORBIS; 48, Joe Raedle/Newsmakers/Getty Images; 49, CORBIS; 50, Bojan Brecelj/CORBIS; 51, (l–r), Louise Gubb/CORBIS SABA; Spencer Platt/Getty Images; 52, (l–r), Bob Sacha; The Granger Collection, NY; 53, Shusei Nagaoka

North America
68, (tl–r), Roger Werth/Woodfin Camp & Associates; Ravi Miro Fry; 68, (b), Chris Stewart/ BLACK STAR

South America
79, (t), Bill Curtsinger; (c), Mattias Klum; (bl–r), Michael Nichols, NGP, both

Europe
88, Bert Blokhuis/Getty Images

Africa
98, (t), Chris Johns, NGP; (b), Paul Zahl

Asia
108, (t), James L. Stanfield; (b), Steve McCurry; 109, (l–r), James P. Blair; Lynn Funkhouser

Australia
120, (l), Reuters/CORBIS; (tr), Gary Bell/Australian Picture Library/CORBIS; (br), Wolcott Henry; 121, (t), Wolcott Henry; (b), David Doubilet

One of the world's largest nonprofit scientific and educational organizations, the National Geographic Society was founded in 1888 "for the increase and diffusion of geographic knowledge." Fulfilling this mission, the Society educates and inspires millions every day through its magazines, books, television programs, videos, maps and atlases, research grants, the National Geographic Bee, teacher workshops, and innovative classroom materials. The Society is supported through membership dues, charitable gifts, and income from the sale of its educational products. This support is vital to National Geographic's mission to increase global understanding and promote conservation of our planet through exploration, research, and education.

For more information, please call 1-800-NGS LINE (647-5463) or write to the following address:

NATIONAL GEOGRAPHIC SOCIETY
1145 17th Street N.W., Washington, D.C. 20036-4688 U.S.A.

Visit the Society's Web site: www.nationalgeographic.com